DIANA TOWNSEND

Summer Days

Me, My Family and the Poltergeist volume 2

USSONS

First published by Ussons 2020

First edition

This book was professionally typeset on Reedsy.
Find out more at reedsy.com

Contents

Preface

Families are complicated, and mine is no exception.

For reasons too complicated to explain here, my brother, David, my parents and I spent many years building a model circus which we exhibited to the public each summer in Torquay.

Then, when David married Phillipa and I married Bob, our whole family decided to buy a derelict school with fifteen acres of grounds and turn it into a tourist attraction called Silverlands.

It seemed a sensible thing to do at the time.

We knew we would face challenges, but we hadn't expected them to include a demolition order, a deranged neighbour with a shotgun, a plague of rats and a resident ghost.

You can find out more in the first book of my series, Me, My family and the Poltergeist – How It All Began.

Chapter 1

When I was a child, I overheard a doctor joking that his hospital would run efficiently if only it wasn't full of patients.

I didn't understand at the time, but years later, when Silverlands finally opened, I discovered what he meant.

"Can you imagine it?" I said to my father. "Won't it be amazing if we have queues of people waiting to get in?"

"Yes," he laughed, his big face cracking into a familiar grin, "it will be amazing, but remember the old saying, 'be careful what you wish for.'"

I scoffed at him. I didn't believe having too many visitors could ever be a problem. We were used to dealing with the public and I was filled with the optimism of youth. I was twenty-seven years old and believed it was possible to achieve anything with enough hard work.

It was the spring of 1987 and the country was preparing for a general election which Margaret Thatcher would win with a huge landslide. Football hooligans seemed a greater threat than the recently discovered hole in the ozone layer and, despite high unemployment levels, rising inflation, and ongoing troubles in Northern Ireland, there was a general air of optimism.

We had worked tirelessly for months to make sure Silverlands opened on time and, after the turmoil of our first weekend, the whole family wanted nothing more than to rest.

It would have been wonderful to lie down and sleep, undisturbed, until the exhaustion inside us faded away, but such a luxury was impossible.

Unexpected expenses had blown our budget, and we had no money left to pay staff except for Martha and Abbie in the tearooms. Instead, we had to face a long summer season fuelled only by adrenalin and the satisfaction of knowing our dreams were still alive.

Gradually, our days settled into a routine.

Each morning was a flurry of cleaning. There were nearly twenty exhibition rooms to prepare, six sets of toilets to clean, as well as three staircases and endless corridors to sweep.

In the giftshop, David, my brother, restocked the shelves while, in the tearooms, my husband, Bob, laid out the counters with cakes and scones, fresh from the local bakers.

David's wife, Philippa, fed the animals and cleaned the cages in the Animal Meadow and, in the main house, Dad and I switched on the exhibitions and made sure everything was running smoothly.

Then, at ten minutes to ten, I would help my mother carry her bags and a supply of leaflets down to the ticket box.

There would often be a few families waiting, but one morning I was surprised to see a mass of mothers and young children crowded around the entrance.

I discovered they were all from the same playgroup in Exeter and had arranged a group visit. Smiling happily, I unlocked the gate and waved them through.

I was about to return to the house when I realised someone had spoken to me.

"I'm sorry, what was that?" I asked as I turned to face a young woman with a toddler in a buggy and a little girl tugging at her skirt.

"Where can I put the buggy?" the woman repeated.

I had no idea.

For months we had planned every aspect of our exhibitions, but now it dawned on me that we may have overlooked a few details.

Like buggies.

We had no excuse. Bob and I had Claire, our beautiful, mischievous, two-year-old, and David and Phil had Michael who was now eighteen months. We used buggies every day, and yet they had completely slipped our minds.

I tried to think of a suggestion as I walked beside the woman.

CHAPTER 1

The sun was shining, and Silverlands looked magnificent. The newly decorated walls of the old house were a warm golden yellow with clean white paintwork around the windows and doors. It was barely recognisable as the neglected wreck we had first seen a year ago.

I couldn't suppress a glow of pride. The transformation really was remarkable.

"Perhaps you can leave the buggy on the tarmac outside the front door?" I suggested, but the woman shook her head. Instead, she heaved the buggy over the threshold and in through the wide doorway.

"I'm not leaving it outside. It might rain."

Other families were following behind us.

"You don't mind if I put it at the bottom of the stairs, do you?" she asked. "There's plenty of room."

I didn't argue. The entrance hall was wide and spacious, and a few buggies wouldn't cause a problem.

* * *

Two hours later, I came to an abrupt halt half-way down the stairs. Ahead of me, the entrance hall was packed with buggies. Parents and small children were squeezing between them, laden down with bags of nappies and baby supplies.

I picked my way through the chaos, pushing the buggies into a line against the wall, trying to clear a path.

Groups of people struggled through but, as soon as I cleared a route, new families arrived with more buggies.

It was a losing battle and, as I glanced at my watch, I realised I should have been in the kitchen helping prepare for the lunchtime rush.

I hurried to the gift shop, hoping David might be able to help, but he was serving a queue of people while Philippa was busy selling brass ornaments to a group of elderly ladies.

I pulled a walkie-talkie from my pocket and called my father.

"Can you spare a minute?" I pleaded. "There's gridlock in the entrance hall."

"OK, I'm on my way."

"Thanks, Dad," I said and rushed off to the tearooms.

As soon as I saw Martha's face, I knew something was wrong. Her lips were pursed into a tight line and she was slapping scones onto a plate with none of her usual finesse.

"Are you OK?" I asked.

"I'm fine," she said through gritted teeth, but her soft Scottish burr was harsher than usual. "You'd better have a word with Abbie. She left her brains at home this morning."

"What d'you mean?"

"Look in there. You'll see."

I hurried through to the kitchen and gasped.

We had acquired an industrial-sized dishwasher from another attraction that was closing down, and I had been delighted by how well it had been working. Now it was hidden from view beneath a billowing mass of bubbles that bobbed gently as they slid down its sides and spread across the wet floor.

"What's happened?" I asked in astonishment.

"I'm sorry."

Abbie was scrubbing dishes in one of the wide, steel sinks, her brown eyes huge and anxious.

"But what's happened?" I repeated. "What's wrong with the dishwasher?"

"It's gone mad. I can't stop it. There's suds coming out everywhere."

"I can see that!"

I wiped away some of the foam and saw the huge glass lid was completely filled with froth.

"By why is it doing it? How many tablets did you put in?"

Abbie dropped her head so her dark hair hid her face as she mumbled something.

"What was that?"

"There weren't any tablets left, so I put in some washing-up liquid."

"Abbie! There's a new packet of tablets in the storeroom. Why didn't you ask me?"

"I didn't want to disturb you. I knew you were busy..."

"How much did you put in?"

"I just filled up the little tray where the tablets go. I wanted to make sure everything was clean."

Martha hurried into the kitchen, her mouth drawn into a tight line.

"If no-one's going to come and collect the orders, I'll have to bring them through myself, won't I? There's four families waiting when you've finish playing bubbles."

She slapped the orders on the work surface and stalked out.

* * *

Dad arrived a little later.

"I've cleared the gridlock..." he began, then stopped and gazed at the mounds of foam creeping across the floor.

"What the hell's going on?"

I was slicing salads at top speed.

"Abbie's been experimenting with washing-up liquid in the dishwasher. Any suggestions?"

"Don't worry, I'll deal with it."

He disappeared and returned a few minutes later with a shovel in one hand and a clutch of buckets in the other. Bob was following him.

"Oh, my God! I see what you mean!"

"Teapots!" Martha's voice rang out from the servery. "I need more teapots!"

"Where are they?" I asked Abbie, but I already knew the answer.

As if on cue, the dishwasher wheezed to a halt.

Bob and I looked at each other. The steel-edged cube that formed the lid of the washer was more than a metre in each direction. Normally, it was possible to see the rotating steel sprayers and the clean crockery inside, but now it was completely filled with foam.

"We can't open it," Bob said. "It'll swamp us."

"We have to," I insisted. "There's a queue of people waiting."

"If we put it through another cycle with just water, it might get rid of the bubbles," Bob suggested.

"But that'll take fifteen minutes. We can't wait that long."

"You two argue it out," Dad said. "I'm going to clear tables. They must have some teapots we can wash in the sink."

"Just open the dishwasher," I urged Bob. "It can't get any worse."

"OK, but don't say I didn't warn you," he muttered.

He slid the lid up and, for a long moment, the huge cube of bubbles quivered in the air, then, very gently, it collapsed in every direction.

I realised at once that I had underestimated the volume of froth.

"I told you," Bob said as a foaming tidal wave oozed across the kitchen, covering our feet and forming drifts against the cupboards.

"It's like those foam parties they have in Ibiza, isn't it?" Abbie babbled. "I've read about them."

Dad appeared in the doorway with a tray loaded with dirty dishes. For a moment, he stared at the white expanse covering the floor, then roared with laughter until the cups on the tray rattled.

"You opened it then," he gasped at last.

"It's not funny!" I wailed, ploughing through the remaining bubbles, trying to find the teapots.

"You're right," Dad agreed, still chuckling. "This is serious. There's a massive queue at the counter, Martha has a face like thunder and all the tables need clearing."

"I'll do the tables," Bob offered and hurried through into the tearooms, leaving a trail of frothy footsteps behind him.

"Here."

I found some teapots and handed them to Dad,

"Can you rinse these and get them out to Martha?"

"Sure," he nodded. "You go on preparing the meals. Don't worry, we'll have everything under control in no time."

* * *

There were still bubbles lurking in the corners of the kitchen when we closed at six o'clock.

Martha had never caught up with the queue of people waiting to be served, and the lunchtime rush had blended with the afternoon tea rush.

Dad hadn't had a chance to release Mum from the ticket box for her lunch break and, by the time we closed, everyone was exhausted.

As usual, we gathered for a cup of tea while Mum counted the day's takings.

"That was a disaster!" I sighed as I sat Claire down with a bowl of macaroni cheese. I felt guilty that I had barely seen her all day while she had been behind the counter in the gift shop playing with Michael.

"Not a complete disaster," Mum corrected me. "We took a lot of money."

"But it was chaos! We have to do better than that."

"Yes," Bob agreed. "Martha wasn't happy. We don't want her walking out on us. That really would be a catastrophe."

"Don't even talk about it," I groaned.

I had already come to depend on Martha's calm head, and the thought of coping without her scared me.

"We ought to sack Abbie, though," Bob said.

"No!" I protested. "It wasn't her fault. She was only trying to help, and she does work really hard."

"I can't see why you defend her. The girl's an idiot."

"No, she's not. She just needs clear instructions."

Bob shook his head in disbelief.

* * *

The next morning, as I vacuumed my way through the upstairs exhibition rooms, David appeared beside me.

"Spare a minute," he said and disappeared out of the room.

"What is it?" I asked. He didn't answer, so I hurried behind him to the other end of the building.

"I need to finish the cleaning," I protested, but David held open the door to Devon Mysteries and waved me inside.

"Notice anything?"

The Devon Mysteries exhibition was housed in four large rooms that had once been classrooms. It contained scenes from macabre westcountry legends and displays about mythical creatures such as the Beast of Bodmin.

"Something stinks, doesn't it?" David asked.

He was right. A rich and deeply offensive smell permeated the air.

"What it is?" I asked.

"No idea."

"Where's it coming from?"

He shrugged.

"I've been trying to track it down, but it seems to be everywhere."

I turned around, sniffing as I went.

"Is it this bad in the other rooms?"

"See for yourself."

The exhibition was laid out along a twisting path so that families discovered strange scenes and apparitions at every turn.

To add to the eerie atmosphere, the displays were lit by dull green spotlights and a soundtrack of moorland winds and peculiar noises played in the background.

I wandered around in the semi-darkness, sniffing as I went. My eyes began to water as the foul smell wafted around me, but I couldn't tell where it was coming from.

"Did you notice it last night, when you switched off?" I asked.

"No, but to be honest, I was so shattered by the time we closed I wouldn't have noticed if the whole place was full of elephant poo."

"Is that what you think it is? Elephant poo?"

"Of course not, but it does smell a bit like poo, doesn't it?"

He was right.

"Maybe people will think it's intentional," I suggested hopefully. "That it's all part of the atmosphere. You know, that it's supposed to stink like a graveyard with rotting bodies."

Even in the darkness I could see the offended look on David's face.

"Don't be ridiculous," he said. "We have to find out what's causing it and we haven't got much time. We're opening in thirty minutes."

We prowled around the rooms, noses twitching, trying to track down the source of the smell. I was concentrating so hard I jumped violently when David's voice rang out from the next room.

"Blooming Hector! That's disgusting!"

I rushed in and saw him leaning against a wall with an arm across his face.

"What is it?" I demanded, but David only pointed into a corner.

From the horror in his voice, I had expected to see a rotting corpse but, as I glanced down, I could see nothing. Finally, as I peered more closely, I noticed a gap between the skirting board and the base of a display case. Something pale was protruding through the gap.

"What is it?"

"No idea," David's hand was still over his face. "I tried to pull it out, and it was like being gassed."

Holding my head aside, I poked the pale object with my finger. It was smooth and flimsy and bent when I touched it. Reluctantly, I grasped it between my finger and thumb and pulled.

Slowly, accompanied by a gut-wrenching stench, the object slid out from behind the display.

It was an overflowing baby's nappy.

"Oh my God!"

The nappy slipped from my fingers and squelched onto the floor.

"I'll have to get some disinfectant."

"And air freshener," David suggested, "lots of air freshener."

"Open all the doors. I won't be long," I shouted over my shoulder as I headed back to the corridor. Then I ran through the house, trying not to panic. There were only minutes left until we were due to open and the vacuum cleaner was still standing, abandoned, in the middle of the Down in Devon exhibition.

Abbie was in the kitchen preparing sandwiches.

"Leave those for now," I ordered. "Finish cleaning upstairs. I'll be back as soon as I can."

Armed with a bucket and an assortment of cleaning materials, I rushed back to Devon Mysteries. As I arrived, David was waving his jumper through the entrance doorway.

"I thought it might disperse it a bit," he explained.

"Here," I threw a can of air freshener at him. "Use that. All of it."

A moment later I was splashing disinfectant over the brown marks staining the bottom of the display case.

"How can people be so disgusting?" I fumed.

* * *

I was still seething when we closed that evening.

"It's not funny," I protested. "We've got a lovely baby-changing room. It's not too much to expect people to use it, is it?"

Dad chuckled at me.

"You look about twelve-years-old when you're indignant. Did you know that?"

I frowned at him.

"I'm being serious."

"I know you are, love, but it's the joy of dealing with the public, isn't it? Most of them are great, but there will always be a few that make you want to kill them."

"I suppose so," I grunted.

"I told you to be careful what you wished for."

He grinned at me. "The problem with tourist attractions is that they attract tourists."

"But we need tourists," I protested. "Loads of them."

"Of course, we do, but you like it much better when they go home, don't you?"

"That's ridiculous," I sniffed, but we both knew it was true.

* * *

Mixing with people has never come easily to me. I have always been the observer, the quiet one in the corner who would rather listen to other people's conversations than join in myself.

Fortunately, the rest of my family love nothing more than entertaining people.

Bob is a natural performer. His mother was an actress, and he spent much of his childhood backstage in a theatre or watching her shows from a spare seat in the auditorium.

He should have been a performer himself, but his father had different ideas and he succumbed to pressure to follow a more traditional career – at least until he met me.

At Silverlands, he was in his element. The circus was a big theme in our attraction and Bob took on the role of ringmaster, welcoming visitors with a wide smile, a red coat and a raised top hat.

David never tired of chatting to visitors, and Philippa welcomed families to the Animal Meadow with a friendly smile.

I tried hard to follow their lead, but I never really succeeded. Painfully shy, I felt awkward talking to people, and I was always afraid they sensed it.

In the tea rooms, I tried to smile all the time, then worried I was smiling too much. I didn't mind working hard. I could wash dishes or clear tables from dawn to dusk without a break, but I found speaking to people nerve-wracking.

Soon, I found excuses to avoid the visitors. If there was a problem with one of the displays, I was the first to volunteer to sort it out. Our main attraction was Silvers Model Circus, the incredible, animated model that my father had started building long before I was born. It ran on an intricate system of belts and pulleys which needed to be tensioned and lubricated at regular intervals. I offered to share the maintenance with Dad and spent many happy hours laying under the model dripping oil onto the miniature bearings.

"Hiding again?" Dad would say as he saw me emerging from under the circus platform.

"Of course not," I answered. "I'll be back in the tearooms soon. I just have to pop down to the office for a bit. I really ought to get the VAT returns up to date."

I made sure I was always back in the tearooms for the lunchtime rush but, by then, I could stay in the kitchen preparing meals. I always felt safe in the kitchen.

I didn't mind clearing tables because people didn't expect me to stop and talk to them, I could just fill up a tray with china and cutlery and move on. In fact, I found the easiest way to avoid talking to the visitors was to make sure I never stopped working.

* * *

Despite feeling uncomfortable with strangers, I did love the energy that flowed through the house when it was busy. It was exhilarating to hear children's voices echoing along the corridors and their excited calls as they discovered something new.

The house felt strangely alive when it was full of people, and there was a wonderful atmosphere that radiated everywhere. When the entertainers were performing on the main lawn the laughter and applause could be heard in the tearooms and the music from the gift shop floated up the main staircase to mingle with the folk songs playing in the Down in Devon exhibition.

Sounds were everywhere. Not intrusive, deafening sounds, but a warm, active buzz like the pulse and heartbeat of a great creature.

I loved Silverlands intensely. It was something we had created from the empty shell of a building listed for demolition, and now it had a character of its own. It was a warm and friendly place and it made me happy to see that other people loved it too.

We soon had repeat visitors. Even in our first season we recognised faces as those who had enjoyed their visits returned.

David spoke to an elderly couple who explained that they had three sets of grandchildren and they had brought each set to visit us when they came to stay.

"It's so lovely," the old lady said. "I can't really put my finger on it but there is something magical about this place. I don't know if it's the exhibitions or the gardens or the entertainers, but it just makes me happy being here."

* * *

But not all our visitors were happy.

One afternoon, as I turned a corner, I heard raised voices and found a woman screaming at Bob. His face was a picture of misery and he was scarlet with embarrassment.

"Is something wrong?" I asked.

The woman rounded on me.

"There certainly is! I have never been so disgusted in my life. You should be ashamed of yourselves."

"Perhaps you can help this lady," Bob backed away as he spoke. "I really need to be somewhere else."

The woman switched her attention to me as Bob hurried off.

"I'm going to write to the newspapers about this! And the radio! And the TV! You can't treat people like this."

"I'm sorry," I managed to break in, "but what exactly is the problem?"

"The disabled toilet! It's disgusting!"

I didn't understand. I had decorated the toilet myself. We had specially adapted a large, ground floor room and provided all the necessary fittings and equipment. There were cheerful pictures on the walls and it was cleaned regularly. I couldn't imagine why she was so upset.

The woman grabbed my sleeve and pulled me along the corridor.

"You see for yourself! It's not decent!"

The moment I stepped into the toilet, I understood.

I had been so concerned with the interior of the room that I had not given a thought to the exterior. The glass in the windows was not frosted.

I was horrified.

The window looked out onto a narrow walkway at the back of the house and the woman told me she had been helping her elderly mother onto the toilet when a man walked past the window and waved at them.

There was nothing I could do but apologise. It had been a genuine oversight, but I felt awful. I refunded the woman's entrance money, apologised to the old lady and offered them both a free meal in the tearooms.

Later, I caught up with Bob. "Thanks for abandoning me earlier."

"I'm sorry."

He had the grace to look ashamed of himself.

"I didn't know what to say to her."

"She was right to be upset about the windows," I conceded. "I've nailed a curtain across the window for the time being and left the light on. I just can't believe none of us noticed."

* * *

After the chaos of the Easter holidays, the children went back to school and our visitor numbers reduced dramatically.

We knew the numbers would go up again as the summer approached but, for a few weeks, it gave us a chance to catch our breath and finish the many tasks we had been unable to complete before we opened.

Without a doubt, the best part of the day was after the visitors had gone. A wonderful peace descended upon the house and gardens and, for a short while, we could relax.

We lifted the children out of their playpens and our dogs, Ossie and Dino, came charging out of the flats, their paws clattering down the stairs as they headed out onto the lawn.

Then Silverlands was ours.

Later, when the children had been fed, played with and tucked up in their beds, the shop had been restocked, the displays checked and everything was ready for the next day, I would take my hoe and go out to weed the flower beds.

I have always loved the special quality of light just before sunset. Those few precious moments when the last rays skim low across the land, outlining every leaf and blade of grass with a magical golden halo.

At Silverlands, the sun dropped below the hills behind the tickets box, sending long purple shadows rolling across the lawns. Robins and blackbirds sang in the treetops and bats appeared to hunt as the day faded to twilight.

I often stayed out weeding until it became too dark to see, savouring the tranquillity and remembering how lucky I was to call such an incredible place my home.

* * *

Each day, after we closed at six o'clock, the family gathered for a cup of tea to discuss how the day had gone.

I usually worked in the tearooms in the afternoon so I would get everything ready and finish laying the tables for the next morning as I waited for the others.

One afternoon, Mum and Dad arrived first, Dad lugging an old hold-all with the day's take from the ticket box. Mum settled herself on the window seat of the bay window and started counting. She entered the figures in a small notebook, then waited expectantly while I made up the tearooms' till.

"Very good," she nodded when I told her how much we had taken.

A few minutes later, David appeared from the gift shop with the cash from the tills there.

Once Mum had tallied up the totals, and Bob and Phil had joined us with the kids, we started chatting about what had happened during the day.

"I had a lovely Irish family in the gift shop earlier," David began. "They were telling me how much they loved the Devon Mysteries. The little boy was giggling his head off describing his Mum jumping at the scary bits. He thought it was the funniest thing he'd ever seen."

"I know the ones you mean," Phil joined in. "They were over in the Animal Meadow just before we closed. They had a little girl too, didn't they? With big blue eyes and no front teeth."

"That's them. They're staying at a caravan park in Paignton and they took some of our leaflets back with them to show the other campers."

"Excellent. There's nothing better than word-of-mouth advertising," Dad beamed.

Claire and Michael were sitting in high chairs. Claire had a bowl of pasta in front of her, but now she upended the lot onto the carpet.

"That's naughty! Don't throw your food on the floor," I scolded her as Ossie and Dino raced across to help clear up.

I slipped behind the counter to grab some kitchen roll and heard a familiar creaking from the corridor upstairs.

Footsteps.

I ignored them.

From the first time we had visited Silverlands, there had always been the sound of footsteps. It had worried me at first, but Bob insisted that all old houses creaked and the builders had joked about a ghost called Fred.

Whenever a tin of paint was spilled or a box of nails went missing, Fred was always blamed. It became a running joke but, as time went on, things happened that were not so easy to explain.

Although I had no proof, at least nothing I could show to other people, I had become convinced the old building was haunted.

Then, one day, a tin of plums disappeared in front of me. One moment it was there, the next it was gone. I had been extremely upset at the time because I knew what I had seen, but I didn't think anyone would believe me.

Mum, Dad and David had all had strange experiences themselves, but Bob was certain Fred was nothing more than a joke played on us by the builders.

Now, as I listened to the distant footsteps, I knew raising the subject again would only end in an argument, so I ignored the sounds and hoped that Fred, whatever he was, would behave himself.

But, as I wiped the last of the pasta from the carpet, I realised the others were listening to the noises too. And it wasn't just footsteps. There were voices.

David was the first to jump to his feet and head into the hall, with Ossie and Dino close behind him.

"Who's there?" he called.

The others followed while I stayed with the children, my heart pounding.

I heard Ossie bark and David telling him to be quiet. It was some minutes before Philippa came back.

"What was it?" I asked.

"Nothing to worry about. Just two old ladies. They didn't realise we'd closed. They were trying to get out, but all the doors are locked."

I breathed a sigh of relief as the rest of the family returned.

"We're going to have to be more careful," Bob said. "Imagine what would have happened if they'd been in the Devon Mysteries when we'd turned the lights off? They would never have found their way out!"

"But I checked all the exhibitions," David protested. "I don't understand how I missed them."

"Did you check the loos?" Mum asked.

"The ladies' loos?" He sounded horrified. "Of course not."

"Well, I think we'd better look more carefully in the future," Mum laughed.

After that, checking the building at closing time became a daily ritual.

As soon as all the tills were emptied, one of us would take up position in the entrance hall while two others, often accompanied by the dogs, went upstairs and worked their way through the various rooms.

There were so many twists to the corridors, hidden alcoves and blocked sightlines, as well as thirteen outside doors and fire exits, that it took a full thirty minutes to make sure the house was empty.

* * *

As the evenings got lighter, I spent more time outside in the grounds. We had hired a local farmer to cut the grass on the lawns, but the surrounding areas were still heavily overgrown. I longed to clear the blackberries and nettles from the woodland areas so that visiting children could explore them but, as we couldn't yet afford any gardeners, I had to satisfy myself with a putting a row of bedding plants around the edge of the tea lawns and hanging baskets under the verandah.

The weather was beautiful, and it was lovely to see families picnicking on the lawns. Over the May bank holiday weekends, Bob arranged jugglers and entertainers each day and the crowds loved them.

Everything was going well.

June arrived and the first day of summer brought black clouds and heavy rain.

I wasn't worried. Silverlands was an all-weather attraction, and there weren't many of those near us. Our visitor numbers went up, and I had to send a message to the bakers in Chudleigh asking them to send more supplies.

"Are you sure we'll need all those?" Abbie asked as the extra cakes and scones arrived but, by the end of the day, the tearooms' counter was empty.

It rained again the next day and the next.

All week, the skies were hidden behind a thick blanket of cloud and we heard from friends who ran a camping site that many of their guests were packing up their tents and caravans and heading home.

We still had plenty of visitors to keep us busy but now, instead of being spread through the grounds and the Animal Meadow, they crowded into the house and the craft block. Picnics on the lawn were no longer possible, and we found families eating sandwiches in every corner of the house.

In the Animal Meadow, Philippa struggled as the rain turned the ground to mud and the animals huddled inside their houses looking wet and miserable.

We weren't the only ones affected by the bad weather. Thunderstorms and hail caused havoc across the country, and the first week of Wimbledon was all but washed out.

Despite the rain and clouds, our visitors were still remarkably cheerful. One afternoon, a man advised me to go and check in the Devon Mysteries.

"I'm afraid there's a bit of a puddle on the floor," he said.

Thinking someone had spilled a drink, I sent Abbie up with a bucket and mop, but she came back a few minutes later with wide eyes.

"I think you'd better have a look yourself. It's a really big puddle."

She was right. The water stretched from one side of the room to the other and I could hear dripping coming from behind a partition. Unlocking an access hatch, I clambered through to the back of the display and found the whole area behind the partition was several centimetres deep in water.

Waving a torch upwards, I could see drips falling from a crack in the ceiling.

Hurrying back downstairs, I found a bucket to put under the leak. Then I mopped the floor as best I could and apologised to the visitors as I worked. To my relief, they were understanding and simply picked their way through the shallowest parts of the puddle.

When I had cleared the worst of the water, I phoned Steve, the builder who had been foreman of the renovations.

"I warned you those roofs were in poor shape," he said.

"I know, but something's changed. We used to get the occasional drip, but now there's a lot of water coming through."

"OK. I'll come over first thing in the morning."

* * *

It was still raining when Steve arrived the next day.

He put up a ladder, inspected the flat roof, then came back and shook his head.

"One of the main joints has let go. I'm afraid the whole thing needs replacing. I told you that when I first looked at it."

"I thought you said it would last for another year."

"I said it might last for another year if you were lucky."

There was a note of exasperation in Steve's voice. I ignored it.

"There must be something you can do?"

His eyebrows furrowed as he frowned at me.

"The problem with flat roofs is they're supposed to be flat. They should only have enough slope for the water to run off, but if they're built of rubbish materials, like that one, they warp over time and the rain gets caught in the hollows. Once it does that, you've got water laying on the roof and it's only a matter of time before it finds its way through."

"So, what's the answer?"

"I told you. A new roof."

"But that means stripping everything off. We can't do that while we're open, can we? Surely you can do something? Just until the end of the season?"

For a moment I thought he would refuse, but then his shoulders sagged.

"OK, I'll try again if you insist, but I'm not promising anything."

Steve spent the rest of the afternoon on the roof and the smell of hot pitch drifted through the rain. Finally, he came down and stood dripping in the kitchen.

"Do you want to borrow a towel?" I offered.

"No, I'm off home for a bath."

He looked exhausted. His wet hair clung to his head and his hands were black with tar.

"Do you think you sealed the leak?"

He shrugged apologetically. "For now, maybe, but it's a mess. If that doesn't hold, I'm afraid there really is nothing else I can do."

* * *

It was only a few days before David burst into the kitchen.

"Phone Steve! Now! The roof's leaking again!"

I was busy unpacking a delivery of groceries.

"There's no point," I said. "He told us there's nothing else he can do."

"He has to do something!" David yelled.

"Calm down," I snapped. "It can't be that bad."

"Can't it? Come and see."

I followed him upstairs and my heart sank. Water was dripping from the ceiling like a shower.

David ran a hand through his hair as he always did when he was stressed.

"We have to close the exhibition," he said. "We can't do that," I protested.

It was David's turn to snap.

"Get real, Diana! There's water spraying over the power sockets. It's not safe. I'll find a closed sign. You get everyone out."

That evening, Dad, David and I met in Devon Mysteries. Dad wanted to see the situation for himself, but David had already made up his mind.

"There's no alternative. We have to close the exhibition. Steve's tried everything."

"Then we need to find another builder," Dad said calmly.

"What's the point? They'll only say the same thing."

"Can you put the lights on?" Dad asked.

David shook his head.

"It's not safe. The exhibition will have to stay closed until we can get the roof replaced."

"We can't do that!" I objected.

"I told you, there's no other way," David shot back.

"Stop shouting, you two," Dad cut across us. "There's always another way. Go and find me a ladder."

By the time David returned with a step-ladder, Dad had opened the access hatch and was standing in the space behind the partition.

"What are you going to do?" David asked as he passed the ladder through to him.

"I don't know yet."

Pulling a torch from his pocket, Dad flashed it above him at the ceiling tiles. Then he climbed up the ladder, pushed a tile out of its frame, and climbed higher so that his head and shoulders disappeared into the space between the ceiling and the flat roof.

A few minutes later, he clambered down.

"Do you have a longer ladder?" he asked.

"Yes, but it wouldn't fit in there," David replied.

"That's OK, I need it outside."

Ignoring our puzzled expressions, Dad began pacing across the floor of the exhibition room.

"What are you doing I asked?"

"Counting. Damn, now I'll have to start again."

He continued pacing across the room, then turned and disappeared out of the door.

* * *

"Can you help hold the bottom?" Dad asked me as David propped a long aluminum ladder against the outside wall of Devon Mysteries.

"OK, but I wish you'd tell me what you're doing," I muttered.

I helped David hold the ladder steady as Dad climbed up with a roll of tools under one arm. When he got to the top, he unrolled the tools on a window ledge and selected a chisel.

He had paced out the distance from the end of the building before he positioned the ladder and now, satisfied that he was in the right place, he began cutting a hole in the fascia board immediately below the flat roof.

"What do you think he's doing?" I asked David.

"Haven't got a clue. You know what he's like when he gets an idea in his head."

I did. Years of experience had taught me not to question Dad when he was in the middle of something.

Finally, he rolled up his tools and came back down the ladder.

"Right," he said calmly, "now all we need is a length of guttering."

Back in Devon Mysteries, David and I helped him slide a length of plastic guttering up into the space between the ceiling and the flat roof. He manoeuvred it carefully between the metal wires supporting the ceiling tiles until it was exactly underneath the crack where the rain was seeping through. Then he pushed it forward until the far end stuck out through the hole he had made in the fascia board.

"There, now I just need to lift this end a little."

He took a piece of wood from his pocket and jammed it under the guttering.

"Perfect."

For a few moments, he listened to the gentle patter of drips, checking that all the rain was landing in the guttering and being safely channelled outside. Finally satisfied, he climbed down the ladder.

"Luckily it only needs to last for a few weeks. Just until we close in September. Like I said, there's always another way."

* * *

By the time the school holidays arrived, the grey skies had given way to a glorious English summer. Visitors queued at the gate every morning, and families filled the grounds and exhibitions. Each day followed the same pattern and, apart from being exhausted, we were all delighted by the way the year was progressing.

The wet summer had given us problems indoors, but it had provided excellent growing conditions outside. The lawn had shot up at an alarming rate and I soon realised I would never cope clearing the weeds along the paths and under the trees by hand.

David and I brought up our concerns with the others, and they agreed that something had to change. David had already done his research and showed us an advert he had found for a second-hand ride-on mower. It would be an investment but, as we were having to pay a local farmer to cut the grass every couple of weeks, it should soon pay for itself.

There were no arguments. Within days, David's new toy arrived, and I became the proud owner of an enormous, metal-bladed strimmer. It came complete with protective gloves, body harness, helmet and ear-defenders.

I adored it.

One evening, after settling Claire down to sleep, I hurried outside and got myself kitted out.

Bob was preparing our evening meal, so I filled the strimmer with petrol, yanked the starter chord and smiled happily to myself as the engine roared to life.

The metal blade sliced effortlessly through the undergrowth and I felt like an explorer clearing a way through an undiscovered jungle.

At the far edge of the lawn, beneath an ancient oak and a magnificent tulip tree, lay an expanse of brambles. As I sliced through it, I found an ornate wrought-iron fence. I guessed it dated from the time the house had been built and was in surprisingly good condition.

Beyond the fence, the land dropped steeply to a lower level, and I found traces of what had once been a gravel path leading down through the woodland.

Closer to the house, an enormous clump of laurel bushes sprawled out across the lawn. Several of the branches were dead, and I spotted something square and angular hidden among them.

Tearing away a tangle of ivy, I revealed a massive concrete block standing on a square plinth. It was considerably taller than me and, while the front and back were flat and smooth, the sides jutted out in odd, irregular, slopes.

I gazed at it for a long time, trying to work out what it was. There were no signs of walls nearby, just the one huge, grey block.

I couldn't make sense of it.

Pulling off the last of the ivy, I noticed two circular holes that went right through the block and were lined with some kind of pipe.

The others were just as confused as me.

"Was it supposed to hold something?" Phil asked. "Something that fitted through the two holes?"

"Like what?" David frowned.

"I've no idea. I was just wondering."

"Maybe there was a lot more to it. Perhaps it doesn't make sense because the rest is missing and this was just the foundation?" Mum suggested.

"But foundations go underneath something," Bob pointed out, "not straight up in the air."

"Whatever it is, it's an eyesore. Can't we just get rid of it?" I asked.

"We can try," Dad said, "but it's enormous and it seems to be one piece. Breaking it up would be a massive job."

The others nodded in agreement.

"We can't do anything about it now," Dad went on. "Maybe we can try in the winter when we're shut."

"Could you grow something over it?" Mum suggested.

"I suppose so," I agreed, "but it will take ages to cover it."

David stepped back and considered the monstrosity from a distance.

"It's a shame you cleared the ivy off it really, isn't it?" he said at last.

* * *

Sometimes, late in the morning when we had finished the tea rush and before we started preparing lunches, I would walk over to the craft centre to make sure everything was running smoothly.

The centre had originally been built as classrooms and consisted of eight units around a central lawned courtyard. The workshops were spacious with huge windows that gave them an airy feel, and each one had been decorated in an individual style.

There was nothing conventional about our craftspeople, in fact, they were an eclectic bunch.

Dougal, the woodcarver, was a tiny man with an enormous shock of grey hair. His small hands appeared too delicate for heavy work and yet he used chisels, axes and even a chainsaw with incredible precision. He was always happy to welcome visitors to his unit and encouraged them to watch him while he worked.

He enjoyed explaining the techniques he used and would stop what he was doing and give demonstrations of how tools were used if someone showed a particular interest.

Opposite him, across the courtyard, were the glass engravers. Elliott was tall, pale and quiet while Marion, his wife, was short, round and bubbly with olive skin, jet black hair and a permanent smile.

They were both accomplished artists and could engrave the most detailed images of animals, flowers or even portraits onto any object made of glass.

In addition, we had a toy maker who produced traditional wooden toys, a knitwear designer who created amazing jumpers, dresses and coats, and a pair of picture-framers who specialised in bespoke frames that often out-shone the pictures they surrounded.

But although the craftspeople were diverse, the one thing they all had in common was their friendly manner. The only exception was Tom Stevens, the potter.

Tom was an excellent craftsman, but he was terrible at dealing with the public. I don't think he meant to be rude, but he often was.

I once heard him tell a family, "If you're not going to buy anything, please leave. I can't concentrate with you standing there watching me."

I was horrified.

"Tom, people are far more likely to buy something if you make them feel welcome," I said as the family shuffled out of the room.

He looked at me in surprise.

"I do make them welcome," he protested, "but that family had been standing there for ages. I don't complain normally, but it's disconcerting when they just stare at me. What more do they want? I'm not going to make them tea and biscuits, am I?"

"Maybe you could talk to them?" I suggested.

"Why? They come to see the crafts, don't they? Not to gossip."

It felt hypocritical of me to say he should spend more time talking to people, but I persisted.

"Perhaps they'd like to know more about you. After all, they only come in here because they're interested in you."

Tom's face darkened.

"I don't want them to be interested in me. I want them to be interested in my pots."

I tried again.

"Then maybe you could tell them how you make them? About your processes? All the steps that go into each..."

"Impossible!" Tom looked at me as though I was mad. "I don't have time for that sort of thing. I'd get no work done at all."

* * *

I was emptying the dishwasher in the kitchen when Mum phoned me from the ticket box. I could tell at once that somebody was with her. She was using her formal voice and sounded like a newsreader.

"There is a visitor to see you," she announced. "It is Mr North from Torrington Bank. Is it convenient for me to send him up to the house?"

"Yes, of course. I'll come and meet him."

As I dried my hands on a towel, I wondered what Mum would have said if I'd told her it wasn't convenient. She could be unpredictable at times and it was easy to imagine her telling Mr North that he should have phoned to make an appointment before coming.

It occurred to me that if I had been in the craft block and hadn't had my walkie-talkie with me, she would probably have sent him away. I winced. Mr North was not like any of the other bankers I had met. We had spoken to many of them while trying to raise the finance to start Silverlands, but it had only been Mr North who had given us a chance.

We owed him a huge debt, but I knew Mum would have seen it differently. She didn't believe in banks, but then, she didn't believe in politicians, or solicitors, or doctors either. I paused for a moment as I realised my mother didn't trust anyone in a position of authority. In fact, she didn't trust anyone except Dad and David and me.

The realisation came as a shock but I knew it was true and suddenly I understood why she struggled to accept Bob. It wasn't about him. It was about her. It wouldn't have mattered who I had wanted to marry. She would not have accepted him.

I had never brought a boyfriend home to meet my parents. Not once. It had not been a conscious decision, but I had always avoided it. Now I wondered why. I had not worried about introducing them to Dad. I knew he would have teased me, but he would have been his usual, cheerful self. Mum would have been a different matter. She would...

A deep voice in the servery cut through my reflections and I jumped guiltily. How could I have let my thoughts run away with me?

I hurried through and held out my hand.

"Good to see you, Mr North. I hope you're keeping well?"

"Yes, thank you. I didn't want to disturb you but I was passing and I thought you might have a few minutes to tell me how things are going."

He smiled down at me and his stiff, upright bearing made me wonder if he had been in the army.

"Absolutely, but would you like a cup of tea, first?"

"Maybe later. I was hoping you could show me around and give me an update on your progress."

Martha was behind the counter and nodded that she could manage on her own.

"I'd love to."

It was mid-morning and Bob was about to introduce the morning show. We had laid out a circle of hay bales on the main lawn and families sat around waiting expectantly.

Mr North followed me across and watched as Bob stepped forward, resplendent in his red coat and top hat. He ran through his patter and the audience cheered.

"And now, are you ready to be amazed?"

The audience shouted back, but Bob held his hand to his ear.

"What was that? I can't hear you? Are you ready?"

"Yes!" the audience roared.

I glanced at Mr North and was pleased to see he was smiling.

"Then let me introduce the greatest juggler this side of the river Teign! The amazing, the talented, the one and only Mighty Max!"

The audience cheered as Max appeared from behind the laurel bushes perched on a six-foot unicycle juggling a rainbow of brightly coloured hoops. Bob stepped back, and I waved to catch his attention.

"Hello, there!"

Bob held out his hand and greeted Mr North with a wide smile. "Good to see you. You've picked an excellent day to visit. We've got a lovely crowd in."

"Yes, I can see that."

I had expected Mr North to move on, but he stayed and watched the show with interest and clapped as loudly as the children.

I showed him through the attractions, pointing out the most popular displays, and introduced him to David in the gift shop, Phil in the Animal Meadow and the craftspeople in their workshops. Finally, we ended up back at the tearooms.

"I won't keep you much longer," he said as we sat down at a corner table. "It seems to me that everything is going well. It's unfortunate that the poor weather has caused you problems, but hopefully the rest of the summer will be better. It's very satisfying to see you at this point, but..."

He broke off as Martha arrived with a tray of tea and a plate of flapjacks. I poured the tea into the cups and waited for him to continue, but he was silent.

I was about to comment on how much people had been spending in the gift shop when Mr North cleared his throat.

"There is one thing I want to bring up with you."

I looked across at him, and his pale blue eyes met mine.

"When you and your mother first approached me about financing this project, I explained that I have great confidence in family-run companies. In my experience, they have much greater resilience than a group of people that have been brought together purely by a business opportunity."

I nodded earnestly.

"But there is one other thing I would like you to consider. Your family are very talented and diverse. They all bring unique abilities to the business. In some ways, they are like the members of a crew. If you want to sail a ship across an ocean, you need lots of different crew members, engineers, officers, caterers."

He paused and sipped his tea before continuing.

"The ship won't run smoothly without all the crew members but, however well each one does his job, the journey will end in disaster if someone isn't constantly on watch checking the ship is navigating properly. It's exactly the same with a business. It's easy to concentrate on the day-to-day activities, but someone needs to keep a long-term view, decide where you want the business to be in five years' time and work out how to get there."

I nodded again and waited for him to go on.

"In my opinion, in your family, that person is you. You're the one that must keep the ship on course. Make sure that everyone is pulling together in the same direction."

He was looking at me, expecting me to agree with him.

"But our family isn't like that," I said. "We make all our decisions together. All six of us have an equal vote in everything."

"Democracy is wonderful," he said quietly, "but please consider what I've said. Now, I think I had better get back to the office."

* * *

As the summer rolled on through weeks of sunshine, a steady stream of visitors kept us busy. Our daily routine became second nature and, in the evenings, Bob, Claire and I ate our meal on the tea lawn while the dogs charged around us.

Life was wonderful.

Finally, when September arrived, and the schools reopened, the number of visitors dropped and the queues in the tearooms shrank.

"Do you remember the last time we had a day off?" David asked one afternoon as we all gathered in the tearooms after closing.

I laughed.

"It was before we saw this place for the first time, so that would be about eighteen months ago, wouldn't it?"

"We did take Christmas Day off," Mum corrected me.

I laughed again.

"Yes, you're right. I'm sorry, I didn't mean to exaggerate."

"Still, it will be nice when we shut," David said. "It's only a few weeks now until the end of September, then we can close the doors until next Easter."

"I am looking forward to having the place to ourselves again," I admitted.

Bob stretched out his legs and leaned back in his chair.

"I saw a report on the news last night," he said. "Apparently, the value of an average house has gone up by twenty-seven percent in the last twelve months. That's incredible, isn't it? It made me think about this place. Last year it was a derelict wreck with a demolition order hanging over it, and now it's renovated and open for business. It would be interesting to know what value the estate agents would put on it now."

"Yes, it would," I agreed. "Whichever way you look at it, the value must have increased hugely."

Mum nodded.

"And property prices never go down, do they?"

"But it's not true to say it's all renovated," Dad chimed in. "We've still got a lot to do. Apart from the roof on Devon Mysteries, there are still two craft units we haven't touched. And don't forget the dormitories at the back, let alone the swimming pool and the sports hall."

"Did you have to remind us of all that?" David groaned. "I was just thinking how well we're doing."

"We are doing well," Dad agreed. "but I don't want you thinking we can take a lot of time off just because we're closing to the public."

"Well, I think we should," Mum cut across him. "We deserve it. We close on the last day of September and, after that, I think we should all take a week off."

Dad looked amazed as the rest of us cheered.

Chapter 2

Claire woke me as usual on the first day of October but, for once, I didn't rush through breakfast and hurry downstairs to start cleaning.

Instead, Bob and I had a chance to relax and Claire squealed with delight as we helped her build towers of wooden blocks then knock them over.

As I looked out of our lounge window, I noticed the magnificent old trees that edged the lawn.

Throughout the summer they had been a vibrant green screen that isolated us from the few houses on the other side of the valley but now, as the autumn days grew cooler, their leaves were touched with orange, gold and red.

"Isn't it beautiful," I said to Bob as he joined me at the window. "We are so lucky."

"I know," he agreed. "I still can't believe we're really here and that we have actually made it to the end of our first season."

"It does feel like a big achievement."

"It is. I think we should celebrate. Let's go out for a meal."

I couldn't remember the last time we had been out together.

"That sounds wonderful," I smiled. "I'll ask Mum and Dad if they can babysit."

"No, I meant everyone. Your parents and David and Phil."

I hesitated. It wasn't that I didn't want to go out with the others. It was just that I was surprised to hear Bob suggest it. He and Mum had never seen eye to eye, and they were often wary of each other. Maybe he was finally warming towards her.

"Great," I said brightly. "I'll see what I can arrange."

The others thought it was an excellent suggestion, and we enlisted some friends to spend an evening looking after the children and the dogs while we all went out to Chudleigh's finest restaurant.

We settled ourselves in our seats and made our choices from the menu.

"Here's to us," Dad said and raised a glass in the air.

"To us," David echoed, raising his glass. "I wasn't sure we were going to get here."

"There were a few times when I thought we hadn't got a hope," Phil admitted.

"But we are here. That's all that matters," Mum said firmly. "From now on everything will be a lot easier."

We clinked our glasses and hoped she was right.

* * *

It was a lovely evening and, by the time we got home, Bob was relaxed and happy. I was relieved to hear that Claire had been well behaved in our absence and, when I crept into her bedroom, I found her sleeping like an angel with her dark curls fanned out across the pillow.

Bob saw our babysitters out and took Dino for his last walk while I made some hot chocolate.

"It's nice that you and Mum are getting on better now," I said as he returned with Dino.

I was curled up on the sofa and Bob kicked off his shoes and joined me.

"Are we? Yes, I suppose so. Maybe she's finally realised how lucky she is to have me as a son-in-law."

I spluttered with laughter and the unexpected outburst made Dino raise his ears in alarm and come padding across to us.

"It's OK, boy," Bob said as he stroked the dog's thick mane. "Nothing to worry about. She's just being silly."

"Seriously, though," I said, "I'm glad you've stopped needling each other."

"Each other?" Bob queried. "Don't blame me. I've always been delightful to her. The needling has been entirely one-sided."

"Really? Even when you suggested we put a padlock on the ticket box?"

"I didn't think she'd hear me."

"Yes, you did. You waited until she was right beside you before you said it."

"You're imagining things. I'm always lovely to your mother."

He sipped his chocolate and considered me over the rim of the mug.

"Are you feeling tired?"

"No, not really."

"Good."

Putting down the mug, he flashed his widest smile and slid his arm around my shoulder. "It's not late yet. There's still time for more celebrating."

* * *

The rest of the week was an oasis of tranquillity. It was wonderful to have Silverlands to ourselves and time to relax and enjoy it.

"This must have been how it felt when the house was first built," I said one morning as I sat on the window seat in the tea rooms eating breakfast.

"Probably," Bob agreed, "except that you wouldn't have made your own breakfast then. It would have been prepared by a cook and served by a footman."

"I like that sound of that."

"And there would have been a butler."

"And a gardener."

"Lots of gardeners for a place this big and chambermaids to make the beds."

"Living here must have been awesome."

"Yes, but I doubt if anyone wandered around in their pyjamas. Not in Victorian times."

"Or threw their weetabix everywhere," I sighed as Claire's breakfast landed on the floor.

"No want eat 'bix," she complained.

"That's very naughty." Bob frowned at her as he passed me a kitchen roll.

"Toddlers wouldn't have been allowed down for breakfast back then, would they?" he said thoughtfully. "They would have been kept up in a nursery somewhere, looked after by a nanny."

"That's true," I agreed as I wiped Claire's hands and gave her a piece of banana.

"Maybe there's something to be said for the old ways. I like the idea of having clean, well-behaved children presented to me once a day so I can pat them on the head."

"Did you hear that, Claire?" I laughed. "Daddy wants to send you to live in a nursery."

Claire stopped with a piece of banana half-way to her mouth and stared at her father. Her bottom lip began to quiver and Bob immediately caved.

"I'm only joking," he grinned and hugged her tight. "Don't cry. You can throw your weetabix on the carpet any time you like."

* * *

The leisurely days flew past, and soon our break was over.

Early one morning, we all met to plan what we wanted to get done before Silverlands reopened to the public the following spring.

Some things, like strengthening the floor in the tearooms or replacing the flat roofs, were priorities, but there were lots of other projects waiting to be done.

Mum wanted a more impressive ticket kiosk at the entrance while Phil was hoping to build the stable that had been postponed so she could add a pair of donkeys to the animal meadow.

Bob thought we should create an indoor area for entertainers to perform on wet days, and I was keen to open up more of the grounds. We agreed to list all our suggestions and get quotes to bring to our next meeting.

I was packing away the display pieces in the tearooms when Bob went past the door.

"Can you spare a minute?" I called out to him. "I want your opinion on something."

"Sure, what is it?"

"Come outside and I'll show you."

Bob followed me through the French windows and across the lawn.

"Where are you taking me?" he asked, but I didn't answer.

During the last weeks of summer, I had cleared a sizeable area that ran around the edge of the main lawn. It was lower than the rest and was separated by a gentle slope in some places and by a sharper drop and a stone wall in others.

I had thought it would be an ideal place for a row of picnic benches as it was shaded by ancient oaks, ashes and aspens and would be a lovely spot for families to relax.

I had scattered boxes of grass seed but it soon become clear that the ground was too overshadowed for grass to thrive. The pale shoots grew frail and spindly before withering or being eaten by snails. In their place, the nettles and brambles I had cleared were already making a comeback.

I didn't want to admit defeat and had been trying to think of a way to make use of the newly reclaimed area.

"Here."

I stopped and threw out my arms dramatically. "Wouldn't this be a brilliant place for an adventure trail?"

Bob looked around him.

"What do you mean?"

"With a bit more work, we could make this into a path that runs along the edge of the woodland right from the entrance all the way around to the craft block."

Bob turned and followed my finger as I pointed.

"We could put in lots of activities. Climbing frames, monkey bars, swinging ropes, balance bridges, all sorts of different things."

"I like it. That would keep the kids busy for hours."

"And we could advertise it as a new outdoor attraction."

"Maybe we should give it a theme?"

A sudden breeze lifted the branches above and the wet leaves spattered drops of water down on us.

"Let's get back inside," Bob said. "I think it's going to rain."

David was in the gift shop with the children. He was packing stock into boxes while Claire and Michael were busy taking teapot stands from a display and lining them up along the window seat.

"Are they supposed to be doing that?" I asked, but David only shrugged.

"If it keeps them quiet, why not?"

David listened as we explained about the adventure trail. I could see he liked the idea.

"We thought it should have a theme," Bob said. "Something that fits in with the other exhibitions."

"Yes, something Devonian," I agreed.

"How about Devon Animals? We could have the Badger Run, the Squirrel Climb, that type of thing," Bob suggested.

"It should be Pirates."

I looked at David blankly.

"Pirates? What have they got to do with Devon?"

"Good grief!"

David pulled a book from a box he had just finished packing.

"You ought to read this."

The book had a black cover emblazoned with the title Pirates of Devon and Cornwall.

"It's fascinating," he went on. "Pirates used to be one of the main exports from these parts. Did you know that Plymouth was a major ship-building centre back in Elizabethan days?"

"Of course, I did," I said indignantly. "The English fleet was based there before it sailed out to meet the Spanish Armada."

"True, but did you know there were just as many pirates in Plymouth as ordinary sailors? Let's face it, Sir Francis Drake and Sir Walter Raleigh, were both pirates really. They came from Devon and they raided wherever they liked as long as they shared their treasure with Queen Elizabeth."

"That's not how they described them when I was at school," Bob cut in.

"But it's the truth," David insisted. "Did you know that when they made the first film of Treasure Island, the actor that played Long John Silver gave him a Devon accent? That's why he went 'Oooh, aargh!' all the time."

I shook my head.

"No, I didn't know that."

David grinned triumphantly.

"Exactly! Everyone knows that pirates go 'Oooh, aargh!', but no one remembers it's because they've got Devon accents."

"OK, I give in," Bob said. "We'll call it the Pirate Trail."

* * *

Our next meeting lasted for hours. Everyone had their own pet project but, even though our first year had been a success, we couldn't afford to do everything at once. We discussed priorities, compromised and argued until, eventually, we agreed a plan.

Bob had already spoken to Steve and arranged for him to have his workmen ready to start the following week. Now he phoned and explained exactly what we wanted done.

"There's one other thing we need to discuss," Mum said to me later. "We have to get back to the solicitor about the water situation."

I groaned.

I knew she was right, but I had been trying to forget the problem with our water supply. It was too depressing.

When we first bought Silverlands, our solicitor had failed to notice that the water supply, for which we were responsible, not only supplied our property but also nine others along the valley. We had no way of charging the other users, in fact, we did not even know who they were, but we were responsible for paying their bills because they were part of the estate the old house had once owned.

We had been in the middle of renovating Silverlands when we had discovered the situation and had been so stretched getting everything finished and coping with our first season that we had simply ignored the problem. Now, we needed to find a resolution.

"We can't put it off any longer," Mum said. "I'll phone the solicitor and arrange a date to see him."

* * *

It was great to have the builders back at work and soon the house was full of toolboxes, voices and blaring radios.

The atmosphere was completely different from the summer when the house was full of families, but there was a new kind of energy that I liked.

The materials for the flat roofs were due to be delivered in a few days but, in the meantime, work started on the floor in the servery.

We pulled the carpet back and revealed the sheet of steel which had lain over a hole in the floor for the last seven months.

"I told you it would hold," Dad said happily. "We could leave it there for another season without any problems."

"But we're not going to, are we?" I asked. "You do know I've been having nightmares about people falling through holes in the floor, don't you?"

Dad laughed at me.

"You worry too much," he teased. "If you really want nightmares, you should look at the state of the floors in the old dormitory block."

"Please don't tell me," I groaned. "I don't want to know."

Dino and Ossie loved the builders. They followed them around the house wagging their tails and soon learned their routines.

They were both large dogs. Ossie was black from head to toe with a silky coat and long feathery tail like a red setter. It was a good thing he had a sweet temperament as he had the largest set of glistening white fangs I ever saw on a dog. When he was happy, he had a habit of pulling back his lips in a 'smile', revealing a row of teeth that would have been perfect for a toothpaste advert.

I loved Ossie because he was a natural clown. He was as lithe as a sea lion, but extremely clumsy. His legs seemed too long and gangly for his body and sometimes, when he raced along a corridor at top speed, he would misjudge his cornering ability and his legs would skid in all directions before he crashed into a wall and ended in a tangle on the floor.

He loved chasing balls but invariably burst them with one bite, then looked surprised and disappointed as the remnants drooped from his mouth.

His coat was so black that when he went outside at night, he simply disappeared. He was usually good at coming when he was called, but in the dark, he seemed to take a perverse pleasure in standing still, knowing he was invisible.

On several occasions I can remember David bellowing "Ossie!" into the darkness and growing increasingly frustrated. It was only when Ossie 'smiled' and his gleaming white teeth appeared that David realised the dog had been sitting quietly in front of him the whole time.

While Ossie was a clown, Dino was an athlete. He could run like the wind and jump high fences without breaking his stride.

He was also a very handsome creature with an intelligent face and deep brown eyes. He had the massive white mane of a Scottish collie and the powerful frame of an Alsatian.

While Ossie was often covered in mud or had leaves entwined in his tail, Dino had a remarkable ability to keep himself clean. The white fur on his legs seemed dirt-proof and, when Bob took him for a walk around the grounds, Dino only needed a quick roll on the carpet to get rid of every trace of mud.

Unfortunately, the carpet was not so easy to clean.

Both dogs accepted the workmen as their friends and whenever they stopped for a tea break or pulled out their lunchboxes, they would appear beside them hoping for a tidbit.

"I'm sure Ossie's putting on weight," Phil said one morning as we started a stock-take in the gift shop. "Every time I see him, he's eating another biscuit."

"Dino's just as bad," I agreed. "He's down by the front door every morning waiting for Steve and the team to arrive."

Phil nodded.

"I know. Dino barks when their van comes in through the gate. I think it's a signal. As soon as Ossie hears him, he starts whining for us to let him out."

* * *

Later that morning Dino was beside me in the office, laying peacefully, his eyes half-closed, while I wrote up the figures from the stock-take into a file.

There was a quiet tap on the door.

"Come in," I called.

A moment later, there was another tap.

"Come in," I called again, louder this time, but the door stayed shut.

Putting down my pen, I crossed the room and opened the door.

There was no one there.

Confused, I looked both ways, but there was no sign of life.

Returning to my desk, I picked up my pen, but an uncomfortable, prickling feeling was running down my spine.

It had been six months since a tin of plums disappeared in front of me on our opening day and, since then, I had deliberately tried not to think about the experience.

We had been ridiculously busy at the time and I had barely slept for days. Could I have been hallucinating? It seemed unlikely as every detail of the event remained etched in my mind but, as time passed, it became easier to tell myself that I must have been mistaken.

Now, the quiet taps on the door triggered a flood of doubts.

Had it been Fred tapping?

What did that even mean?

I had not believed in ghosts before I moved to Silverlands, and I still didn't really believe in them, but I hadn't imagined the taps. Something must have caused them. I wished I had a simple explanation, but I couldn't think of anything that made sense.

Suddenly, I jolted upright as Dino exploded in a frenzy of barking, throwing himself forward, his claws scraping against the back of the door.

"Excuse me, is it all right if I come in?"

It was Steve's voice.

"Of course."

I grabbed Dino's collar and made him sit as Steve opened the door. I was irritated to find I was shaking.

"Is everything OK?" I asked.

"Yes, I just wanted to let you know we're off," Steve said. "We've removed the damaged joists and fitted new ones. The floorboards are back in place and we just have to finish levelling and put the carpet back down in the morning."

"That's great."

"See you tomorrow, then."

"Yes, night, Steve."

Dino barked again, and Steve patted his head as he left.

* * *

The next morning, I was getting Claire dressed in our lounge when the doorbell rang downstairs. Dino charged across the room and jumped at the window, barking loudly.

"Quiet!" Bob bellowed, but the dog was enjoying himself too much to stop.

"Loud!" Claire put her hands over her ears. I wasn't sure if she was complaining about Dino or her father.

"Enough!" Bob shouted as he grabbed Dino by the collar and dragged him, still barking, into the bedroom.

"It's probably the postman," he said as he hurried downstairs.

"Loud," Claire protested again as Dino's barks rang out from the next room.

"He's a silly dog, isn't he?" I said.

"Silly dog," she agreed.

Bob returned a few minutes later with an armful of mail.

"Anything interesting?"

"No," he sighed as he let Dino back into the room. "It's junk, all of it."

The doorbell rang again.

"I don't believe it," Bob muttered.

"Do you want me to go?" I offered.

"No, you stay with Claire."

It was only when Bob returned that I realised Dino was laying quietly by the sofa, watching me.

"Who was it?" I asked.

"No one. It must have been those kids from the stable," Bob muttered. "Their parents let them run wild."

"Did you see them?"

"No, but it must have been them. Who else could it have been?"

I looked across at Dino.

"This is going to sound far-fetched," I began, "but have you noticed how Dino barks at everything?"

"Of course, I have. He's an absolute menace."

"Would you say he barks every time the front doorbell rings?"

"Yes."

"And every time there's a knock on the door?"

"He never misses."

"That's what I thought... but he didn't bark just now when the doorbell rang."

"Didn't he? Maybe he didn't hear it."

"He must have done. He was right here beside me."

"What are you saying?"

"I'm not sure. It was as if he knew there was no one there."

Bob looked at me, and his expression changed.

"Wait, a minute. You're not starting all that Fred nonsense again, are you?"

"Hear me out. It wasn't the first time. Yesterday there was a knock on the office door and he didn't react at all."

"Maybe he's getting deaf. He's not a puppy anymore."

"It wasn't like that. It was a definite tap, but when I opened the door, there was no one there. Dino must have heard it. He just didn't take any notice."

"It was probably the door frame creaking. He would have known the difference. Dogs don't have overactive imaginations like people."

"It wasn't a creak. It was a tap."

"Then someone was playing a trick on you. Don't you think it's a bit of a coincidence that this is all kicking off again the moment the builders are back?"

"But if it was one of the builders, Dino would have barked, wouldn't he?"

"For Christ's sake!" Bob's voice rose in frustration. "This is ridiculous. I'm telling Steve to sort his guys out."

"No! please don't mention it to Steve."

"Why not? I'm not having them upset you."

I tried another approach.

"If it is someone trying to wind us up, maybe it's better to ignore it. That way they'll get bored and let it drop."

Bob hesitated for a moment, then relented.

"All right, if you're sure, but if it happens again, tell me and I'll deal with it."

* * *

The appointment with the solicitor was on a Wednesday morning but, by midday on Tuesday, it was clear Mum was coming down with a heavy bout of flu.

Bob and I were in the office when she pushed the door open.

"I'm sorry," she croaked, "you'll have to phone the solicitor and postpone tomorrow's visit."

"There's no need," Bob said. "I can go in your place."

Mum frowned at him.

In the past, Mum had always dealt with anything official. While I was a child, my father had often been ill and was prone to severe headaches that sometimes lasted for days. Mum worried they might be triggered by stress so she had always made sure that she was the one who paid the bills, made appointments, dealt with tax returns and spoke to the solicitor.

I couldn't see her giving up her responsibilities willingly, but her face was pale and drawn. I could tell she felt really ill.

"Maybe it would be best," I ventured. "I can go with him and find out what the solicitor has to say. We won't make any decisions."

"Of course, you won't," Mum rasped. "Remember, there are six partners in this business and we all have to agree before anything is decided. There's no room for anyone doing anything impulsive."

"Of course not," I agreed. "We'll just find out what he has to say."

* * *

"You'd think I was a trainee on work experience!"

Bob was still muttering the following morning as he parked the car and we walked to the solicitor's office.

"I've been running companies for over twenty years. I've been responsible for dozens of shops and hundreds of employees. Why did she even want me in the business if she doesn't trust my judgement?"

I sighed.

"She does trust you. I know she does. She just wasn't feeling well."

"She said I was impulsive."

"No, she didn't. Not exactly... Look, we're here now."

The solicitor's office was situated in an elegant Georgian terrace in the centre of Exeter. Outside, the walls were made of rich, red brick fired from the clay of the surrounding hills. Inside, the decor was cool and calming, a mixture of muted greens and soft greys. I wondered if the colours had been chosen to have a calming effect on waiting clients. It occurred to me that the last time I had spoken to Mr Barbary I had threatened to sue his company for negligence.

Bob spoke to the receptionist, and we settled ourselves in the waiting area. Before long, Mr Barbary appeared and ushered us into his office.

"Thank you both for coming," he began formally once we were seated. "As it happens, I have just received a missive from the water board."

"Really? What's it about?" Bob asked.

The solicitor pushed a file of papers across the desk to us.

"Basically, they've outlined why they believe you are responsible for the entire water supply. We can go into it in more detail in a moment, but they are demanding you pay all outstanding amounts immediately or they will issue court proceedings."

Mr Barbary waited as we looked through the papers.

"How much is outstanding at the moment?" he asked.

I opened my handbag, pulled out a statement and handed it to him.

He scanned the page and gave me a puzzled look.

"I don't understand."

"It came as a shock to us too," I said. "As you know, when we first discovered there was a problem with the water supply, we were rushed off our feet getting everything ready to open and, since then, we've been working seven days a week."

"Yes, but that doesn't..."

"I didn't open the bills," I blurted. "I just put them to one side and ignored them."

"Let me get this clear. You are saying you have paid nothing at all to the water board?"

"Not a penny."

"Then why does the statement show nothing owing on your account?"

"We didn't understand either," Bob said, "but then we went down to have a look at the water meter. It's ancient, and it seems to be broken."

"You mean it's been vandalised?"

"No. There's no sign of any damage. The mechanism must have jammed."

"I don't think it can have been working since we arrived," I added.

"Oh, dear."

The solicitor leaned back in his chair. "This makes things even more complicated. The water board will want to charge an estimated amount. We can challenge it, but that will mean more time in court and more legal fees. Ultimately, if you lose, this could prove very expensive."

"Then what do you suggest we do?" Bob challenged him.

"As I explained to your wife last year, the only real solution is to install a new water main."

"But we don't have that sort of money," I protested.

Bob was still studying the papers Mr Barbary had passed us.

"I don't understand why the water board sent us a bill for zero pounds in the first place. Surely, they can see that makes no sense? Can't we just send them a cheque for zero pounds and leave it at that?"

"I wish it was that simple. The bills will have been sent out automatically, but that really isn't the issue. Their legal department will expect an answer to their letter. I'm afraid you can't just ignore the situation."

"We're not ignoring it," Bob said firmly. "You can write to the water board today and tell them we intend to fight them every step of the way. If they won't back down, we will see them in court."

* * *

"I told you we should have postponed the appointment," Mum exploded when I repeated the conversation to her that afternoon. "We can't afford to take this to court. He had no right to tell the solicitor to go ahead."

"I know," I said uncomfortably, "but I'm sure Mr Barbary will find a more diplomatic way of phrasing things."

Mum shook her head.

"This is serious. Put the kettle on."

A short while later we were all gathered together in Mum and Dad's flat. David was looking worried, and Phil gave Claire and Michael a packet of crisps each to keep them busy.

Bob explained what had been discussed with the solicitor and there was an uneasy pause when he finished.

"I still don't understand why we can't have a separate supply," Phil said at last.

"We can have one. The question is who will pay for it," Bob replied.

"Not us. It's so unfair," David burst out.

"Exactly. That's why we have to fight," Bob fired back. "We have to make a stand."

"Or we could look for a compromise," Dad suggested. His voice was calm, but I knew he was worried.

"Even if we agreed to split the bill, it would still be huge," David insisted. "I don't see why we should pay any of it."

"Mr Barbary said if it goes to court the costs could go through the roof," I warned.

"We have to fight this. There's no other way," David protested angrily.

"Isn't there anyone else we can...," I began, but David's voice was loud.

"I'm with Bob. We have to fight..."

Suddenly Mum cut across us.

"Stop it! All of you! Can't you see what you're doing?"

She was looking at Dad and I realised the colour had drained from his face, leaving his skin grey and waxy.

"Are you OK?" I asked.

Dad flapped a hand at me, but his eyes were half closed.

"Don't make a fuss. I just need to lie down."

Mum took his arm and the rest of us waited awkwardly as she helped him out of the room.

"Is there anything I can do?" David asked, but Mum shook her head. "Just calm down. All of you. You're not kids anymore."

She shot a look at Bob as she helped Dad out of the room.

When they had gone the four of us sat in silence. Claire and Michael were taking books from a shelf and stacking them on the floor.

"Maybe we can stall things a bit longer," I suggested, "until we agree what to do."

The others said nothing, so I continued. "I could write back to the solicitor saying we need more time to consider."

"You know what I think," Bob said.

"And me," David added.

"OK... I'll tell him we'll get back to him soon."

* * *

Dad's headache lasted well into the following day, and he was still in bed with heavy shadows under his eyes when I called in to see him.

"Feeling any better?" I asked.

"Don't worry about me," he said. "I always bounce back. Always have, always will."

"I know you do, but I can't help worrying."

His face broke into a smile.

"So, you still love your old Dad then?"

"Of course, I do. I hate it when you're ill."

"Don't be daft, love, I'm fine. The headaches don't mean anything. I've had them since I was a nipper. There was an accident when I was about Claire's age and my Mum had poured a jug of boiling water over me. It was probably my fault. I expect I pulled her skirt or something. I can't remember that part, but I do remember having bandages and cream all over my head for months."

"That must have been awful."

"I used to throw up a lot, and the headaches were terrible. They lasted for weeks sometimes. I don't know how my mother coped with me."

"Couldn't the doctors do anything to help?"

"They tried. God knows how many doctors I've seen over the years. I spent weeks in hospital being tested, and I've been on every headache medicine known to man. Nothing ever stopped them. Most of the pills just made it worse."

He reached out and took my hand.

"But I've learned to live with them. These days I can feel when they start and if I just lay down and let them pass, they go much quicker. Your Mum's been a star. I never wanted to be a burden to her, but I honestly don't think I'd be here without her."

"I know. She's very special."

"She is. She's a good girl. Even if she can be a bit protective of her own."

"Protective?" I laughed. "Is that what you call it? Even now that we're adults, she's still like a lioness with cubs."

"She does like to look after us all, doesn't she?"

We were still laughing when the door opened and Mum walked in with Dad's lunch on a tray.

"What are you two giggling about?" she asked.

"Not a thing." Dad winked at me as he struggled to sit up.

"Turn the TV on, Diana, we might catch the end of the news," Mum suggested, and I obediently crossed and pressed the button on the set.

"Too late, it's finished," Mum sighed as Michael Fish, the weather forecaster, appeared.

"Earlier on today, a woman rang the BBC and said she's heard there's a hurricane on the way," Michael Fish announced. "Well, if you're watching, don't worry, there isn't."

"That's a relief," Dad smiled. "The last thing we need right now is a hurricane."

* * *

Later that afternoon, I headed down to the office. I hated bookwork, but I felt I ought to make sure the accounts were up to date to keep the pressure off Mum.

As I passed the Down in Devon exhibition, I glanced through the window and noticed ominous clouds scudding across the sky. The wind ruffled the treetops and flaming leaves tumbled across the lawn.

Grabbing a mug of tea and some biscuits from the kitchen, I settled myself at my desk. The office was tucked away between the kitchen and the tearooms. It didn't have a window, so it was really a very large cupboard with thick walls and a solid wooden door.

I worked my way through a pile of receipts, entering the figures by hand in a ledger and calculating the VAT due on each item, until, at last, I leaned back in my chair and stretched my arms over my head.

Reaching for another biscuit, I noticed the wind sounded much stronger. I could hear the windows in the tea rooms rattling and the hum of the electric cables outside.

Suddenly, a shuddering thud reverberated through the building. I couldn't tell where it had come from, but I was on my feet in a moment and ran out through the tea rooms onto the lawn.

My hair whipped around my face, and gusts of wind buffeted me. Leaves were flying everywhere. Looking around, I saw an enormous branch had come down from the oak tree by the front door, narrowly missing the building. It lay across the tarmac, bare twigs stretched out like fingers.

"Thank God the cars weren't there," Bob shouted above the roar of the wind.

I jumped. I hadn't heard him come up behind me.

"Yes. D'you think any more branches will come down?"

"Hard to tell..."

He looked up at the old tree, its branches flailing wildly above us.

"Let's get back inside."

* * *

David had been watching us through the gift shop window.

"Has it done much damage?" he yelled out.

"No," I called back as we walked through to him. "Luckily it came straight down. If it had swung around a few feet, it would have gone right through the porch."

David looked worried.

"Can you stay with the kids?" he asked. "I want to check Phil's all right. She might need a hand closing the animals down."

"Sure, no problem," Bob replied. "I'll get them their tea."

We took Claire and Michael to the kitchen and I settled them into their high chairs while Bob prepared their food.

Although it was still early, the heavy clouds looming overhead blotted out the afternoon light and the children were subdued, listening, wide-eyed to the wind howling around the house. For once they were not interested in eating, and Claire put her arms out to me for a cuddle.

"It's all right, honey," I reassured her. "It's just the clouds rushing around in the sky. Nothing to worry about."

I was still trying to get Claire to eat her vegetables when the kitchen door crashed open and David and Phil burst in.

"Mumma! Dadda!" Michael cried excitedly.

Phil was pale and shocked, her face streaked with mud, but David was full of animated energy.

"Another inch and she'd be dead!" he yelled. "That was the closest thing

I've ever seen!"

"What happened?" Bob demanded.

"I'm fine," Phil mumbled, but her voice trembled.

I pulled out a chair.

"Come and sit down."

"It's a miracle she's alive," David gasped. "It's crazy out there, unbelievable."

"Calm down. Tell us what happened."

Phil lowered herself into the chair, and David flopped down on the window seat beside her.

"I couldn't find her. I thought she'd be in the stable, but there was no sign of her. It turns out the water carrier had blown away. You know, the big five gallon one, half-full too, but it flew right across the field."

David sucked in a huge breath and rushed on.

"I'd just spotted her in the meadow and was going across when this almighty shape came over the hill. I thought it was a plane at first. It was massive. Then the wind got under it and it flipped. Turned it right over. It was a roof! Can you imagine it?"

"What do you mean, a roof?"

"It was a roof! A complete roof, rafters and all! I screamed at Phil, but she couldn't hear me. It was heading right for her then, at the last minute, it twisted. I thought it hit her. She went down on the ground like a log and I was sure she was dead."

Bob turned to Phil.

"Jesus! Are you hurt?"

"No." Phil looked as though she would be sick.

"Sit still for a bit."

She nodded.

"I'm OK. It was just a shock. I didn't see it coming. The first thing I knew was when the shadow went over me. I must have ducked because the next thing I knew was I was on the ground and the roof, or whatever it was, crashed down next to me."

"It was so close," David wrapped his arms around Phil and blinked back tears. "I really thought I'd lost you."

* * *

The storm raged all night. The slates rattled, Dino howled, and Claire woke every few minutes.

In the morning, news reports showed that the entire country had been ravaged. Seventeen people had been killed by falling trees or collapsing masonry, and railway lines and roads were blocked from Cornwall to Scotland.

Substantial damage had been done to properties, and an estimated fifteen million trees had been brought down, including a third of those at Kew gardens. At Sevenoaks in Kent, six of the seven oaks that gave the town its name had been lost.

Hundreds of thousands of people were left without power, and some supplies would not be fully restored for more than two weeks.

At sea, many small boats had been wrecked, a cross-channel ferry had been driven ashore at Folkestone and a bulk carrier had capsized at Dover.

After watching the reports, we ventured outside to survey the damage to our little own world.

The black clouds had vanished and the roar of the wind had been replaced by an eerie stillness broken only by a robin singing in the distance.

Overnight, the golden leaves of autumn had been ripped from the trees and lay scattered across the lawn or piled in heaps against walls and fences.

Without them, the trees seemed naked, their bare branches exposed, pale wounds showing against the bark where boughs had been torn away.

Everywhere I looked, there was evidence of damage, but none of it was major. Branches lay strewn across the ground, fencing had been blown over and a few slates from the roof lay shattered on the path, but that was all. We had been lucky.

In the Animal Meadow, the roof that had narrowly missed decapitating Philippa lay forlornly on the grass. It was enormous. One corner was shattered where it had impacted the ground, and huge splinters stuck up like porcupine quills.

"Where did it come from?" I asked.

David pointed.

"That way. The only buildings up there are the riding stables."

"It looks too big to have come from a stable."

"It's from a double stable. Look, you can see where it joined the walls."

Bending down, I tried to lift the edge of the roof, but it was firmly embedded in the ground.

"Wow! That's seriously heavy. It's hard to imagine it flying all the way down the hill."

"Believe me, it did."

"I know. Look, it must have caught the fence as it came down."

David let out a disappointed gasp.

"I hadn't seen that. Bugger. The whole run is down. We'll have to do something about that before we can let the goats out."

"Do you think the stables know what happened?"

David looked at me in disbelief.

"Do you really think they won't have noticed their stable roof is missing?"

"I mean that it came down here? They may not know which direction it went."

"I suppose. Maybe I'd better go and have a word with them."

* * *

I was helping Dad clear a drain at the back of the house that had been blocked by leaves and falling debris when David returned. He didn't look happy.

"How are things at the stables?" Dad asked.

"Apart from the stable roof, there doesn't seem to be much damage."

"Were the horses OK?" I asked. "Were they in the stables when it happened?"

"I don't know."

"Didn't you ask?"

David glared at me.

"No. They weren't exactly pleased to see me, if you must know. As soon as I mentioned their roof had landed in our meadow and nearly killed my wife, they got all defensive."

I tried to imagine the conversation. David always enjoyed a bit of drama, and he rarely missed an opportunity to embellish a story. It was easy to see how his description might have sounded like an accusation.

"They seemed to think I wanted to sue them," David went on.

"That does seem to be the way around here," Dad laughed.

"I was going to ask if they needed any help but they just blanked me. They weren't exactly rude, but they said they were busy and if I wanted to speak to them, I should contact their solicitor."

"Seriously? They didn't even offer to come down and take the roof away?"

"No. His wife looked a bit embarrassed, but he just turned his back on me and walked off."

"What is wrong with people round here?" I muttered.

Dad shook his head and blew out his cheeks.

"Damned if I know, but let's not start another range war. We've got enough problems with neighbours as it is."

* * *

I had expected a quick response from Mr Barbary but it was over a week before he answered my letter and his reply said little except that he would await further instructions.

I showed the letter to Mum, but she only shook her head and tutted.

I knew if I raised the subject again with Bob or David it would cause more arguments, so I decided to take the coward's way out and say nothing for the time being.

Dad was the only one to question me.

"I really wouldn't worry about it," he said cheerfully when I showed him the solicitor's letter. "It will all sort itself out somehow. The water board won't want to go to court either. These cases always cost a fortune and they won't want to risk having to pay the expenses."

"I hope you're right."

"Of course, I am," Dad said. "Just put it out of your mind for now. We've got far more important things to worry about."

Chapter 3

Before the storm we had intended to delay work on the buildings at the back of Silverlands, but now, we changed our priorities.

"The wind came from behind us and the hills gave us a bit of protection," Dad pointed out, "but if we get another night like that, we could lose all the flat roofs in one go."

A huge dormitory block ran along the back of the original house and its roof was little better than the one on Devon Mysteries. If the roof was damaged and water seeped into the fabric of the building, the whole block could become unsalvageable.

Doing the renovations now made sense, but it would be expensive and we would have to cut back our plans to improve the exhibitions.

David was reluctant to accept any delay.

"We can't!" he insisted. "There are still things we didn't finish before we opened. We can't leave them for another year."

I tried to sound reassuring.

"It won't stop everything. We can still go ahead with the painting in the Enchanted Forest and put in the extra displays in Down in Devon. It's just the bigger things that will have to wait, like the stables and the Pirate Trail."

Mum didn't like the situation any more than the rest of us and reacted in her usual way by calling the family together to discuss the situation. When we were all settled, she asked if any of us had any suggestions.

"There has to be something we can do," she said. "We've come this far. If we have the roofs repaired, we'll have lots of unused buildings. There must be some way of capitalising on them. I've read in the papers about people setting up all sorts of money-making schemes. There must be something we can do."

She was right. It was 1987, the era of the Yuppies. Young, Upwardly mobile People who were only interested in money. Thatcher's children were widely condemned for their selfishness, but they had a Puritanical work ethic that drove the economy. Magazines ran as many features on 'how-to-run-a-business-from-your-spare-bedroom' as they did on fashion or cooking.

If other people were building fortunes out of nothing surely, we could raise the money we needed?

"You're right. We have to use all our assets," David said seriously. "Particularly the swimming pool and the sports hall. There must be something we could do with them straight away."

Ironically, the sports hall was the only building from the last phase of the school development that was in good condition.

Instead of having a flat roof, the building was similar to an industrial unit with a huge, steel-framed roof and concrete block walls. It was enormous and the dark red floor was marked out with two long rows of tennis courts.

It was an impressive building, but I couldn't imagine anything that we could do with it that would give us an immediate income.

"I've got an idea..." Phil began hesitantly. "David mentioned the swimming pool. Couldn't we open it up to locals? I'm sure lots of people would love to use it. There's not much for teenagers and families around here in the winter."

There was an awkward pause.

"It's a nice idea," Dad agreed, "but the pool has a crack in it."

"Oh, I didn't know that." Phil sounded deflated.

"I wasn't suggesting we open it as a swimming pool," David said. "Even if it didn't have a crack, it would cost a fortune to heat, and we'd have to pay for lifeguards..."

"OK, I get it," Phil said quickly.

"... and local people wouldn't want to pay much so we couldn't..." David continued but Mum cut across him.

"Any other ideas?"

"Actually, I don't think it's such a silly suggestion," I said. "Maybe we can't use it as a swimming pool but Phil's right, there's hardly anything for youngsters to do around here. I remember Abbie got excited when she was talking about foam parties. Don't you think they might be worth a go?"

The others looked at me blankly.

"We could fill the pool with foam and put in a lighting system and some big speakers. It wouldn't cost much. I'm sure no one would notice there was a little crack in the bottom."

David snorted loudly.

"Have any of you actually looked at it?" he demanded. "It's not just a little crack. It's massive. It's big enough to put your hand into and it goes from one end of the building to the other."

Dad nodded.

"I don't think they built the foundations properly. I'm not even sure the building's safe. We certainly couldn't use it until we'd checked it was structurally sound."

"Then we can forget about the swimming pool and foam parties," Mum said flatly. "There has to be something else."

"OK," I conceded. "No foam parties for now, but let's leave them on the Maybe-One-Day list."

I smiled hopefully, but Mum only raised an eyebrow.

"Any other ideas?"

There was a lengthy silence, and rain began pattering against the window.

"We don't seem to be making much progress," David said at last. "Why don't we meet again on Friday and let's try to come up with some sensible ideas by then?"

* * *

On Friday we gathered in Mum and Dad's flat, which was at the far end of the main building and had a window overlooking the front lawn. It had once been the top floor of the carriage house and the rooms had high ceilings with ornate metal supports that echoed the shape of the gabled roofs.

Despite the high ceilings, the rooms were small enough to keep warm with a single gas fire and we huddled together with our mugs of tea. Since Silverlands had closed to the public, we had turned off the central heating system and now the bulk of the house felt as cold as a fridge.

Claire and Michael were sitting on toddler-sized chairs colouring in comic books.

"The children are being very good today," Mum commented. "Maybe we'd better get on while the peace lasts."

She handed Claire and Michael a biscuit each and passed the packet around the rest of us.

"Who wants to start?" she asked.

The silence was broken only by the sound of munching.

"Surely someone has come up with a something?"

Bob was the only one to speak.

"Actually, I have got a plan. How about converting the sports hall into a motor museum?"

The munching stopped as everyone looked at him.

"How?"

"What about cars?"

"Wouldn't that cost a fortune?"

Bob grinned.

"Slow down. Give me a chance to explain. It won't cost anything, in fact, it will give us a healthy income. I've been working on this for a while, but I didn't want to say anything before…"

"Why not?" I demanded.

"Let me finish, will you? I've been putting out feelers for months, trying to find someone who needed a large exhibition space, and I've made contact with a guy called Eric Davies. He's a farmer, and he renovates vintage cars. He's got dozens of them crammed in a row of old barns. It's been his passion all his life but now he's getting close to retiring he wants to put them on display to the public."

"That's perfect!" David couldn't control himself. "When does he want to move in?"

"Hang on, it's not that simple. He's a farmer, like I said, and most of the cars are half buried under piles of old machinery and garbage. It will take a while for him to get everything sorted, but he wants to do things properly. He plans to fit out the hall with partitions and information boards and have demonstrations. He's very enthusiastic, and he seems to have plenty of money to spend."

"That's incredible!" David was bouncing. "It's exactly what we need. A second attraction on the same site. We can both work together and he'll be paying us rent!"

He stopped abruptly.

"He is going to pay us rent, isn't he?"

"Better than that. He wants to take a three-year lease, and he's offered very generous terms."

"I don't believe it!"

I was as happy as David. Only Mum wasn't smiling.

"But who is this man?" she asked. "Why didn't you tell us what you were planning?"

"I didn't want to get everyone's hopes up," Bob said. "It all seemed too good to be true at first but I've checked him out and he's genuine. I thought you'd be pleased."

"We are," Dad assured him. "It's fantastic news. Well done."

"Yes, it sounds promising," Mum admitted, "but let's wait and see how it works out."

* * *

"Are you worried about the motor museum?" I asked Mum later. "You didn't seem very excited about the idea."

She looked at me in surprise.

"I'm not worried. It just came as a bit of a shock. I thought we were going to talk about ideas, not have a fully formed plan dropped on us."

"But it is good news, isn't it?"

"Yes, it's wonderful. It's exactly what we need. I can't believe Bob managed to arrange it all so suddenly."

"Then, you're impressed?"

"Yes, I suppose I am. In fact, it's more than that. I'm really rather relieved. I'd been worrying a lot about how we were going to get through the next few months."

"I'm glad you're relieved. To be honest, I've been worrying too."

I gave her a hug, and she smiled up at me. She seemed to grow shorter by the day.

"So, can I tell Bob you're impressed?"

Her face straightened at once.

"Is that really necessary?"

* * *

Once the lease for the sports hall was signed, we contacted Torrington bank, and they agreed to increase our loan by enough to carry us through the winter. They insisted that we had another surveyor's report done on the entire site and we were pleasantly surprised to discover the property was now valued at nearly three times what we had paid for it.

"That's ridiculous," David said when I told him. "I know we've done a lot of work but the place hasn't changed that much."

"It's crazy, isn't it? But it's nice to feel rich."

"I guess so," he agreed, "but I won't feel rich until I can afford a car that doesn't break down all the time."

I laughed.

"Don't get your hopes up. We're only rich on paper, remember!"

We were all delighted when Steve and his team finished laying the new roof on the Devon Mysteries and started work on the other buildings.

The dormitory block disappeared under a framework of scaffolding and skips quickly filled with debris as the builders tore off the old roofs and began work.

"I know we hadn't planned to get all this done so quickly but it's good to know we won't have to worry about any more storms," I said to Dad one morning.

I was helping him do some maintenance work on the circus and we were both laying on the floor underneath it checking the belt tensioners.

"I suppose so," he agreed, "but I wish we hadn't had to borrow any more money. It doesn't sit well with me."

"Why not? It's only to cover us until we start getting payments from the Motor Museum."

"I know. I suppose it's just the way I was brought up. Your grandfather didn't believe in borrowing. He always taught me that if you wanted something, you should work hard and save up until you had enough to buy it."

"But that's a bit old-fashioned, isn't it? We'd never have been able to buy this place if we'd had to wait and save all the money ourselves."

"That's true, but it's hard to break old habits. It doesn't feel right to be too indebted."

He seemed unusually serious, so I changed the subject.

"Do you have any idea what Mum wants for Christmas?" I asked.

* * *

Early in our relationship it became clear that Bob and I have very different approaches to Christmas shopping. Bob likes to go out with nothing more than a mental note of the people he needs to buy for. Then he goes into a shop, buys a collection of things that he would like to be given himself, and comes home an hour later blissfully happy that his task is complete.

I prefer to scour every shop in the vicinity, make endless lists of possible presents, and spend days comparing costs, aesthetics and novelty value before actually buying anything. Then, when I finally make up my mind, I discover that my perfect choices have all sold out and I have to begin all over again.

We soon realised that joint shopping trips were doomed to end in disaster and Bob made the wise decision to stay at home and entertain Claire while

I undertook the task single-handed.

As usual, I waited until the shops were about to close on Christmas Eve before deciding on my final purchases and made it home with bulging carrier bags to find that Bob had a delicious meal waiting for me.

I smiled happily at my good fortune. Claire was bathed and ready for bed and I knew I was lucky to have such a thoughtful husband. The shopping trip had left me exhausted, but now I could look forward to a relaxed evening and a good night's sleep before all the excitement of Christmas Day.

When we finished our meal, I wiped Claire's face and hands.

"Time for bed now, Honey. Say goodnight to Daddy."

But Bob shook his head.

"You're forgetting something. We have a special job to do tonight."

"Of course! We have to hang up a stocking, don't we? You go with Daddy and clean your teeth and I'll see what I can find."

Giggling happily, Claire grabbed Bob's hand and dragged him towards the door.

By the time I had pulled a giant striped stocking from the bottom of my wardrobe, Claire was running in excited circles around her bedroom.

"Remember, Santa can't leave any presents unless you're a good girl," Bob reminded her.

"And you have to go to sleep," I added.

Claire raced past me and bounced on the bed.

"Santy Claws! Santy Claws!" she giggled as her curly hair bounced around her face. "Presents! Me want presents!"

I tried to sound kind but firm.

"Remember, Claire, Santa can't leave any presents unless you're asleep."

It made no difference. Weeks of anticipation fuelled her excitement, and she bounced higher and higher.

"Santy Claws! Santy Claws!"

"I think I'll leave you to it," Bob said as he escaped out of the door, "by the look of those carrier bags you'll need me to start on the wrapping."

I groaned inwardly.

One of my failings is forgetting that buying presents is not enough. They need to be wrapped as well.

"But you can't wrap them until I've told you who they're for," I protested, "and you can't go rummaging through the bags because there are things in there I don't want you to see."

"OK. I'll wait for you but try not to be too long."

I did try. I spoke seriously. I put on my strict expression. I even frowned, but calming an over-excited three-year-old is not an easy matter.

Claire ran and jumped and giggled until, at last, she collapsed in a heap on her pillow.

I straightened her out and smoothed the duvet over her.

"Night-night, sweetie," I whispered.

In the lounge, Bob was relaxing in front of the TV with a large brandy.

"What are you watching?" I asked as I sorted the presents into piles.

"It's a Christmas ghost story. I thought it might be good for a laugh."

"Really? You don't fancy something funny?"

"It is funny. You can't take this stuff seriously. I thought you liked ghost stories?"

He was right. In the past, I had always enjoyed spooky films and stories about the paranormal. I had grown up watching Hammer Horror movies, but since moving to Silverlands my tastes had changed.

I knew Bob wouldn't understand, but I couldn't escape the feeling that Fred might be somewhere nearby. If anyone outside the family had asked me, I would have said that I didn't believe in ghosts. The truth was that I still hadn't made sense of my experiences. Sometimes, when I was alone in a room, I had a powerful feeling of being watched. It was such a subjective thing that I had never told anyone. I was sure they would think I was being hysterical and, in any case, I didn't know how to explain it.

It wasn't a frightening feeling. Sometimes it even felt comforting. It was like having Dino asleep in the room with me, but it wasn't something I wanted to explain.

Now I felt uneasy. Would Fred appreciate us watching a ghost story? Would he be offended?

Suddenly, I recognised the absurdity of my thoughts. Was I really letting a superstitious belief in ghosts dictate my choice of television programs?

I was being ridiculous.

I poured myself a drink and fetched some more wrapping paper.

"Yes, I'd love to watch a ghost story. In fact, there's a late-night horror film on ITV, why don't we watch that afterwards?"

It was well after midnight before the last presents were wrapped and Bob and I stumbled happily to bed.

A few hours later, we were woken by a crash that reverberated through the house. My eyes flew open and, as I struggled to sit up, a black shape emerged from the darkness and rushed towards me.

Dino barked from the corner of the room, and Bob scrambled to reach the bedside lamp. He flicked the switch, and the room filled with light just as the shape reached me.

"Presents!"

I dropped back against the pillow as Claire hurled a bulging stocking on top of me.

"Yes, Santa brought you presents. Isn't that wonderful?" Bob laughed as he looked at the clock. "Imagine that. Presents at half-past three in the morning."

I was still trying to focus my eyes.

"Tell you what, Claire, how about you open your presents now, then go back to bed?"

"Forget it, darling," Bob laughed, "there's no way she's going back to sleep."

I nodded and yawned.

"Never mind. At least we can make an early start on the vegetables. Happy Christmas!"

* * *

The rest of the day was wonderful. We had decorated the tearoom with an enormous Christmas tree and tucked sprigs of holly behind all the pictures on the walls.

Carols played, the central heating had been turned on for the day, and the smell of roast turkey and Christmas pudding filled the air.

Claire and Michael ran around showing us their new toys and munching their way through a never-ending supply of sweets.

Once all the vegetables had been prepared, the turkey had been basted, and the pudding was steaming, we sat down by the tree to hand out the pile of presents waiting beneath it.

"More presents!" Claire announced.

"Here, you can help me give them out," Mum said. "And you, Michael. No, that's not for you. Let me read the labels and I'll tell you who they're for."

The children worked hard distributing the presents one by one then, when everyone was ready, Bob counted down to zero and the unwrapping began.

Paper flew everywhere. Dino and Ossie joined in, joyously tearing at the empty wrapping paper, and the air was filled with laughter and the happy cries of the children.

When everyone had finished, Bob announced the meal was ready to serve. While Mum, Dad and David hurried to the kitchen to help carry the food through, Phil and I grabbed the piles of paper scattered around the floor and stuffed them into a carrier bag.

Realising I was running low on wet-wipes, I decided to run up to the flat for a new packet. I took the bag of paper and left it at the bottom of the stairs, ready to go out to the dustbin. Then I raced up, grabbed the wet wipes and ran down again.

As I reached the bottom step, my heart missed a beat. The carrier bag was torn to shreds and tiny pieces of wrapping paper were scattered from one end of the hall to the other

The paper had been in large clumps when I put it into the bag, but now it was more like confetti. It was as if it had been through a mincer.

Was this someone's idea of a joke? I took a deep breath and tried to calm myself. The others were all busy, and I had only been gone for a few moments. It could only have been Fred.

I could hear laughter coming from the tearoom. Should I say something? If I mentioned Fred now, would Bob get annoyed?

"Diana! Where are you? It's on the table!"

I left the devastation and hurried back to join the others.

I decided to say nothing. After all, no harm had been done. Someone else would spot the mess soon enough and no one would be upset if they thought the dogs had torn up a bag of old wrapping paper.

* * *

Christmas was lovely and when it was over, it was hard to turn off the central heating and get back to work.

I was delighted that the extra money from the bank meant we could go ahead with the donkey stable and the Pirate Trail.

The stable had been ordered from the same company that made the other buildings in the Animal Meadow, and we had found a wonderful playground engineer who was designing the various elements for the Pirate Trail. It was due to be installed in late March so we needed to have the whole area prepared before then.

Dad and David were busy working on the interior of the First World War exhibition which had been rushed before our opening last year and it was already looking much more atmospheric.

My personal ambition was to landscape the concrete at the back of the house.

Silverlands was built on the side of a hill and although the original house stood on a level area with a huge flat lawn in front of it, the land behind it rose steeply.

The previous owners had added a dormitory block when they extended the school in the 1960s and had built it on a series of terraces tucked away behind the main building.

Unfortunately, at the same time, they had concreted over a large section that ran from the dormitories to what was now our craft workshops.

The concrete had weathered badly, leaving a cracked, gravelly surface, and the whole area was an eyesore.

The builders called it the bunkers, and the name suited.

I longed to replace the bleak, ugly concrete with tiers of flowerbeds and picnic tables, but I knew I would have to settle for something less ambitious. I had asked Steve if it would be possible to remove some concrete and expose the soil below, but he warned me against the idea.

He thought the concrete had been intended to stop the soil moving down the hill towards the back of the house and was worried that removing it might result in a landslip.

Reluctantly, I took his advice but as I looked at the grim, grey expanse I vowed that I would find a way to make it attractive one day.

For the moment, I had managed to put aside a small budget for plants and materials, but I couldn't see how it would be enough to disguise such a huge area.

* * *

By the beginning of February, the work on the roofs was complete. It was wonderful to know all our buildings were weatherproof, but some of them were still in a very poor condition.

The units at either end of the craft block had been left with water running through them for so long the floors had disintegrated and were not safe to walk on. Parts of the dormitory block were no better.

"It's probably a good idea to do the renovation in stages," Steve said encouragingly. "The walls and floors are completely sodden at the moment. It will make things much easier if they have a chance to dry out for a few months before we move on to the next stage."

"I suppose so," I agreed, but I hated the delay and longed to have all the units finished and open.

Some days, it felt as though we were making no progress at all, but when I got frustrated, I thought back on how far we had come already. At this time last year, we had not even known if we would be able to open Silverlands on time. It was hard to believe how much had changed.

I remembered how exhausted I had felt working long into the night and the frustration of never being able to deal with one crisis before another appeared. I recalled how upset I had been when I had forgotten Valentine's

Day. This year I vowed to do better.

On 14th February, I crept out of bed early and woke Claire. Together, we tiptoed down to the kitchen and prepared a lavish breakfast for Bob.

I filled two plates with bacon, eggs, sausages, mushrooms, beans, tomatoes and onion rings and was loading everything onto a tray when the kitchen door opened and Bob appeared with a worried look on his face.

"Are you all right?" he asked.

"Daddy! Me helping Mummy!"

"So, I see. Is something wrong?"

I burst out laughing.

"Everything's fine. Is it really that unusual for me to get you breakfast?"

He looked at me for a moment, then started laughing too.

"Let's just say, I don't remember it ever happening before."

"Don't be mean! I wanted to surprise you."

"Well, you certainly did that. Here, let me take the tray."

We made our way back up to the flat, and I unloaded everything on to the table by the window. It was a crisp winter morning and a light frost shimmered on the lawn outside.

"There." I lay a single rose beside Bob's plate with a dramatic flourish. "Happy Valentine's Day!"

"Thank you," he smiled and kissed me. "This year I'm the one who hasn't got a card for you."

"That's all right," I said smugly. "I don't need a card to know you love me."

I cut Claire's breakfast into pieces while Bob poured the tea.

"Actually, I have got you something. It's a surprise. It's not very romantic, but I hope you'll like it."

"That's sweet of you! What is it?"

"A team."

I waited for him to explain, but he just watched me with an amused expression.

"What sort of team?"

"It's a team to help you with all the things you need to finish."

I had no idea what he was talking about.

"Let's enjoy breakfast first then I'll explain about it to everyone."

* * *

By the time I had got the others together I was filled with curiosity and a little apprehension.

"What's this all about?" Mum asked.

"I'm not sure. Bob's got something he wants to tell us."

"But what is it?"

"I told you, I don't know."

We had gathered in Mum and Dad's flat again and were waiting for Bob to come up from the office. I wished he would hurry up and explain what was going on. I didn't know why, but I felt an uncomfortable tension in my stomach.

"Morning all," Bob grinned as he burst through the door. "Has Diana explained what this is all about?"

"No," Mum said.

"Then I'll start at the beginning. I had a phone call yesterday from a man called Ian Baker. He runs a business providing government training schemes."

"Does he have courses on how to start a tourist attraction without any money?" David asked.

"No, nothing like that," Bob laughed. "He's setting up a training scheme. It's sponsored by the government and it's intended to help people who don't have any qualifications develop skills that will help them get jobs."

"But what's that got to do with us?" Mum asked.

"I was coming to that. The subjects he's going to teach are basic building skills and gardening. He's looking for somewhere that he can give his students some hands-on experience and was asking if we might have any projects, like pruning trees or laying paths, that they could do for us."

"I can't see how that would work," Mum interrupted. "We can hardly afford to pay our own builders at the moment let alone take on students."

"But that's the whole point. We won't have to pay them. It's an amazing opportunity. All Ian wants is somewhere to store equipment and a room he can use as a classroom. Then he can give the students practical experience working in the grounds. It's perfect, isn't it? A win-win situation."

It was obvious from Bob's expression that he was expecting me to be delighted by the idea but, instead, my stomach tightened into knots.

"I'm not sure. Maybe we need to think about it..." I began, but David had no hesitation.

"It's brilliant!" he cried. "You've been saying you need a gardener. Now you can have lots of them."

"But..."

"Could they prepare the paths for the Pirate Trail?" David asked.

"Yes, that's just the sort of thing," Bob nodded happily.

"And what about the concrete base for the donkey stable?" Phil suggested.

"Good thinking, that would be perfect for them."

"But who would be responsible?" Dad interrupted. "If they're students, they'd need a lot of supervision."

"Don't worry, they only work in small groups and they'll always have a tutor with them. Ian explained everything. He got so excited on the phone that he called in on his way home. He thinks there's huge potential to set up a scheme here, and he left me some of his brochures. Look."

Bob handed around leaflets with photos of smiling young men wearing safety helmets and hi-viz waistcoats.

"Because it's part of a government scheme, they all have to be fully insured and everything's strictly monitored."

"Why didn't you tell us yesterday when he was here?" I asked.

Bob waved a leaflet dismissively.

"Everyone was busy. Ian only had a few minutes so there didn't seem any point in disturbing you."

I caught Mum's eye and I could tell she was as unhappy as me.

"When would they want to start?" she asked.

"Officially, the next course doesn't begin until next month but I said they can move in on Monday to get everything sorted out."

"What!"

Mum was rarely lost for words, but now she stared at Bob in silent outrage.

"Move in where?" I asked.

"They're going to use the ground floor of the dormitory block. It's mainly to store stuff."

"We can't have people in there. The building's not safe," Dad said firmly.

"The upstairs may not be safe, but there's nothing wrong with the ground floor," Bob persisted.

"But we don't know anything about these people," I burst out.

Bob looked at me in surprise.

"I thought you'd be pleased. This is what you wanted, isn't it? Free labour to finish the things you want to get done?"

"But you can't just make a decision like this on your own! It should have been discussed with everyone first!" Mum exploded.

Everyone fell silent, and Bob drew himself up to his full height.

"Clearly, I've made a mistake. You don't think we need any help. I'll phone Ian now and tell him the whole thing's off."

"Wait a second," David jumped in. "Let's not be hasty. I think it's a brilliant idea."

"But we should have discussed it!" Mum shouted.

"Discuss it as much as you like," Bob said coldly. "You know my opinion. When you make a decision, I'll be downstairs in the office."

He stalked out of the room and there was silence as the rest of us tried to make sense of what had happened.

"What do we do now?" Phil asked at last.

"I think we should give it a go," David said stubbornly. "What have we got to lose?"

I sighed.

"It's true that I was hoping to get a gardener, but I wanted to choose someone I could get on with, someone that understood what I wanted do."

The thought of unknown tutors and a class of students hacking down the bushes or re-landscaping the flowerbeds while I was busy in the tearooms filled me with dread.

I looked to Dad for support.

"If the building's not safe, it wouldn't be possible anyway, would it?"

"Not without a little work," Dad agreed. "It wouldn't take much though. We'd have to block off the staircase, but Bob's right, there's not much wrong with the ground floor if they don't mind it being a bit scruffy."

"So that's not a problem," David said triumphantly. "I can't see why you're all being so negative."

"I'm not being negative!" I snapped.

"How do you feel about it?" Dad asked Mum. "Do you have any real objections?"

She hesitated before answering.

"It's not the scheme I object to. It's the way Bob went ahead without consulting us."

"I don't think he meant to upset you," Dad said. "Remember, he's spent years working as an executive in a big company and making whatever decisions he thought were right. It can't be easy for him adjusting to being part of a family business."

Mum took off her glasses and wiped them with a tissue.

"You're probably right. It's difficult for all of us sometimes, but the question is, what are we going to tell him?"

* * *

Bob was tapping away at the computer in the office. He glanced at me as I came in but went on typing. I sat down beside him and waited. Eventually, he stopped and turned to face me.

"Well," he demanded, "do I have my instructions?"

"What's that supposed to mean?"

"Isn't it obvious? I'm not allowed to make any decisions. I'm just expected to follow orders and do what I'm told."

"That's not true! You know it isn't."

"Isn't it? It wouldn't matter what I come up with. Your mother always finds fault with it, doesn't she?"

"That's not fair. You didn't give anyone a chance to think."

"What is there to think about? It's an amazing offer. Free labour, a team of people waiting to do whatever you ask of them. Anyone with a brain would have jumped at the idea, but it's too late now."

"What do you mean? Have you spoken to Ian?"

He waved a hand at the computer screen.

"I'm emailing him."

"Don't send it. We want to go ahead."

He looked at me, and his eyes were dark with hurt pride.

"I told you. It's too late. I can't work in this atmosphere."

"What do you mean?"

"Your mother hates me. She'll never accept me and I'm not going to spend my life asking her permission for everything I do."

"She doesn't hate you. She's can be unreasonable at times, but she's like that with everyone."

"Really? Because it feels very personal to me."

"I'm, sorry. It's just that you two are so different."

Bob snorted.

"You can say that again. She's critical and disapproving and completely impossible. We have absolutely nothing in common."

"Yes, you do."

He frowned, and I took the opportunity to stretch across and kiss the tip of his nose.

"Me. That's what you have in common. You both love me."

* * *

"So, is he going ahead with the scheme?" Mum asked.

"Yes, but that isn't really the problem."

"Then what is?"

"He thinks you hate him."

Mum looked genuinely shocked.

"Whatever gave him that idea? I've never been unpleasant to him."

I chose my words with care.

"You can be a bit fierce sometimes."

"Me? Certainly not. Even if I don't approve of something, I never let it show."

I couldn't stop myself.

"That's rubbish! You're the most transparent person on the planet! If you don't like something it's written all over your face."

To my surprise, her eyes welled with tears.

"How can you say such a thing? I would never upset anyone."

"But you do. I know you don't mean to, but you do. Couldn't you try being more open? Tell people how you feel about things?"

"What good would that do? It would only end in an argument and I couldn't cope with it."

For the first time, it occurred to me that Mum had grown up in a family where arguments were terrifying. My grandmother had been violent and, as a result, Mum had spent her life trying to avoid confrontation.

"This isn't about arguing," I said. "It's about talking."

"But Bob's always so certain about everything. He thinks he knows what I'm going to say before I open my mouth so he doesn't listen."

"That's not true!"

"Isn't it?"

She looked tired and hurt, and I wanted her to be happy again.

"To be honest, Mum, you can both be unreasonable at times."

She sniffed and pulled out a tissue.

"I'm sorry, dear."

When she finished blowing her nose, I gave her a hug.

"You'll always be my Mum and I'll always love you but life would be so much easier if you and Bob could get along."

She hugged me back.

"I know dear. I'll do my best."

* * *

Within a week Ian had set up his base in the dormitory block. He was younger than I had expected, with a round baby face and endless energy.

As mobile phones were still in their infancy, he carried a folder the size of a paperback book containing pages divided into sections for day-to-day activities, accounts, contact details and notes. It was called a Filofax.

Bob fell in love the moment he saw it.

"It's ingenious!" he enthused. "Everything you need is in one place. It's like being able to carry your office around with you."

"Why would you want to do that?" I asked. "Surely the whole point of having an office is that you can leave all the boring stuff there and go out and do other things?"

Bob tutted at me.

"You don't understand. It's efficient. Filofaxes are the future and I'm going to get one."

We were watching the team arrive from the window of our flat.

"When are they going to start work?" I asked, trying to change the subject.

"Tomorrow. In fact, Ian was hoping you could spare some time this afternoon to talk through what you want them to start on."

"Great," I tried to sound enthusiastic. "I've made a list. I'll go and talk to him now."

The inside of the dormitory was almost unrecognisable. The mouldy walls and ceilings had been cleaned and painted with magnolia emulsion and the windows had been transformed by the addition of slatted blinds. Even the missing fluorescent tubes had been replaced.

The floor was still mottled and discoloured but it had been swept and was covered with a selection of chairs, two tables, a cupboard and a large whiteboard ready for lessons to begin.

By the door, a row of hooks waited for coats and a set of pigeonholes was ready to hold boots or shoes.

"What do you think?" Ian asked as I looked around.

"I think you've done a great job," I said honestly. "How many students are you expecting?"

"Thirty-two in total," he replied, "but we prefer to call them clients."

"Really? OK, I'll remember that."

"I've heard there's an old tennis court at the top of the hill. Is that right?"

"Yes, but it's ancient. The surface is full of potholes and it's half covered in blackberries."

"I was wondering if we could use one end of it? It sounds like a perfect place to teach bricklaying. Would that be possible?"

"I don't see why not? Let's go and have a look."

Leaden clouds scudded across the sky as we walked up the hill and I pulled the collar of my coat tightly around my neck.

On our right, the goats trotted across the meadow to see us, hoping we had some food for them.

"Nothing for you today, boys," I said as I patted George on the nose.

He shook his ears, bleated disapprovingly and wandered away.

It had rained overnight and rivulets of water were running down the road, gathering in cracks in the rough surface and carrying gravel as they went.

At the top of the hill, the land flattened out and the bulky shape of the sports hall sat on our left. To the right was the old tennis court, and immediately ahead of us a wooden gate across the road marked the end of our land.

It had been months since I climbed to the top of the hill and the blackberries had grown even larger than I remembered.

"You'll have to clear it back a bit but there's plenty of space here if it's suitable," I said.

"It's perfect."

Ian turned around and looked back at the view.

"Look at that. It's fantastic. On a clear day, I'll bet you can see right across to the coast."

"Maybe. I've never had time to look."

The lush Devon countryside stretched away in front of us, mile after mile of rolling hills, rich farmland, ancient woods and scattered villages. Even in the grey light of a February morning, it was undeniably beautiful.

"We won't be in anyone's way if we do some practical work up here then?"

"No, not at all." I tore myself away from the view. "Make yourselves at home."

"Thank you. We'll be covering the basics first, of course, health and safety and all that. Then I want to get everyone straight into some practical work."

A creak sounded behind me, and I swung around to see Duncan Matthews opening the gate.

I was about to shout across to tell him to keep off our land when I realised that he was already on our land and was letting himself out.

"Bastard," I muttered under my breath.

"Someone you know?"

"A neighbour. He owns the caravan site next to us."

I marched over to the gate and saw the padlock was missing. I glared at Matthew's back as he strode towards the stables.

"This gate has to be kept locked," I told Ian. "I'll bring up another padlock but if you see that it's missing, please let me know."

"No problem. I take it your neighbour's not welcome?"

"Excuse my French, but he's an asshole. If you see him down here again, please let us know straight away."

I gave Ian a brief outline of the problems Matthews had caused us as we walked back down the hill.

"I can see why you don't want him around," he said.

Phil was cleaning the rabbit hutches as we drew level with the entrance to the Animal Meadow.

"Did you see Duncan Matthews?" she called. Her voice was unsteady and I could see from her expression that she was upset.

"Yes. Was he down here?"

"He was really rude. I only asked him what he was doing, and he started shouting at me. He called me a... well, I'm not going to repeat it."

"What did he want?"

"I think he was just trying to pick a fight. He said he's found there's a public right of way across our land and there's nothing we can do to stop him using it."

"Are you all right?"

Phil's lip was quivering, but she nodded.

"Don't let him get to you," I said. "You're right, he's looking for trouble. He cut the padlock off the gate. If you see him again, don't say anything to him just come and tell the rest of us."

* * *

The following day David and I were working on the murals in the Enchanted Forest when a group of men walked past the window.

"They must be the first of Ian's students," I said, but David shook his head.

"No, they must be the teachers."

"I don't think so. They're too scruffy to be teachers."

"And they're too old to be students."

Another group wandered past.

"They must be students. There's too many of them to be teachers."

David pointed with his paintbrush.

"Look at that one. He must be nearly sixty, and the one behind him's built like a wrestler. This can't be right."

"Maybe I'll go and check with Bob," I said.

"I'm sure there's a simple explanation," Bob sighed, when I found him, "but I'll have a word with Ian if you really want me to."

He came back looking uneasy.

"What did he say?"

"It seems none of us read the details on the leaflets he gave us. We missed a few things."

"Like what?"

"Well, the scheme isn't aimed at students for a start. It's for people who've been out of work for a while."

"You mean unemployed?"

"Yes, that sort of thing."

"That would explain why they're older than we expected. Perhaps you'd better explain it to the others when we meet up. Just so that everyone knows what's going on."

Back in the Enchanted Forest, I explained what Bob had said to David. He didn't seem pleased with the news.

"I don't have anything against them being unemployed," he said. "If they're here, that must mean they want to work but I am worried about Phil. She's never been very good at standing up for herself. It was one thing telling a group of students what to do, but these guys are a different thing altogether."

I understood his concern.

"Maybe you'd better stay with her for a while," I suggested. "Just until we see how things work out."

* * *

"How did things go today?" I asked David later as we passed in a corridor.

He stopped, and his expression was gloomy.

"Not great, if I'm honest. Most of the things Phil needs help with aren't allowed."

"What d'you mean?"

"It turns out the team can only do practical work that relates to their training. They can't touch anything that's classed as maintenance. It means they're allowed to build something, but they can't clean it out once it's in use."

"What about the grounds? Can they do any gardening?"

"It all rather complicated and I don't think Ian knows the rules himself yet. Every time I asked him a question, he had to look it up. I think they'll be able to do some things like planting trees but not cutting the grass or weeding."

"That's not much use," I grumbled. "We've got plenty of trees already. What does Phil think about it?"

"She just went quiet. Ian agreed a few of the guys could use the rocks from the pile at the top of the field to make a rockery. You remember the old guy with the bald head?"

"Yes."

"He's called Arnold and Ian put him in charge. He seems quite sensible, but some of the others are pretty rough and I'm not sure how Phil's going to get on with them."

The next morning, I was in the office when David burst in.

"You're not going to believe this!" he shrieked. "They're not unemployed at all! They've been banged up!"

I didn't understand.

"Didn't you hear what I said? The guys in Ian's team are straight out of prison."

The penny dropped.

"Oh, my God! I don't believe it!"

"They've got to go!" David yelled. "We can't have a lot of villains roaming around in a family attraction."

"Slow down, let's not over-react." My heart was racing. "How do you know?"

"From the greengrocer. He told me all about it. A few of the team called into the pub in Chudleigh on their way home last night and the locals recognised Arnold."

"So?"

"They recognised him because he used to live around here. He was in all the papers when he strangled his wife."

When we confronted him, Ian admitted the rumour about Arnold was true.

"But it wasn't murder. It was only manslaughter," he explained.

"So? His poor wife is just as dead," I protested.

"I don't think you understand..."

"No! You don't understand!" Bob exploded. "This is a family attraction. You'll have to leave. At once."

"Immediately," David added for good measure. "Today. Now..."

"Wait," Ian interrupted. "Please, let me explain. I'm not allowed to share confidential information, but Arnold's case was all over the press. You've met him. He's a gentle soul."

"He killed his wife!" I yelled.

Ian held up his hands.

"It's not that simple. He claimed it was self-defence, and even his wife's family supported him."

He looked at each of us.

"Domestic abuse can affect men too, you know. He was the quiet one that got hurt for years. He even called the police when he ended up in hospital, but they didn't take him seriously. Then, one night, his wife tried to drown their son and Arnold lost it."

Ian hesitated before going on.

"The little lad was six years old. Arnold snapped, but he's not a violent man. He's served his time, and he's not a danger to anyone. If people had listened to him when he asked for help, perhaps he wouldn't have ended up doing what he did."

We were silent.

"What about the rest of them?" Bob asked at last.

"There are a few others who have been in prison," Ian admitted, "but not for anything violent and they're certainly not a risk to anyone. They've admitted their mistakes and all they want is a chance to rebuild their lives."

"Well, that's reassuring," David muttered.

"I can't blame you for being concerned," Ian said earnestly, "but there is a huge need for courses like ours. It's so difficult for people to find a second chance. Please don't back out now."

Bob looked at me.

"We're going to have to think about it," he said.

"Do you still want to make them leave?" David asked Bob as we walked across to the Animal Meadow.

"Me? You were as keen to chuck them out as I was."

Phil was feeding the goats.

"What did he say? Is it true?" she asked.

"Yes and no," David said evasively. "It's complicated."

"But what's going to happen?"

Bob explained what Ian had said, and Phil listened attentively.

"Does that mean we're going to let them stay?"

"Possibly."

"I don't feel as worried about them as I did," I admitted.

David nodded.

"I find it hard to think of Arnold as a murderer. It sounds like he had a pretty rough time."

"I wonder what happened to his son?" Phil asked.

"I vote we let them stay," David said.

"Me too," Bob agreed then turned to me with wide eyes. "Oh, my God. Who's going to tell your mother?"

* * *

"Mum, have you got a minute?"

She looked up from a list she was copying into a file.

"Yes, of course. What is it?"

"I just wanted a word. David found out something about the people on the course and I thought it was better if everyone knows."

I explained what we had discovered about Arnold, then gritted my teeth and waited for the explosion.

"Right, well thanks for letting me know," she said and picked up her pen.

I looked at her blankly.

"You're not upset?"

"Why should I be upset?"

"I thought you might object to having him working here."

Mum looked puzzled.

"You're talking about the one with the bald head, aren't you?"

"Yes, that's him."

"And he's not likely to kill anyone else?"

She couldn't have been calmer if she had been asking about the weather.

"I don't think so."

"Then why should I object?"

"It's just that... you get a bit funny about things sometimes..."

She looked straight at me.

"Have you forgotten Granny?"

"No, of course not."

"I tried to be a good daughter to her, you know I did, but I watched her wear my father down year after year. Domestic abuse affects men too. I didn't realise that's what it was at the time, but I do now. She bullied him, ridiculed him and reduced him to a nervous wreck."

She paused and twisted the pen with her fingers.

"He didn't deserve it. He always tried to please her but, if he'd lost his temper, just once, and done something stupid... I'd like to think someone would have given him a second chance too."

I waited, but she was silent.

"That's OK, then."

I didn't know what else to say.

* * *

David needed to go to Torquay to collect some special lighting for the First World War exhibition but he was worried about leaving Phil to deal with the Ian's team so he asked me to keep an eye on her.

"Yes, everything's fine," she assured me when I called in at the Animal Meadow. "I asked them to make a sign for the goat enclosure and they've done a fantastic job."

She was right. The words PLEASE TAKE CARE - OUR GOATS EAT ANYTHING! were beautifully painted on a wooden board.

"They're going to put it up on a post. I'm really pleased with it."

"Excellent. I'm popping over to see how they're getting on with the Pirate Trail. See you later."

I found Ian surrounded by eager workers levelling the pathway around the edge of the lawn. A light, drizzly rain was falling, but they were all wrapped in waterproof jackets and seemed to be enjoying themselves.

"That's going well," I smiled.

"Yes, they're doing a terrific job," Ian beamed back at me.

"Great. In that case, I'll leave you to get on."

* * *

A couple of hours later I walked back to the Animal Meadow.

"How's things?"

For a moment, I thought Phil was upset, but then I realised she was giggling.

"What is it?" I asked.

"You remember the sign?"

"Of course, what about it?"

Phil took a breath to steady herself.

"I'll show you."

I followed her around to the goat enclosure.

"There,"

She waved a hand at a sturdy wooden post standing in the middle of the grass.

"But why's the post in the field?" I asked.

Phil stifled another bout of giggles.

"I told the men to put it outside the gate but they must have thought it looked better there."

"Really?"

"Then a delivery arrived, and I had to put everything in the feed store. By the time I got back they'd put the sign up and gone."

"So, where's the sign now?"

Phil pointed to the corner of the field.

"The goats thought it was delicious!"

I looked across to where George and Ted were standing in a circle of splinters chewing the remains of the wooden board.

"Oh dear! What a pity they didn't read the sign," I gasped, and we both roared with laughter.

* * *

The bricklaying lessons on the tennis court gave me an idea. Each day, the team spent hours laying a long, low wall of bricks then took them down, washed the mortar off the bricks and stacked them up ready for the next day.

It seemed a sad waste of effort, so I asked Ian if he would like to move his lessons down to the bunkers.

"The walls you're building would be ideal for flower beds. It doesn't matter if they're not perfect. I'm happy to pay for the materials and it will save you having to clean the bricks off every day to reuse them."

"That's a great idea," Ian agreed, "and it will be encouraging for the guys to feel they're achieving something."

I ordered the bricks and marked out where I wanted the flower beds. I could already imagine them bright with flowers.

The preparation work on the Pirate Trail was nearly finished, so the following day Ian split his workforce into two groups and set one to work on the bunkers.

I explained exactly what I wanted done, then left them to it.

At the end of the day, I went to check on their progress and was delighted by what I saw. More than half of the flowerbeds were finished, but there was one mistake. The walls should have had drainage holes at the bottom to let rainwater run away.

Ian looked crestfallen when I pointed out the error.

"Don't worry, we'll fix it," he assured me.

The cement was still wet, so I assumed it would be easy to knock out a couple of spaces in the bottom row of bricks but when I passed the bunkers the following morning I was astounded to find the walls had disappeared and the bricks were standing in a neat pile.

"I'm sorry," I said when I saw Ian. "I wasn't complaining about the walls. I didn't mean you to knock them all down."

"It's no problem," he said brightly. "It's all good practice, isn't it? We'll have another go later."

That evening I walked around to the bunkers, but the bricks were still standing in their neat piles.

The following morning, I asked Ian if the flowerbeds were on his daily schedule.

"No, not today, I'm afraid. We're going to be building a flight of steps."

I was confused. I hadn't heard anything about steps.

"Where's it going to be?"

"Leading down on to the main lawn."

"Does Bob know about it?"

"Oh yes," Ian smiled, "it was Bob who suggested it."

"Did you tell Ian to build a flight of steps down to the main lawn?" I asked Bob the next time I saw him.

"No. Well, not exactly. I was talking to him and I suggested it might be nice."

"But his men are supposed to be building my flowerbeds!"

"Don't get cross with me. I was only chatting with him."

I fought to control my frustration.

"Well, please be careful what you say. We haven't got much time left and I don't want another panic like last year."

Later that morning I was helping David put up the new blackout boards on the windows of the First World War exhibition. Instead of being plain black on both sides, they now had figures painted on them that could be seen from outside.

Below us, a group of men were dragging wheel barrows and a cement mixer.

"Do you know what they're doing?" David asked.

"They're building steps down to the lawn when they're supposed to be doing my flower beds," I grumbled.

"Should someone go and check on them?"

"Not me. Bob suggested it so he can sort it out."

"Are you sure?"

"Yes. I'm doing this, aren't I? No one seems to have noticed but there's less than two weeks left until we open."

"All right, don't bite my head off. I was only asking."

When we stopped for lunch, I couldn't resist wandering over to see how the steps were going.

There was no sign of Ian or his team, so I guessed they too had stopped for a break.

The cement mixer was positioned on the side of the road and a pile of paving slabs and bricks waited nearby. A large amount of turf had been cut from the slope that led down onto the main lawn and the red earth had been hacked out to leave a rough set of steps.

Something about the uneven levels filled me with doubt.

"Have you spoken to Ian about the steps?" I asked Bob later.

"No. I told you it's nothing to do with me."

"But he's going ahead with it. Don't you think someone should keep an eye on him?"

"Why? He's the expert."

"But what happens if it goes wrong?"

"For goodness' sake, Di, it's a few steps down onto the lawn.What could go wrong?"

I didn't answer. It was clear Bob thought I was looking for problems that didn't exist. Reluctantly, I went back to the Fist World War exhibition.

* * *

"Come and see this."

I could tell from Dad's voice he was amused.

"What is it?" I asked.

"See for yourself."

David and I dropped our tools and hurried after him.

"I've seen some clever things in my life but this takes the biscuit," Dad grinned over his shoulder.

"What is it? Where are we going?"

He didn't stop, so we followed him downstairs, through the tearoom and across to the main lawn.

"There. What do you make of that?"

David and I stared in disbelief.

"What on earth were they thinking?" I demanded as Dad's laughter echoed around the grounds.

"Bloody hell!" David didn't sound so amused.

"You couldn't make it up, could you?" Dad gasped.

From the road level, three steps of bricks and paving slabs led down. From the lawn, three more steps led up. Unfortunately, they did not meet in the middle.

"Maybe they thought it would save time to have two teams working at once," I said, struggling to make sense of the scene.

"They've been out here all day," David groaned. "I can't believe this."

Dad was still bellowing with laughter, and I found myself grinning. The absurdity of the situation appealed to me.

"What I can't understand is why they didn't stop. They must have realised what they were doing?"

"Maybe not." David began to smile too. "Perhaps it was some kind of race."

"Are they still here?"

"No. They've all gone home," Dad chuckled.

"But the mortar will have set by tomorrow." David's face straightened. "Should we try to take it all up?"

"No way! They made the mess. They can clear it up," I said firmly.

"Oh dear," Dad snorted. "That'll keep them busy for a while."

"This really isn't funny, you know," David complained.

I tried to look serious, but as I turned away, Dad caught my eye and we burst into giggles like naughty schoolchildren.

* * *

Ian was full of apologies the next morning. He tried to explain what had gone wrong with the construction of the steps, but nothing he said made sense.

"Don't worry, I'll sort it out," he assured me.

"Will there still be time to build the flower beds?"

"Yes, it's all in my schedule. The flower beds are the next project after the base for the donkey stable."

"Has Phil given you the details for that?"

"Yes, she gave me the phone number of the man who's installing it and he was very clear. They need a square of concrete with nice clean edges.

I've ordered some timber to make a frame and all we have to do is pour the concrete inside. It couldn't be easier."

All that day, heavy thuds sounded from the lawn as the men took turns chipping at the mortar holding the bricks and paving slabs in place.

"They must have got the mix wrong," Dad chuckled as he watched them from the tearooms. "They should have finished ages ago."

"They probably used concrete by mistake," David said gloomily. "I'm beginning to think they're all idiots."

"You can't blame the men. They're only doing what the tutors tell them," I pointed out.

"Then the tutors are idiots," David corrected himself. "Either way, they're making a right mess of it."

"How's the stable base going?"

"Surprisingly enough, it looks good," David admitted. "They finished it before lunch so it's ready for the stable to go up on Tuesday."

"That's great," I agreed. "Maybe now they can get on with my flowerbeds."

* * *

Phil was like an expectant mother awaiting the arrival of the donkeys. She bought herself a series of books on donkey welfare and read them at every lunch and tea break.

"It's a big responsibility," she explained. "Although they're coming to live here, they won't really be ours. They will still belong to the donkey sanctuary and if there are any problems, they can come and take them away."

"There won't be any problems," Mum reassured her. "They are going to be very pampered donkeys and I'm sure you will look after them beautifully."

"I hope so, but I won't be happy until they're here and settled in."

The weather was improving as April approached and we had taken to eat our lunches in the tearoom again. It was still cold, but we were used to wearing several layers of jumpers.

"Have you checked all the arrangements for tomorrow?" David asked.

"Yes, I've been over it all a million times," Phil assured him. "The builders will be here by 9am and they should have it all finished by late afternoon. That gives us Wednesday to get the electricity and water connected and put down the bedding."

"Perfect. Then the donkeys arrive on Thursday?"

"Yes, that's right. They'll have two days to feel at home before we open on Sunday."

* * *

I always feel uncomfortable when plans are too well organised. It seems to be tempting fate.

When the stable builders arrived on Tuesday morning, I wondered if everything was going to go as smoothly as we hoped. It didn't take long to find the answer.

I was finishing the last of the murals in the Enchanted Forest when I heard shouts coming from the Animal Meadow.

Putting down my brushes, I went to see what was happening. I could make out an angry voice before I reached the end of the main building.

"No, you clot, I told you it had to be an eleven, eleven square!"

Ian's voice was equally indignant.

"And that's exactly what it is! Eleven foot by eleven foot."

As I turned the corner, I saw the builders had unloaded the sections of the stable from the lorry and laid them out around the concrete base. Now their leader, a tall man with ginger hair scraped into a ponytail, was standing with his shoulders back and his head thrust forward until his nose was only inches from Ian's face.

"You still don't get it, do you?" he barked. "I said an eleven, eleven square. That's eleven feet eleven inches by eleven feet eleven inches."

Ian's shoulders sagged.

"Then why didn't you say so?"

The ginger haired man squared his shoulders threateningly.

"Because no one told me I was dealing with an idiot!"

As I hurried across, I saw Phil appear behind the men and her voice cut sharply across them.

"What I want to know is what are you going to do?"

I stopped in my tracks and watched as the two men turned to face her.

"I can't do anything until the base is extended," the builder said flatly.

"And how long is that going to take?" Phil demanded.

Ian looked at her and rubbed a hand across his forehead.

"Even if I get a team straight on it, the concrete won't be set until tomorrow."

"Then you'd better get started, hadn't you?"

Phil turned back to the builder and her voice held an authority I hadn't heard before.

"I've got two donkeys coming on Thursday. I don't care what the problem is, this has to be ready by then."

"What's going on?" David demanded as he puffed up behind me.

The builder grunted, then nodded.

"All right. I'll have to rearrange a few things, but we'll come back at 10am tomorrow. We may be a bit late finishing, but we'll get it done."

"Should we go over?" David asked, but I shook my head.

"No, I think Phil's doing fine on her own."

* * *

The builders were as good as their word and turned up on the dot of 10am the following morning.

Ian had supervised the extension to the concrete base, and this time everything went smoothly. By the end of the afternoon, the stable was assembled. It was built of rich, honey-coloured timber with a gabled roof and a traditional split door. I was sure our donkeys would love it.

As I watched the builders fit the hinges on the doors, I heard the scrape of the bottom gate being opened. At once, I remembered I had removed the padlock to let the builders' truck in but had forgotten to replace it.

Swearing under my breath, I hurried down the hill to see Duncan Matthews swing his Range Rover in through the gate.

Bursting with indignation, I planted myself in the middle of the road. The Range Rover climbed steadily up the hill and Matthews' blonde head poked out of the driver's window.

"Get out of my way," he growled.

"You have no right to be here," I called back, fighting to keep my voice steady.

The car slowed to a crawl.

"This is a public right of way. Ask your solicitor if you don't believe me," Matthews sneered.

Beads of sweat rolled down my spine. I wanted to run but instead I clenched my hands into fists, took a deep breath and stepped forward.

"GET OFF OUR LAND!" I bellowed.

To my surprise, the car jerked to a stop. I glared at Matthews and saw his eyes were not on me but on something farther back. Swinging around, I found the builders, most of Ian's team and even two of the craftspeople were lined up behind me.

Without another word, Matthews reversed down the hill and drove out of the gate.

"Thanks guys," I said and let out a long breath.

* * *

The following day the Pirate Trail was installed. It was wonderful to see all the elements we had planned come together. David had made some cutout pirate figures, and we had fun standing them around the trail.

As the installer was leaving, Bob and I went to tell him how pleased we were with his work.

"I'm glad you like it," he smiled. "It should be popular with your visitors if your neighbour is anything to go by."

"Our neighbour?"

"Yes, a big blond guy in a Range Rover. He pulled up just now and asked all about it. He said he thought it looked great. He has a son, apparently, and he can't wait to bring him down to try it out."

I looked at Bob but he only shook his head.

The next day, Martha and Abbie returned to prepare the kitchen for opening on Easter Sunday. It was lovely to have them back.

Abbie was beside herself with excitement when the donkeys arrived and asked if she could go over and watch them being unloaded.

Glad of the excuse, I walked across with her. The donkeys were adorable. Moses was a soft, smoky grey with a black cross over his shoulders and Victor was earthy brown with deep, liquid eyes and a creamy muzzle. They were both quiet and friendly and I was sure they would be popular with our visitors.

When we got back to the house, the phone was ringing. To my surprise, it was Mr Turner, the head of the local planning department.

"It's good to hear from you. Is everything OK?" I asked.

Mr Turner had visited us so often while we were renovating Silverlands that I had come to think of him as a friend, but now his tone was formal.

"Have you built an adventure trail through your grounds?"

"Yes. That's not a problem, is it?"

"It might be."

"But I didn't think we needed planning permission."

There was a moment's hesitation.

"Actually, it's a bit of a grey area. Technically, you don't have to have planning permission unless anyone objects to what you've done."

"So that's OK, isn't it?"

"It would be except we've received a complaint."

I couldn't believe it.

"But the trail was only installed yesterday. It isn't even open yet. Who's complained?"

"I can't tell you that."

"But what does it mean?"

"It means we will have to investigate the complaint and if the objection is upheld you will have to remove the adventure trail."

My stomach twisted into knots.

"Are you serious?"

Mr Turner sounded apologetic.

"Yes. I'm afraid I am."

Chapter 4

"What are we going to do?" I asked as I looked around the row of faces.

Bob and David were frowning, Mum and Phil looked worried and Claire and Michael were squabbling over a toy. Only Dad seemed relaxed.

I felt irritated. Dad should have been taking the situation more seriously.

"This is really important. We've advertised the Pirate Trail on all our leaflets, but there's a real chance the planners will uphold this complaint and make us take it down," I said earnestly.

"You don't have to remind us!" David snapped. "If they do, it'll be an absolute disaster. The kids will be disappointed and the parents will complain. We'll have people demanding their money back and..."

"All right, I just wanted to make sure everyone understood."

"Of course, we understand. But sitting here moaning isn't going to help," Bob muttered.

"I still don't see why the planning department is taking it seriously. It's obvious who's behind it."

"I know, Mum," I said. "I'm sure the planners realise it's Matthews as well as we do, but they have to investigate."

"Isn't there anything we can do to change their minds?" Phil asked.

I shook my head.

"It's not like that. I spoke to Mr Turner yesterday, and he said the only reason the department would support the complaint is if the adventure trail is visible from outside our property."

"But how can it be visible?" David asked. "Surely it's hidden by the trees?"

Bob shrugged. "It might not be. There's no way of telling without going out and having a look."

David was on his feet in a moment.

"Right. I'm going to find out. Anyone coming with me?"

"Can you keep an eye on Claire?" I asked Mum.

She nodded, and I turned to Bob.

"What about you?"

"I can't. I'm expecting a call back from a coach company."

"I'll tag along," Dad offered.

He smiled at me, and my irritation grew. I knew I was being unreasonable. It wouldn't have made things any better if he had been chewing his fingernails, but my stomach was churning and I wanted to know he shared my concern.

It didn't make me any happier when David insisted on driving and I had to squeeze into the back seat of his car with a huge box of leaflets, a toolbox and several of Ossie's dog towels.

"Where will we get the best view of the grounds?" Dad asked.

"If anything's visible, we'll see it from the road into Chudleigh or the little back road that runs towards Gappah." David replied.

"OK. Let's take a look."

I sat in the back, gnawing at my bottom lip, imagining how satisfying it would be to throw an oozing cowpat at Duncan Matthews.

A few minutes later, David pulled the car onto the grass verge half-way up the hill to Chudleigh and we climbed out.

"There you are. I told you we wouldn't be able to see it!" David crowed. "Not a trace. It's completely hidden by the trees."

"Let's check the other road too," Dad suggested.

I relaxed a little as David drove the car towards Chudleigh and turned off along the back road. It was a beautiful drive at any time of year, but now the view across the valley was spectacular. Every tree branch was tipped with vibrant new leaves and the hedgerows were full of golden primroses, bluebells and bright pink campions.

The road twisted and turned along the side of the hill, and each bend revealed a magnificent new panorama.

"I'd forgotten how pretty it is up here," I said.

David swung the car around a corner, and my heart dropped. Ahead of us, across the valley, a row of cutout pirates and climbing frames were clearly visible.

"That's it. We're finished," David groaned.

"Wait a minute," Dad said, "it might not be that bad."

"How could it be any worse?" David demanded.

I sighed. He was right.

"There's no way they'll accept that. We haven't got a hope."

Dad opened the car door and climbed out.

"Stop being so dramatic. How much can we see?"

"Too much! There's the log cabin at the entrance, the A-frame, the crow's nest and about six pirates."

"Is that all?"

"Surely it's enough?" I snorted.

Dad took off his glasses, cleaned them with the bottom of his jumper and put them on again.

"The pirates aren't a problem. We just need to move them to the other side of the path, turn them to face the house and paint their backs green. No one will see them if they blend in with the bushes."

I couldn't believe he still didn't understand.

"But what about the rest of it? The three climbing frames! We can't hide them!" I wailed.

"Why not? We could plant some trees in front of them."

I struggled not to shout.

"It would take years for trees to cover that lot. The planners are coming on Tuesday."

"True, but do you remember last year when David used branches to hide the holes in the wall for the advertising video?"

"Of course, I do."

"Then why can't we move a few trees?"

I stared at him in amazement.

"Seriously? Could we even do that?"

"There's only one way to find out."

* * *

On the way home, we called in to see David's friendly farmer.

The car bumped along the rutted track into a muddy yard surrounded by ancient stone cattle sheds. A wooden barn stood at one end and a figure in wellies and a green waxed jacket was heaving a sack from the back of a Land Rover.

"Hello, Alan, are you busy?" David asked hopefully.

"I'm always busy. What d'you want?"

David explained our problem and what we were trying to do. When he mentioned Duncan Matthews, Alan's expression changed.

"No problem, my friend. If that bastard's causing you trouble, I'll be straight there."

Alan was as good as his word. In less than an hour, his tractor chugged through the entrance and David directed him to the wide bank of laurels growing behind the craft block.

"Try to get as much of the roots as you can," I called out above the roar of the engine.

David nodded, and I hurried across to where Ian and his team were waiting by the entrance to the Pirate Trail.

"We'll put the first one here," I said, pointing to a spot by the first climbing frame. "That should hide it nicely."

It took the rest of the afternoon to move the laurels but, by the time we finished, everything was hidden.

"That what I call a good afternoon's work," Dad grinned. "Feeling happier now?"

"I'm sorry I was grumpy earlier."

"Come here."

He put out an arm and hugged me until I gasped for breath."Yes," I sighed, as I laid my head on his shoulder. "I'm happy now."

* * *

At 10am on Easter Sunday we opened the gates and Silverlands filled with visitors once more.

Compared to the chaos of our first opening day a year earlier, everything ran smoothly. The weather was beautiful, the grounds were alive with spring flowers and the animated displays ran without a hitch.

The Pirate Trail proved to be an enormous success, and it was lovely to hear laughter floating across the lawn as families tried out the various challenges and activities.

When we had a lull in the tearooms, I walked across to see how everything was going. It was wonderful to see families enjoying themselves, and I was amused to watch fathers competing with each other on the monkey bars while their children looked on in amazement.

By the time we closed, we were all tired but happy. As usual, we gathered in the tearooms as and were about to start our evening search when a familiar figure walked through the French doors.

It was Mr Turner.

"I'm sorry to disturb you," he said, "but I was passing so I thought I might as well call in."

"No problem, but we weren't expecting you until Tuesday. Is something wrong?" I asked.

"No. Quite the contrary," he said with a smile. "I've been visiting my family in Chudleigh and it seemed silly to come all the way over from Newton Abbot again. I thought I might as well do a quick inspection while I was here."

"Of course. Is there anything you want us to show you?"

"No. I've already done it. You'll be glad to know there is no sign of your activity trail from the A38 or the other side of the valley, so the planning department won't be supporting the complaint."

There was a murmur of relief from the rest of the family.

"That's wonderful news," I beamed.

"Would you like a cream tea while you're here?" Bob offered.

"No thanks. I can't stay. I just thought you'd like to know."

"You're right. We've been wondering what was going to happen."

"Well, you can stop worrying about it now. And I hope the bank holiday goes well tomorrow."

"What a lovely man," Mum said as soon as he was gone.

* * *

The weather held and the rest of the Easter holidays were busy but once the children returned to school our visitor numbers dropped.

"It's a shame we can't get more visitors during the low season," Bob said as we ate our evening meal one night.

"It's just the pattern, isn't it?" I said through a mouthful of pasta. "Some months are quieter than others."

"I know, but we still have the same overheads. I've been wondering about doing something special to draw locals in on the weekends."

"You mean special events?"

"Yes, I suppose I do."

"Do you have anything in mind?"

"I haven't worked out the details yet, but I was wondering about having a Clown Convention."

I stopped eating and looked at him in surprise.

Before we bought Silverlands, when our exhibition was still in the Spanish Barn in Torquay, we had been invited to take Silvers Model Circus to the first International Clown Convention in Bognor Regis.

It was an amazing experience. Hundreds of clowns from all over the world had converged on the town for a weekend of fun and mayhem. It had felt as though everyone in Bognor was involved. The shops put clown displays in their windows and there was an enormous procession through the town with clown bands, clown cars and hundreds of local children in clown outfits.

Clown performances took place in the theatre, in the convention centre and on every street corner. Even the local policemen joined in the celebrations and wore red noses.

Silvers Model Circus was on display in the convention centre and was at the heart of everything. To join in with the atmosphere, we all wore matching clown outfits. Even Claire had her own little outfit. She was only five months old at the time and quickly became known as the youngest clown in Bognor.

To Mum's amazement, even Dad agreed to dress as a clown with the rest of us. He was usually rather self-conscious, but he looked amazing in an old dress suit with a red shirt, a spotted bow tie, a battered top hat, and a painted face with a massive red smile.

Bob was the only one who didn't dress as a clown. Instead, he wore his red ringmaster outfit and was soon enlisted to be the Master of Ceremonies at various clown performances.

The convention was opened by Ron Moody, who played Fagin in the original musical Oliver! Ron was fascinated by the model circus and when Dad offered to show him the mechanism that drove it, the two of them ended up laughing and swapping stories for hours.

It was an amazing weekend, and I loved every moment of it, but my chief memory of the clowns was that they were wildly unpredictable and totally incapable of sticking to any schedule or arrangement.

I didn't want to discourage Bob, as he was convinced that inviting our clown friends to hold a convention at Silverlands was a great idea, but I hoped he wasn't going to regret his decision.

* * *

One morning an official-looking letter arrived from a firm of solicitors in Exeter.

"I don't want to open it," I groaned. "It's going to be about the water supply."

"It might not be. It might be something wonderful," Bob said optimistically.

I put the letter on the table.

"I'll open it later. I should be checking the exhibitions by now."

"Give it to me. I'll open it. You'll only worry about it otherwise."

I handed Bob the envelope, and he tore it open. I waited as he unfolded the letter and began to read.

Suddenly his expression changed.

"It is about the water supply, isn't it?" I asked, but Bob kept reading.

Finally, he dropped the letter on the table.

"It's Matthews. He's suing us. He claims there's a legal right of way along the back road and we've got no right to keep it padlocked. He's insisting we open the road and says he's going to put up signposts from the caravan park so their visitors can use it as a shortcut to Chudleigh."

My anger burst out in a torrent of words.

"That's ridiculous! No one ever uses that road. The gates were locked for years before we arrived. How can we run a tourist attraction with cars driving through the middle of it?"

"I think that's the point."

I wanted to scream but struggled to stay calm.

"Surely we would know if there was a right of way? Shouldn't it be on the deeds?"

Bob nodded.

"You would think so, but since we moved here nothing seems straightforward."

"I'll phone Mr Barbary."

"Do you want me to speak to him this time?" Bob offered. "It won't help if you start shouting at him."

I gritted my teeth.

"Don't worry, I'll be polite this time."

* * *

"Did you get through to Barbary?" I asked Bob later. I was stabbing jacket potatoes with a knife and lining them up on a baking tray ready to go in the oven.

"No. He's in a meeting, but he's supposed to be calling me back."

"I didn't really shout at him, you know. Not much."

"I was in the room, remember? I know it's difficult, but you have to keep calm when you're dealing with solicitors."

I wanted to tell him that some solicitors deserved to be shouted at, but instead I nodded and changed the subject.

"I think we're going to be busy today. We've gone through a whole tray of flapjack already."

"Great. It's always a..." He broke off as the phone rang in the office. "That's probably Barbary now."

He hurried off, and I went back to stabbing the potatoes.

A moment later Abbie arrived with a pile of trays loaded with crockery.

"Martha says, can you take over the counter so she can have her break?" she panted as she deposited the trays by the dishwasher.

I shunted the potatoes into the oven and wiped my hands.

"I'll be right there."

The servery was full of customers as I slipped behind the counter. The smell of fresh-baked cakes filled the air and the morning sunshine reflected from the mirrored wall behind me, making the room feel bright and airy.

I waited for Martha to finish serving a family, then took her place.

An elderly couple asked for two coffees with extra milk, and I was reaching for the coffee jug when I heard something rise above the cheerful background music.

Bob's voice was coming from the office.

"I hope you're enjoying your visit," I said to the couple. "Would you like anything with your coffee?"

"No thank you," the man replied. "We're saving ourselves for lunch."

"Very sensible. We have a lovely range of salads."

Bob's voice was rising. I couldn't make out the words, but he didn't sound happy.

The man turned and looked towards the office.

"Here, I can give you a menu, if you like," I said loudly.

I reached beneath the counter for a menu and turned up the volume of music at the same time.

"There you go, I'm sure you'll find something to tempt you."

The next family wanted tea and toasted teacakes.

I made the tea and stacked cups and saucers on to a tray, then hurried through to the kitchen with the order for the teacakes. As I passed the door to the office Bob's angry voice was unmissable.

"... that's ridiculous! You can't expect us to..."

I pulled the door shut with a bang. Bob must have got the message because the volume reduced considerably.

When Martha came back from her break, I found Bob waiting in the kitchen.

"Barbary's an idiot!" he fumed. "He didn't even sound concerned when I told him what's happened. He seems to think we can sort it by giving Matthews a key to the padlock and asking him to lock the gate when he goes through."

"I told you he's an idiot. What are we going to do? There has to be some way to fight back."

"Not according to Barbary. He's going to check everything, but if there really is a right of way our only choice is to move the road."

I didn't understand.

"Is that supposed to be a joke?"

"No. We'll have to build a new road around the edge of our property."

"But that would cost a fortune!"

"I know. But it seems we don't have any choice."

* * *

David knew something was wrong the moment he saw my face.

"What is it this time?" he demanded.

I told him the news and waited for the inevitable reaction.

Once he had calmed down, David sat with his head in his hands.

"It's just one disaster after another, isn't it?"

I tried to sound encouraging.

"That's not true. We keep facing challenges, but we haven't been beaten yet."

"Really? This place is supposed to be somewhere people can bring their kids. Somewhere they can relax and have fun and be safe. How is that going to work if Matthews can roar through in his Range Rover whenever he feels like it?"

"We have to stop him," I said simply. "If a new road's the only answer, we'll have to build one, but not yet. Barbary says he can stall things for a while and even if it does go to court, it will take months."

"But where does that leave us now?"

"We have to fight back. Matthews has been cutting the padlocks off the gates. Can we get anything stronger? High security ones?"

David nodded.

"Yes, there must be something. I'll see what I can find."

* * *

I was still thinking about Matthews when we searched the house that evening. The sun was slanting through the windows and Dino paced beside me as I walked through the exhibitions. The house felt calm and peaceful as I turned everything off and checked there were no visitors lurking in corners.

I wondered what Matthews had been like when he was little. Was he a spoiled only child? Or had his siblings been mean to him? Or had there been some terrible trauma that had turned him into a bully? It was hard to imagine him ever being happy.

Crash!

I jumped violently at the sound of smashing china. It had come from behind me and I spun around to see a large Victorian milk jug lying in pieces on the floor.

Dino ran across and sniffed at the shards spread out across the carpet.

"Come here, boy."

I patted Dino's silky head as he returned to my side and was glad of his company.

The jug had been standing on a shelf as part of an exhibition of butter-making in the Down in Devon display. I couldn't see any reason for it to have fallen to the floor.

As I stood and listened, all was silent except for the distant rumble of traffic on the A38, and yet I had a strange sense that there was something I could not hear. As if someone close to me was holding their breath.

For a long moment I struggled to control the impulse, but finally I gave in.

"Is that you, Fred?"

I waited, half expecting another jug to come hurtling through the air, but there was nothing.

"Come on," I said to Dino at last, "we'd better get going."

I met up with David and finished the search, then went back to where Mum was waiting at the bottom of the main staircase.

"All clear."

"Are you all right, dear? You look pale."

It was hard to hide anything from Mum.

"I'm fine. A jug fell over upstairs, that's all."

She waited for me to go on and I sat down beside her on the bottom step.

"It just seemed odd that it fell over for no reason."

"These things happen sometimes," she said. "There isn't always a reason. At least, not one we can see. Sometimes it's best not to think too much about it."

I turned and looked her in the eye.

"Do you mean Fred?"

"If that's what you want to call it."

"You believe there's something here, don't you?"

She hesitated before answering.

"Yes, I think there is. I've no idea what, but I've decided I don't mind because it doesn't feel threatening."

It was a relief to know she felt the same way.

"I wish I understood more about it."

Mum smiled.

"I do too, but if there is something here, then it was here before we arrived so I guess it has more right to be here than we do."

"I suppose that's one way of looking at it."

"Does it bother you?"

"No, not really."

"Good. A lot of people get upset if you mention ghosts."

I nodded.

"I've tried talking to Bob about it but he won't listen. He gets cross if I even mention it."

"Is he religious?"

I was surprised by her question.

"No. That is... I don't think so. We've never really talked about religion. I know he was a choirboy when he was little, but he's never suggested going to church. Why?"

"I've found that people with strong religious beliefs don't like the thought of ghosts. I think it contradicts their idea that people go to heaven when they die."

"I suppose that makes sense," I agreed, "but whatever it was that broke the jug, I'd better go and sweep up the pieces."

* * *

After that, I spent a lot of time cleaning up. I never saw anything break, but I would find a cup lying on the kitchen floor with its handle broken or a vase tipped over on one of the tearoom's tables with the flowers scattered everywhere.

Sometimes nothing would happen for days and I would find myself waiting to see what would be next. At other times, I scolded myself for letting my imagination run away with me.

Nothing was ever definite. There was always a plausible explanation for the things that happened. Abbie must have dropped the cup. The last customers must have tipped over the vase. A child must have unrolled the toilet paper and scattered it everywhere.

Most of the incidents happened in the kitchen and, inevitably, Abbie took the blame. She had a pleasant nature and was so aware of her clumsiness that she never took offence and often blamed herself before others could blame her.

One morning, I was preparing salads when Abbie came back from the tearoom with a tray of dirty dishes.

"Oh dear. I must have spilled the milk."

She was standing in the doorway, and a white puddle covered the floor in front of her.

I felt bad as I watched her get a mop and start cleaning up. It hadn't occurred to her that, unless she had splashed through the milk when she left the kitchen, it must have been spilled after she left.

I wanted to tell Abbie that she shouldn't be so hard on herself, and I felt even worse when Martha complained about her.

"That girl hasn't got a brain in her head," she said one morning. "I told her to tidy up in the servery before she left last night, but when I came in this morning, there were sugar sachets scattered all over the floor behind the counter. I really don't know why you put up with her."

"Maybe she didn't see them."

"You're too patient," Martha scolded me. "The girl will never learn if you mollycoddle her."

I caught David on his own one evening and explained what was happening.

"But have you actually seen anything?" he asked.

"No. I haven't seen anything tip over, or fall off a shelf, if that's what you mean."

"Do you think it would be worth setting up a camera? We could leave it running overnight."

"No!" I was horrified by the idea. "Why would we do that?"

David looked at me in surprise.

"I thought you wanted to prove Fred exists?"

"Of course not. Nothing like that. I just want him to behave himself so we can get on with running this place. I feel bad about Abbie taking the blame, that's all."

"Do you have any idea how insane that sounds?"

I glared at him.

"Of course, I do. That's why I'm only telling you. I know you've got enough sense to keep it to yourself."

"OK." David looked disappointed. "No cameras."

* * *

One evening, after we closed, Eric Davies came over to meet us all. It had been agreed that the Motor Museum would open on the late May bank holiday weekend and work was due to start any day on converting the sports hall.

As soon as I saw Eric, I liked him. From Bob's description, I had expected him to be a round, cheerful man with red cheeks and a loud booming voice, and I had been curious to see if the real man matched the image in my head.

Apart from his voice, which was warm and friendly rather than loud and booming, he was exactly as I had pictured him.

From his flat tweed cap to his wellie boots and thick knitted jumper, Eric was a typical Devon farmer. His hair was gingery and his eyes were the palest blue, but his skin had the unmistakable ruddy complexion of a man who had spent his life working outdoors.

He beamed and nodded as Bob introduced him to each of us.

"It's a real treat to meet you at last," he said.

"Come and have a seat. Would you like some tea or something stronger?" Bob asked.

"A year ago, I would have said a beer, but now I'll just have tea, if you don't mind. I've had a few health problems recently and I've promised my wife I'll stick to the new rules."

He winked at me.

"Us men have to do what our wives tell us, don't we?"

I laughed.

"Perhaps you could tell Bob that."

"Or David," Phil added.

"I'm sure you have them running around after you all the time," Eric chuckled. "And these must be the little ones I've heard so much about.

Claire and Michael, isn't it?"

Claire looked up at the sound of her name.

"Are you going to say hello to Eric?" I asked, but her only response was a shake of her head and a stubborn frown.

"Eric's going to be bringing lots of cars here for his Motor Museum, Michael," David said.

"Cars!" Michael repeated excitedly and held up a toy fire engine.

"That's not a car, is it?" Eric said as he held out a hand to Michael. "That's a fire engine. Can I see? I've got a fire engine too, but mine's bigger than that. If you like, you can come and see it once we're open."

To my surprise, even Mum liked Eric. He was wonderfully uncomplicated and said exactly what he thought, but he was never unkind.

We soon learned more about him as he had a wealth of stories about his life as a farmer and his passion for restoring old vehicles. Inevitably, he and Dad became firm friends.

* * *

As May progressed, lunchtimes became busier, and I wondered if we would need to take on another girl in the kitchen earlier than we had planned.

One morning, I was about to put a pile of mixing bowls away in a cupboard when the cupboard door swung shut.

I jumped, and a shiver ran down my spine, but I took a deep breath and told myself I must have caught the door with my elbow.

I was holding the bowls in both hands so I put them on a work surface, opened the door and was just about to put the bowls away when the door swung shut again.

This time I knew I had not touched it.

My heart was racing, so I took another deep breath to calm myself.

"Abbie, can you help me," I called. "There must be something wrong with this hinge. The door won't stay open."

Abbie left the dishwasher and hurried across.

"I expect it's Fred," she said.

"Please, don't joke about Fred. It's not funny."

"I'm not joking. It's just how he is. He likes playing tricks."

I was flabbergasted.

"Do you believe in him?"

"Of course, I do. Everyone knows about Fred."

There was no hint of sarcasm or ridicule in her voice.

"But aren't you afraid?"

Her eyes opened wide in surprise.

"Why would I be afraid?"

"The green grocer won't deliver here after dark. I thought everyone in Chudleigh was frightened of ghosts."

Abbie smiled at my naivety.

"Some people are just daft. My auntie's a spiritualist. She talks to dead people all the time. They're still just people, aren't they?"

She held the door open, and I put the bowls away while my mind absorbed what she had said.

"I mean, they were all somebody's son or daughter, or Mum or Dad or whatever, weren't they?" Abbie went on. "I wouldn't be frightened of them if I'd met them when they were alive, so why should I be frightened of them just because they're dead?"

I couldn't fault her logic.

Suddenly, I felt a ridiculous sense of relief. It was true. If Fred was the ghost of someone who had died, why should I feel any more frightened of him than I would have felt when he was alive?

I began to smile, then to laugh.

"Are you all right?" Abbie asked.

"Yes," I replied. "I'm fine. Absolutely fine."

A few days later, David asked me if Fred had done anything.

"No," I replied. "All's quiet on the kitchen front."

"Right."

I could sense his disappointment.

"I like it much better when he's behaving himself, don't you?" I asked, but David only grunted.

* * *

Abbie never ceased to amaze me.

She struggled with things other people found easy, like carrying a bowl of soup without spilling it or remembering to put the lid on a bottle of sauce before turning it upside down, but she had an instinctive understanding of what was important in life. She was full of innocence and wonder. Sometimes I envied her.

She was busy scrubbing baking trays one afternoon just before we closed.

"Abbie," I said quietly, "some people aren't as relaxed about ghosts as you are."

She must have read my mind.

"You mean Bob, don't you? He doesn't think Fred's real."

"No, he doesn't."

"And he gets cross."

"Sometimes," I admitted. "He thinks someone's playing tricks on him."

Abbie frowned.

"He doesn't think it's me, does he? Because I would never do anything like that."

"I know you wouldn't, but it's hard to explain sometimes."

She sighed, and I took the baking tray from her and stood it on the drainer.

"Maybe it would be better if we don't mention Fred," I suggested. "If anything happens, let's just clear it up and keep it to ourselves."

Abbie smiled and, as I smiled back at her, I had the strange feeling of being drawn into a conspiracy.

* * *

"That's a surprise."

"What is?"

Bob was reading his post over breakfast while I tried to insert a wriggling Claire into a pale pink romper suit.

"We've been invited to join the Devon Association of Tourist Attractions."

I held Claire's arms with one hand and struggled to do up a row of poppers with the other hand.

"That sounds impressive. D'you know what it is?"

"Of course, I do. It's an association of tourist attractions based in Devon."

"Wow. Thanks for explaining that," I grinned, "but what do they do? And why do they want us to join?"

Claire slithered out of my grip and undid all the poppers with one smooth tug.

"Naughty girl! How am I supposed to get you dressed?"

"I expect they've noticed what a fabulous attraction we have here," Bob said happily. "They're having a meeting next Wednesday at the Shire Horse Centre and they've invited me to go to lunch to meet the other members."

Grabbing Claire's ankles, I attacked the romper suit from the other end.

"Then you'd better go. We can manage without you for one day."

"Are you sure?"

"Yes. We'll be fine, won't we, Claire? Unless Daddy wants to take you with him?"

* * *

Bob returned from the meeting with a pile of leaflets from the other attractions and a huge smile on his face.

He waited until we had closed and the evening search was finished, then recounted every detail of his visit.

"It was brilliant. The owner of the Shire Horse Centre gave us a guided tour and told us all about their history and how they came to develop the site, then each of the other attractions told us a bit about themselves."

He stopped for breath as I handed around cups of tea.

"How many others were there?" David asked.

"The association only has eight members at the moment, but they want to expand so they can do more joint advertising. That's why they invited people from other attractions like us."

"I like the sound of that. The more publicity we can get, the better."

"Exactly!"

I could tell Bob was excited. His eyes were bright and his hands flew through the air as he spoke.

"They want new members who are keen to work together to promote each other. The main thing is going to be a joint leaflet. The cost will be divided between everyone and they're talking about having adverts on the TV and radio."

"That's awesome! Absolutely brilliant!"

David was bouncing, and Mum, Dad and Phil were smiling too.

"I take it everyone's happy to go ahead then?" Bob asked, and there was a chorus of agreement.

"There's one other thing," Bob went on. "The Shire Horse Centre put on some entertainment for us and one of the things was a Clairvoyant from Teignmouth. She's called Madam Valerie and I couldn't resist going to talk to her."

He hesitated, and I wondered what was coming next.

"I wasn't sure what to expect, but she turned out to be very impressive."

"How? What did she do?" Phil asked.

"That's the weird thing. She didn't do anything. She just talked to me. She told me all sorts of things and I've no idea how she could have known them."

"It was an act," Mum said flatly. "My mother used to love having her palm read. She believed everything she was told, but fortune tellers are nothing but charlatans."

"No, it wasn't like that," Bob protested. "She didn't predict the future. She just told me things about myself and they were all true. She knew where I had grown up, how many children I had, all sorts of things."

Mum shook her head.

"You didn't realise it but you must have given her clues. That's how those people work. I've seen it before. They say something general, then pick up any little clue in your answer to find out more about you. They're very clever, but it's all an act."

Bob looked deflated.

"It really wasn't like that," he insisted.

"They can be very convincing if you're gullible," Mum said smugly. "If she had tried it on me, I wouldn't have given anything away."

Bob glared at her.

"Well, you can make your mind up yourself when you meet her. She's offered to come and do a session here as part of a clairvoyance day."

There was an awkward silence and Mum's disapproval radiated from her.

"Is that really a good idea?" I asked.

"Of course it is! The visitors will love it," Bob said.

"But is it suitable for a family attraction?" I persisted. "Some people take things like that very seriously."

"Don't be ridiculous. It's just a bit of fun," David jumped in. "No one really believes any of it."

"Don't they? Bob said this woman seemed to know…" I began, but Bob interrupted me.

"I said she was impressive. That doesn't mean I believed her. I'm not stupid!"

"Well, I think it's a bad idea. We shouldn't risk offending people," Mum sniffed.

"No-one's going to be offended. She's a lovely lady and I'll tell her not to say anything outrageous," Bob insisted.

There was another uneasy silence.

"Why don't we have a show of hands?" Dad suggested.

David's hand shot up at once and Bob and Phil raised theirs too.

I was torn. I didn't want to upset Mum, but I was intrigued. Slowly, I raised my hand.

"Well, I can see I'm outvoted." Mum clasped her bag firmly under her arm and marched out of the room.

* * *

I caught up with David later as he let Ossie out of the kitchen door for a last run before bed.

"Why do you think Mum is so opposed to having a clairvoyant here?" I asked.

"Probably because it was Bob's idea," he replied. "She still seems to think he's taking over."

"Do you feel like that?"

"Of course not. He's doing a great job. Joining DATA is just what we need and holding special events makes perfect sense. The problem is Mum."

"Why do you think she's being so difficult?"

David leaned against the kitchen door.

"Maybe she feels left out. After all, she's stuck in that little shed every day from ten in the morning until five in the afternoon. It's a long time to be on her own. I know Dad takes her a cup of tea now and then, but she must feel a bit abandoned."

"You might be right. I hadn't really thought about it before, but she must get lonely down there. And I'm sure she thinks the rest of us spend our time sitting around in the tearooms chatting."

David laughed.

"I wish!"

"Do you think it would help if we mixed things up a bit?" I suggested. "Maybe she could do a turn in the gift shop now and then?"

"Yes, that's a good idea." David nodded. "But not on the day Madame Valerie comes."

"No, definitely not!"

"We want everything to go well. I'm really looking forward to it."

He sounded excited, and I wondered why he was so keen to meet a clairvoyant.

"I thought you didn't believe in that sort of thing."

"I don't. But then, I didn't believe in ghosts until I came here. You never know. If there is a ghost then maybe..."

He looked at me strangely.

"Maybe what?"

"Maybe she could get in touch with it. Tell us what it's all about."

I felt a surge of apprehension.

"But we don't know anything about her!" I blurted out. "She could tell us anything and we wouldn't know if it was true or just a load of garbage!"

"I'm not saying we have to believe everything she says. But wouldn't it be amazing? If we could make contact with a ghost?"

"You mean hold a seance?"

"Yes. I suppose so..."

"No!" I was outraged. "That's a terrible idea! Firstly, there's no such thing as a ghost and secondly, we should leave him alone!"

I knew I wasn't making sense.

"OK, calm down. There's no need to bite my head off. Maybe this isn't the right time to talk about it."

I turned away as David called Ossie back inside.

"See you in the morning," he said.

I didn't reply, but listened as his footsteps receded along the corridor.

For a long time, I stood still while my heart raced.

Why was I so upset?

I was being ridiculous. What difference did it make if there was a seance? If Fred really did exist, wouldn't it be a good idea to find out about him?

Suddenly it dawned on me that I was feeling jealous. Fred was my ghost. I didn't want a stranger to come in and talk to him. And what would happen if he didn't want to speak to a clairvoyant? Would he get upset? If he did, what would happen?

Dear God! Was I really standing in an empty kitchen having this conversation with myself? The absurdity of the situation hit me and I laughed out loud.

"This is insane," I said to myself. "I must be losing my mind after all."

* * *

Every afternoon Dad came into the tearooms and made up a tray of tea for two, which he carried down to the ticket box to share with Mum.

"Is it OK if I take that for her today?" I asked.

Dad looked at me in surprise.

"Of course, if you've got the time."

"Yes, it's pretty quiet at the moment. Bob's in the kitchen so he can keep an eye on things."

I added a couple of scones and some jam and cream onto the tray and carried it carefully down to the ticket box.

I waited outside until Mum finished serving a family before tapping on the door.

There was a scrape of a bolt, and the door swung open.

"Hello, dear, this is a nice surprise," Mum said as she saw me.

I squeezed inside and put the tray on top of a cupboard. Mum was sitting on a cashier's stool with tall legs and a back support. Beside her, a folding chair filled the rest of the space. Bending down, she lifted her handbag from the chair and dropped it onto the floor.

"I'm afraid it's rather cramped in here, dear."

I poured the tea and passed Mum a cup and a plate of scones.

"Thank you, what a treat."

A family arrived outside, and she slid the scones out of sight until she finished serving them.

"Has it been busy today?" I asked when they had gone.

"Not too bad. It was steady this morning, but it's slowed down since lunchtime."

She bit into a scone, and we munched in amiable silence. When we finished, I put the plates back on the tray.

"I was chatting to David last night, and we thought you must get lonely on your own here sometimes. Would you like it if we changed things around and you could take a turn in the shop?"

I expected Mum to look pleased, but instead her face fell.

"It's very sweet of you to think of me, but I'd really rather stay here."

"Are you sure? It must feel awfully cut off down here all the time."

Mum reached out and took my hand.

"You're not the only one who likes privacy, you know. If I was in the shop, I would have to talk to people. Be nice to them. Here, I just have to sell people a ticket, smile at them and they go away. Then, when it's quiet, I can take out a notebook and get on with some writing."

"You're impossible. You know that, don't you?"

"Of course, I do, dear. After all, like mother, like daughter, isn't that the expression?"

* * *

"Have you heard of Reiki?" Bob asked me one evening.

"Is it some sort of coffee?"

"I don't think so. It says here it's an alternative therapy."

"Alternative to what?"

"It doesn't say."

He was sitting on the sofa next to me reading a leaflet and he looked confused.

"Madam Valerie suggested I might like to invite some of these therapists to take part in our special event."

"Can I see?"

He passed me a handful of leaflets, and I glanced through them. Most had flowing letters and line drawings of lotus blossoms or white doves.

"How do these relate to a clairvoyant?" I asked.

"I'm not really sure, but she told me they often do exhibitions together. There's six of them in all and they give people free taster sessions of things like Reiki, Tai Chi, Shiatsu and self-hypnosis."

"Do we have to pay them?"

"No. She said they do it for publicity."

"Then I guess we've got nothing to lose."

I handed the leaflets back to him.

"Are you sure this special event is a good idea?"

"Of course, I am. Anyway, it's too late to cancel it now. I've booked the adverts. I decided to call it a Day of Discovery."

* * *

Mum refused to discuss the Day of Discovery, but as it grew closer, she made her disapproval clear.

Everything she said began with "Not that anyone cares what I think, but..." and she insisted on referring to Madame Valerie as 'that fortune-telling person.'

Bob kept his distance from her, and there were no major confrontations.

On the appointed day Mum disappeared to the ticket box much earlier than usual and left the rest of us to make the necessary preparations. Bob had printed signs to show people where the various therapists would be based and had made a large information board to stand in the entrance.

"That must be the first of them now," he announced as a car was heard pulling up outside the house. "I'd better go and meet them."

Madame Valerie was tiny. I have never been good at guessing people's age, but I'm sure she was old enough to have been a grandmother. Her skin was well hidden beneath a smooth layer of beige foundation, but her eyes were bright and lively.

"You must be Diana. It's lovely to meet you."

She smiled widely and reached out to grasp my hand.

Instinctively, I pulled away from her. She seemed friendly and open, but I had a ridiculous fear the contact might allow her to drain my innermost secrets through some mystical power exchange.

With an effort, I controlled myself and gave her hand a quick shake.

"I'm glad you to meet you too."

Bob was busy unloading Madame Valerie's props from her car and carrying them inside.

There was a large alcove beneath the staircase with a tall window that looked out onto a bank of ferns. Bob had put a table and two chairs there, and the clairvoyant trilled happily when she saw it.

"This is perfect! So beautifully grounded. The very spot I would have chosen myself."

Bob laid an old leather suitcase on the ground and Madame Valerie began unpacking candlesticks and crystals and arranging them on the table. At last, she was satisfied.

"There. Now all I need is a curtain or a screen to shield my clients and I will be ready."

Bob and I looked at each other.

"Do we have a screen?" Bob asked hopefully.

"Not that I know of," I whispered.

I found David helping Phil with the donkeys.

"Can I borrow you for a moment? I need a curtain. Or a screen."

He looked at me blankly.

"When do you need it?"

"Now."

"Oh."

He emptied a bowl of food into a trough, then rinsed his hands under the outside tap and dried them on the sides of his trousers.

"Where does it have to go?"

"Under the main stairs. Apparently, our clairvoyant needs something to shield her clients."

"Right. I'll see what I can find."

"Thanks. I'll be in the kitchen if you need me."

* * *

I ventured into the hall shortly before opening time and was impressed to see a large silk curtain with embroidered leaves and dragon heads hanging across the alcove.

David was screwing a hook to the wall so the curtain could be held back by a silk tassel.

"Wow. That's awesome."

"I thought you'd like it," David beamed. "I've had it tucked away for years. I knew it would come in useful eventually."

"Where's Madame Valerie?"

"Bob's taken her to say hello to the therapists. He's got them spaced out all over the building."

"Everything's ready to go then?"

"Yes, I think so."

"Good. All we need now is lots of customers."

As we were now in our second year, we could compare our daily take with the previous year's figures. Every evening, as Mum added up the figures, we waited to know whether the day was up or down. So far, our figures were not great. Mostly we were a little up, but not as much as we had hoped.

Last year we had attracted a lot of publicity when we had the advantage of being a novelty, but it was much harder to get any press coverage in our second year.

Bob was convinced that running regular special events would help get us noticed, and I hoped he was right.

It was important that today went well.

* * *

I was decanting clotted cream from a massive enamel bowl into individual serving pots when Martha burst into the kitchen.

"You'd better come. There's a customer at the counter and he's not a happy bunny."

I followed her into the servery and was confronted by a middle-aged man wearing a T-shirt with a drawing of a sheep and the words I AM NOT LOST written beneath it.

"Can I help you?" I asked.

His mouth opened and words poured over me like a tsunami. It would have been futile to interrupt, so I closed my ears and waited. I didn't need to hear what he was saying to know he was upset. A few words registered in my mind. Satan, Charlatan, Defile, and Corrupting-God's-Innocents were among them.

At last, the flow subsided.

"Did you hear what I said?"

"Yes, I did and I'm sorry you are upset. Clearly you didn't see the advertisements for today's special event..."

Another torrent of words crashed over me.

"It's clear you feel very strongly about this. Is there anything I can do to make you feel better?"

I gave the man his admission fee back and watched as his wife and young sons walked meekly away behind him. As he went, I saw the words FOR HE IS MY SHEPHERD printed on the back of his T-shirt.

As soon as he had gone Martha reappeared from the kitchen.

"He was a character, wasn't he?" she said grimly.

"Yes. What a lovely man. I hope we don't get many like him."

For the rest of the day, I flinched at every sound. When Dad came to make up Mum's tea tray, I told him what had happened.

"I tried to warn you. Some people take these things very seriously."

"I know. But lots of other people seem to be enjoying it. The queue for Madame Valerie was half-way along the hall at one point."

"Are you going to see her?"

"Me? No, I don't think so."

"Why not?"

I didn't know what to say. Dad knew me too well to accept a glib answer. Was it because I believed she was a fraud? Or was I afraid of what she might tell me?

"I think it's because I don't want to be influenced," I said at last. "It doesn't matter if she's genuine or not. The moment someone makes a prediction or tells you something about yourself, it changes the way you think. Even if you know it's not true, it leaves a question in your mind."

"Fair enough. That's pretty much how I feel."

* * *

To my relief, we didn't have any other difficult customers.

By the time Mum came up from the ticket box, the queue of people waiting to see Madame Valerie had shrunk to one young woman.

"The curtain looks brilliant, doesn't it?" I whispered as we watched from a distance. "David had it tucked away somewhere."

"It looks very mysterious. I'm glad to hear it's all gone smoothly."

"Yes, no problems at all," I lied.

At that moment, the curtain was pulled back, and Dougal the woodcarver appeared. He waved the young woman through to take his place and dropped the curtain behind him.

"She's very good, isn't she?" he said as soon as he spotted us. "Most of the others from the craft block have been over, so I didn't want to miss out. Have you had a reading done?"

Mum looked at him in amazement.

"Certainly not."

"But you must! That woman has a real talent. Quite remarkable. She has an incredible eye for an aura. Spot on."

Mum looked at me imploringly.

"We're just going for a cup of tea..." I began, but Dougal cut across me.

"It would be a real shame to miss an opportunity like this. I've had lots of readings done in my time, but I've never had such a sense of transparency. Of connection..."

He explained at length the different techniques Madame Valerie used, and Mum's eyes grew wider and wider.

"It could be the strength of the ley lines here that boost her accuracy. They really are a great help with transmissions," Dougal concluded.

"I see." Mum's eyes were glazing.

"So, are you going to have a go?" Dougal asked as the curtain lifted and the young woman appeared.

"Well, I suppose it wouldn't do any harm," Mum said and stepped inside to meet Madame Valerie.

I was amazed.

I waited until she reappeared and whisked her into the tearooms.

"What did she say?" I asked.

"Nothing really. She hardly got anything right. The only thing she knew was that I live here in the house and anyone could have told her that."

"Did she say anything about a ghost?"

"Yes. She started talking about a white lady. Absolute nonsense. She asked if I'd ever felt her presence. Of course, I said no. Then she told me that this white lady was standing on the stairs when she arrived."

She laughed.

"I've never heard such nonsense. Now I'll have to say 'excuse me' every time I walk upstairs in case I'm walking through her."

"But we did see a white figure, didn't we?" I reminded her. "When we first moved in."

A shadow flitted across Mum's face.

"Did we? I don't remember. Everything was so confused back then."

I found it hard to believe she didn't recall the incident as she had been quite upset at the time.

"It was at the other end of the building in the Enchanted Forest. You thought it was Lyn at first."

"You're right. We did see something," Mum conceded, "but it's such a cliché, isn't it? The White Lady. Why are ghosts always white? Why can't they ever be orange? Or purple?"

She settled herself on the window seat and, as I made her a pot of tea, I felt what I can only describe as a sense of relief. I had no idea whether Madame Valerie was genuine or not, but I was certain of one thing. She knew nothing about Fred.

Chapter 5

The morning after the Day of Discovery, I was unpacking a delivery of groceries in the kitchen when I heard footsteps behind me. I looked over my shoulder and was not surprised to find the room was empty.

"So, you're back, are you?" I said quietly. "You didn't want the clairvoyant to see you yesterday, is that it?"

I turned back to my unpacking when a voice spoke behind me.

"But she did see me."

My heart leapt into my mouth, and the hairs on the back of my neck stood to attention.

"I had a session with her during my break."

Swinging around, I saw Abbie standing in the corner tying an apron around her waist.

"Are you all right?" she asked. "You look a bit strange."

My shoulders sagged as the tension inside me unwound.

"I'm fine. You surprised me, that's all."

"Sorry. Shall I start on the salads?"

Abbie opened the fridge and took out a stack of plastic containers. She laid them out along the worktop, ready to start the morning preparations.

My heart was still pounding, so I took out a tissue and pretended to blow my nose.

"Can you do the fillings for the jacket potatoes as well?" I asked.

"No problem. It's an exciting day, isn't it?"

"Yes," I said, trying to remember what was in the diary. "Why is that exactly?"

"The first cars are arriving for the Motor Museum today, aren't they? My Dad's ever so excited. He loves old cars."

I finished sorting the groceries and passed Abbie a box of lettuce.

"In that case you should tell him to come on the opening day. Eric's invited a lot of car restorers and they're going to be doing displays. I expect your Dad would enjoy that."

Water splashed everywhere as Abbie turned on the taps to wash the lettuce.

"And he might learn something too," she said earnestly. "He's always taking cars to pieces, but he's not so good at putting them back together again. Our garden's full of bits of engines and things."

"I'll bet your Mum loves that."

Abbie shook the lettuce leaves vigorously and a shower of water sprayed across the floor.

"She's used to it. If she complains, Dad always says, 'you knew what I was like when you married me. It's too late to change me now.'"

Abbie wasn't the only one who was excited about the vintage cars arriving. Over recent weeks, Dad and David had spent increasing amounts of time at the top of the hill advising Eric how best to convert the sports hall into a museum.

They had reported back to us regularly, explaining how the work was progressing and passing on stories of where Eric had discovered his favourite cars and how he had restored them.

It was clear Eric enjoyed talking about his collection and Dad and David made an eager audience.

When post arrived addressed to the Motor Museum, the postman delivered it to our letterbox. Even after Eric visited the post office to explain the new arrangements, we still received letters or parcels most days.

David always insisted on taking the post up to the museum himself.

"After all, it might be something important," he told us.

Inevitably, it was an age before he reappeared with another collection of stories from Eric.

Dad was just as bad. Normally, if I couldn't find him in the ticket box with Mum, or helping in the Animal Meadow, I could be certain he would be in his workshop, but now he disappeared for hours at a time.

"It's supposed to be women that gossip, not men," Phil grumbled. "I needed David to help me move the feed sacks earlier. I couldn't find him anywhere, but I know where he was."

"It's not good enough," I told David when I saw him later. "What are Phil and I supposed to do in an emergency? We can't drop everything and run all the way up the hill to find you, can we?"

He dropped his head and looked ashamed of himself.

"Sorry. But I have to check on Eric occasionally. He is our tenant, after all."

"Occasionally? You've been up there every day this week."

"That's not fair. I was only there yesterday because there was a problem with the electricity."

"Really? Dad told me he went up to check if Eric needed anything and the two of you were laying on the floor under a T-Model Ford."

"What was I supposed to do?" David asked sheepishly. "He wanted to show me how he'd welded the chassis. It would have been rude not to have shown any interest."

I glared at him.

"You should be interested in what's happening down here! It will be the start of the season soon. We need you."

* * *

Ian's gardening team were busy cutting a pathway from the end of the Pirate Trail down through the woodland to the craft block. It would open up a whole new area for people to walk and enjoy the peace of the countryside and had the added benefit of keeping the men away from the public.

I had visited the work regularly and was delighted with the way it was progressing. I wasn't sure if the men were getting more skilled or the tutors were giving clearer instructions, but the end results were much improved. The steps they made were cut evenly into the hillside and reinforced with well-laid wooden boards. It was an excellent job and Ian told me that once the path was finished, they would put in handrails.

In addition to the new path, Bob had a brainwave and asked Ian if his building team would like to practise on the two flats at the end of the dormitory block. They had dried out since the new roofs had been put on and the walls needed to be re-plastered. Ian was delighted with the opportunity. We only had to provide the materials, and the team did all the work.

Bob even persuaded them to do the decorating.

* * *

Saturdays were always the quietest day of the week, so I was not surprised when David popped into the tearooms one Friday and asked if we could manage without him the following morning.

"Why? Has Eric got something new arriving?" I teased.

David looked offended.

"Certainly not. I have to pop over to Newton Abbot to collect something."

"That's fine, as long as you're back to cover for lunchtime."

True to his word, he arrived back halfway through the morning and his face gleamed with excitement.

"Spare a minute. I've got something to show you," he said as he plonked an enormous cardboard box on the kitchen table.

"What on earth's that?"

"You're going to love it. This is our new communications system."

I eyed the grubby box doubtfully. The words CAPE BANANAS were stencilled along one side.

"I think you'd better explain."

He lifted the cardboard flaps and revealed an assortment of dark green objects. I had no idea what they were until he took one out and held it to his ear.

"Walkie-talkies!" he announced proudly. "There are twelve of them altogether and a control box. I got it from the army surplus store. It will take a bit of sorting out but they've got a range of half a mile so we should be able to talk to each other from all over the site."

"Really? That's amazing!"

I picked up one of the walkie-talkies and examined it with interest. It was too big to carry in a pocket, but there was a clip on the side to fit onto a belt. A knob at one end pulled out to provide an aerial and the front panel had three switches and a circle of wire mesh which I guessed must be a speaker.

"No more problems," David said happily, "from now on, whenever you need help you just have to call."

"That's brilliant! We can have one each and carry it with us. Is that right?"

"Yes, that's it. Of course, the batteries in the receivers only last for ninety minutes so we can't keep them with us all the time. The man in the shop said it's best to leave them plugged into the charger and only take them out when we want to use them. What do you think?"

"I think they're awesome! But how much did they cost?"

"They weren't cheap," David admitted, "but I thought we could see them as an investment."

"Absolutely," I agreed. "They're really sturdy too, so they'll last for years."

David grinned.

"I bet we'll still be using them next century!"

* * *

"How are the arrangements going for the Clown Convention?"

I had expected Bob to give me an update, but instead he just frowned.

"Not good?" I asked.

He wrinkled his nose and shrugged.

"I've heard back from lots of clowns and they all say what a wonderful idea it is, but only three have actually said they're coming."

"Oh, dear."

"Some others have said they'll come if they can, but it depends on whether they get any paid bookings for that weekend."

"That's not very helpful."

"No," Bob agreed. "I can't make my mind up whether we should advertise it or not. I don't want to get the public here expecting clowns and then have hardly any turn up."

I nodded.

"That would be awful."

We discussed the matter with the others and asked what they thought.

"My vote is that we take the risk. There's no point in putting the event on if we don't advertise it," Dad said.

Mum nodded.

"From what I remember, even three clowns would make a big impression."

"But what happens if they let us down?" David asked. "Do we know for sure they're going to turn up?"

"They've said they'll come, but they're clowns. They're not famous for being predictable, are they?" Bob replied.

"Then I guess we have to be brave and take the risk," Dad said simply.

Bob nodded.

"OK. I'll go ahead and book the advertising. There's still a month to go. We'll just have to keep our fingers crossed."

* * *

The summer half-term week marked the start of the main tourist season, and it was vital that it went well. Half-term started with the Late May bank holiday, and this year it would finish with the Clown Convention.

Since we opened at Easter, Bob had arranged live entertainment each Sunday. The shows took place on the lawn in front of the main house and had proved so popular we decided to extend them and now planned to have live shows every day.

Our main entertainer was Max, an outstanding young juggler who could make balls, hoops or clubs twist through the air in impossible arcs and return to his hands with effortless grace.

His performances were mesmerising and the range of tricks he could perform was remarkable, but Max was not always good at communicating with his audience. As a result, although teenagers and adults appreciated his skills, smaller children sometimes became bored.

To cater for the youngsters, Bob engaged an older entertainer who called himself Uncle Waldo and performed traditional Punch and Judy shows and simple magic tricks.

The public loved both performers, and we were delighted by the positive comments we received, but it soon became clear that Max and Uncle Waldo did not rate each other at all.

It wasn't long before Max told David he thought Uncle Waldo's act was 'anachronistic and irrelevant' while Uncle Waldo described Max as an 'opinionated young upstart.'

In an attempt to keep the happy family atmosphere, Bob decided to introduce the acts himself at every performance rather than leave them to introduce each other as they had done in the past.

Soon Bob, in his top hat and red jacket, became the symbol of Silverlands. We used his photo on all our advertising and I found myself waiting for an objection from Mum.

To my surprise, she was gathering up a pile of our leaflets in the ticket box one afternoon when she paused and looked at the image on the front.

"Bob makes a good ringmaster, doesn't he?" she said. "He has a way with people."

I was tempted to ask her if she was feeling well, but instead, I agreed with her.

"There's something about him," she went on, "people always seem to like him."

She must have realised I was staring at her because she looked up at me and frowned.

"Well, they do, don't they?"

I laughed.

"Yes, people like him because he's a lovely, friendly person. He's also kind and patient and long-suffering and..."

"All right, that's enough," Mum cut across me. "I was just commenting. You don't have to make a song and dance about it."

* * *

"What are we going to do if it turns out to be another wet summer?" I asked Bob one morning as I fastened his white bow tie.

"It's not going to be wet. It's going to be beautiful," he said confidently.

"I hope you're right."

"Of course, I am. Don't look for problems."

It worried me that we had nowhere big enough to hold the live shows indoors if it rained. When we first decided to have live entertainment, we had tried to find a suitable room, but it had proved impossible. There were still a number in the main house that had not been brought into use, but they were all too small. In the end we had decided to go ahead anyway.

So far, we had been lucky, but I found myself looking at the weather forecast each day and my heart sank every time I saw a little cloud symbol.

To give the entertainers somewhere to store their equipment, David assembled a small shed among the bushes at the side of the lawn. It was just big enough for a table and a couple of chairs, although we knew that Max and Uncle Waldo would never choose to be in it at the same time.

We had grown used to Uncle Waldo complaining about his colleague.

"That young man has no respect," he protested. "I left my props laid out on the table and he's swept them all into a pile. It's so unprofessional."

"Never mind, I'm sure he doesn't mean to upset you."

"Yes, he does. He knows I have to use the same space as him, and yet he insists on smoking in there. He sprays the place with air freshener and thinks I won't noticc, but it's disgusting. It was so strong last week it gave me a headache."

"You're going to have to do something about Max," I said to Bob later. "I can't cope with Uncle Waldo moaning all the time."

"I already have. I think he may not be as reliable as we'd hoped."

"Really? Why?"

"He lost his patience with a little boy this morning. The lad kept running up to him in the middle of the show and finally Max shouted at him."

"That sounds embarrassing."

"It was. I had to apologise to the family afterwards."

* * *

The next morning, the sky was heavy with clouds and Uncle Waldo's mood matched the weather.

He appeared in the kitchen just as we were about to open.

"Is it all right if I help myself to some black coffee? I need something to fortify myself."

"Of course," I said, "but please don't put your bag on the chopping board. I'm just about to start preparing."

"Sorry," he said and dropped the bag to the floor. "I don't mean to get in your way but there's nowhere else I can go to escape the public. Are we expecting Max today?"

"Of course."

Uncle Waldo scowled as he spooned coffee granules into a mug.

"I was hoping yesterday's outburst might have changed things."

"Not at all. I'm sure it was just a thoughtless moment."

"Perhaps. But there is something about that young man I don't trust."

By mid-morning the air was damp with the threat of rain. A few families were still clambering over the Pirate Trail, but others were looking up at the sky and making their way inside.

Bob was standing in the corner of the kitchen in his ringmaster's outfit, drinking a quick coffee.

"Do you think it's worth starting a show?" I asked him. "It's going to pour down any minute."

"We might as well. I don't want to disappoint anyone. If it gets too bad, we'll have to stop."

"OK. I'll keep my fingers crossed," I said as he slipped out of the kitchen door.

Through the window, I could see Max standing behind the bushes waiting to be announced.

"They're just about to start the first show," I told Uncle Waldo.

"All right, my dear, I'll get out of your way. I don't mind waiting in the shed as long as Max isn't in there."

By the time I had finished in the kitchen, heavy raindrops were rattling against the window. The tearooms were overflowing with families and Martha was passing through a steady stream of orders.

"At least it's busy in here today," Bob grinned as he let himself into the kitchen and shook the rain from his top hat.

"Did you manage to finish the show?" I asked.

"Pretty much. Max cut the last couple of tricks, but I doubt if anyone noticed."

"That's good. What's happening with Uncle Waldo?"

"He's in the shed for now. He said he didn't want to be under your feet, so he's staying there until the rain stops and we can get started again. Any hope of a quick bite to eat?"

"Of course," I grinned, "but you'll have to get it yourself. I've got a queue of orders waiting."

The lunchtime rush had eased by the time the rain stopped and Bob disappeared to start Uncle Waldo's show.

Dad was helping clear the tables and the usual backlog of china was waiting to be put through the dishwasher.

"Do you want to grab some lunch?" I asked Abbie.

"If that's OK."

"Sure, take a break while you can. When you've finished, I'll take over from Martha."

Dad and I worked steadily, and in the distance the sound of children's laughter floated up from the lawn.

"They're loving Punch and Judy today," Dad commented.

"Yes," I agreed. "Never loses its magic, does it?"

I had taken over from Martha and was serving teas when Bob and Uncle Waldo appeared in the servery.

To my surprise, Uncle Waldo blew me a kiss and headed unsteadily into the kitchen. Bob gave me a strange look that I couldn't decipher and followed him.

I was tempted to rush after them but there was still a crowd of people waiting to be served so I controlled my curiosity and stayed at my post. To my relief, Martha soon returned from her break and I hurried into the kitchen.

Uncle Waldo was leaning against the sink. He had a pasty in one hand and was waving it through the air as if conducting an orchestra.

Abbie was watching him in amazement.

"Is he all right?" I asked Bob.

"God only knows!" Bob looked bewildered. "There's something wrong with him. That was the weirdest Punch and Judy I've ever seen. The baby started arguing with the crocodile and Judy hit the policeman with a banana."

"What?"

Abbie sniggered as Uncle Waldo began waltzing around the room with an imaginary partner.

"Did the audience notice?" I asked.

"If they did, they didn't seem to mind. They certainly laughed a lot."

"He reeks of something," I grimaced as Uncle Waldo pirouetted past me.

"I was magnificent!" he trilled. "That show was... the highlight of my career."

"The shed reeks too," Bob nodded, "I noticed it earlier when Max was in there."

Uncle Waldo stumbled and crashed to the floor. He lay staring up at the ceiling as I rushed across to him.

"Are you hurt?"

"No, dear, I'm just having a little rest."

Bob came up beside me and we both looked down at Uncle Waldo.

"He must be drunk," Bob said.

"What are we going to do?" I wailed. "He's got another show at three o'clock."

Uncle Waldo climbed slowly to his feet.

"Never fear, I am here! I will dazzle them. My audience will be amazed!"

Suddenly, Abbie burst into giggles.

"He's not drunk. He's high!"

I stared at her.

"What?"

"He's high. It's cannabis. I can smell it from here."

Bob was appalled.

"Oh, my God. She's right! It's Max. He must have been smoking pot in the shed."

It took ages for us to persuade Uncle Waldo to go up to our flat and lay down. The afternoon show was cancelled and Bob sacked Max on the spot.

We couldn't let Uncle Waldo drive home, so I had to phone his wife and tell her that he had a bit of a headache and would be late getting home.

Bob went to check on Uncle Waldo and found him asleep on the sofa cuddling one of Claire's teddies. When he woke up, we gave him a large drink of water and sent him home in a taxi.

* * *

"What are we going to do without Max? We can't manage with just Uncle Waldo for the whole summer."

I was trying to hide my panic, but failing miserably.

"It will be OK," Bob reassured me. "There are lots of other entertainers around. I met a lad called Zac recently. He's quite young, but he's brilliant. I was thinking of giving him a chance to see how he gets on."

"Don't we need someone experienced?"

"We'll still have Uncle Waldo. I'm sure he'll be fine by next weekend."

"I hope so!" I still felt bad about what happened. "Don't you think we should tell him what was really wrong with him?"

"Why? He'd die of embarrassment. You know what he's like. He such a dignified old fellow. How do you think he'd feel if we told him he'd been waltzing around the kitchen singing to a pasty?"

"I suppose you're right."

"You know I am. I'll see if Zac is available this weekend and if he is, we'll find out what he's like in front of an audience."

Zac arrived promptly at ten o'clock on Sunday morning. He was young and extremely thin with a serious expression and long black hair scraped neatly back into a ponytail.

He wore tight striped trousers, a black waistcoat, and carried a large canvas bag filled with juggling equipment.

Bob took him off to show him where he would be performing, and Abbie watched him go with interest.

"He's not much older than me, is he?" she asked.

"No, I don't think he is," I agreed.

"I wonder how he learned to be a juggler?"

"You'll have to ask him."

Abbie's cheeks flushed immediately.

"Oh no, I couldn't do that. I'd be shy."

"Why? I've never known you be shy before."

Abbie didn't answer, and I was distracted by Uncle Waldo's arrival.

His face was a picture of misery and his shoulders drooped as he apologised profusely for his 'unprofessional behaviour.'

"Don't be silly," I told him. "You weren't well, that's all."

"My wife thinks I must have been dehydrated. Delirious."

"She's probably right," I agreed. "What matters is that you're better now."

He blinked and blew his nose.

"Thank you for being so understanding, my dear. It was all most upsetting."

* * *

"How did Zac's show go?" I asked Bob when I saw him.

"Brilliantly. You could tell he was nervous, but the audience loved him. I think he's going to be great."

"Excellent. Let's hope he gets on with Uncle Waldo."

I need not have worried. Later that morning I found Zac and Uncle Waldo settled on stools at the far end of the kitchen discussing the history of juggling. Uncle Waldo was listening intently to what Zac was saying, and it was clear the young man took his profession seriously.

"He's an interesting lad, isn't he?" Uncle Waldo said later. "A bit shy, but there's nothing wrong with that."

It was true that Zac didn't like mixing with the public when he was not performing. As soon as his show finished, he would slip in through the door from the yard and settle himself at the far end of the kitchen. Fortunately, it was a large room. When Silverlands had been Stokelake school, it had housed several hundred boys and the kitchens would have been full of cooks. Now Abbie and I only used one of the six massive ovens that lined the far wall of the kitchen and there was plenty of space for a juggler to relax without getting in our way.

The following day Zac must have felt more at home because he began practicing new tricks between his shows.

Abbie was enthralled.

"Don't watch him," I scolded her as I strapped yet another plaster around a cut finger.

"I can't help it."

"I'll tell him not to come in here if you can't concentrate on what you're doing."

"Please don't," she begged. "He's so clever. Did you see what he was doing earlier? He had a bowl on his head and was flipping saucers up with his foot and catching them in the bowl."

"He wasn't using our saucers, was he?" I asked, looking along the room to where Zac was balancing a spinning plate on a pole on his chin.

"No, of course not. They were metal ones he brought with him. He's awesome, isn't he?"

"Yes, he is," I admitted.

"And he likes steak and kidney pie."

"Does he? How do you know that?"

"I gave him the last portion that was left over from lunchtime."

"Abbie! You're not supposed to give away food without asking me."

"I know. I'm sorry, but he looked so hungry."

She looked at me with huge brown eyes and I understood. The young juggler was worryingly thin and there was a puppyish quality about him that made me want to feed him too.

"All right. I don't mind you giving him stuff that would be thrown away, like jacket potatoes, but nothing that we can save for tomorrow. OK?"

"Yes, of course," Abbie beamed happily, "he'll do a much better show this afternoon if he's been fed, won't he?"

Zac fitted in easily. The audiences loved his performances, and Uncle Waldo took him under his wing.

Abbie was delirious when I told her that Zac would be performing all through the summer.

"That's the best news ever," she beamed. "Now I'll be able to watch him every day. It'll be like having my own little shows."

"No, it won't. You're here to work, not to stare at Zac," I tried to sound stern, but she looked so happy I couldn't stop myself smiling.

* * *

"It's great that we've got Zac as well as Uncle Waldo, but is that going to be enough for the whole summer?" I asked Bob as we ate our evening meal.

"No," Bob admitted, "we can't expect them both to work seven days a week. I need to find someone to fill the gaps."

The following morning, we were woken by a horn blaring outside our window.

"What the hell's that?" Bob demanded as he leapt from bed and threw open the curtains.

As he peered out of the window, the horn stopped. Dragging on his dressing gown, he hurried out of the door and I was left to stumble across the room and peer out of the window myself.

Our bedroom was immediately above the front door and a bright red camper van was parked on the tarmac below.

Moments later I heard the scrape of the front door being opened, and Bob appeared.

As I watched, a slim blonde woman climbed out of the car and held out her hand to him. They talked for a long time before the woman climbed back into the van and Bob retreated inside.

I waited, expecting the van to drive off, but it stayed where it was.

"What was that all about?" I asked as Bob returned.

"She's a clown," Bob said as though it explained everything. "She heard there's a convention here next weekend, and she's turned up early."

"You're joking."

"I wish I was. Her name's Liza. She's been working at a caravan park in Cornwall, but she had a disagreement with her boss and walked out. Now she has nowhere to stay, and she's living in her camper van, so she's asked if she can put it in the car park here for a few days until she sorts herself out."

"But how would that work? What about a loo? Or water? Or electricity?"

I waited for Bob to answer, but he only yawned.

"What are we going to do?" I asked.

Bob looked at the bedside clock.

"The alarm's not due for another forty minutes. I don't know about you, but I'm going back to sleep."

And he did.

By the time we had dressed and come downstairs, David was outside talking to Liza. "She's very grateful we let her stay," he said when he came in. "She's offered to do a show for us every day if we want her to."

"But we don't know if she's any good," Phil pointed out.

Bob shrugged.

"I guess there's no harm in giving her a chance."

* * *

"Are you busy?" Bob's head popped around the kitchen door. "I thought you might like to watch this woman's show with me."

"Do I have to?"

"Yes. You might as well suffer too."

"I suppose. Unless you want to go for your break now, Abbie?"

"No, I don't mind waiting."

Bob grinned.

"Good. You have no excuse. Follow me."

* * *

Bob had put up a blackboard announcing CLOWN SHOW – 11AM and a small crowd had gathered on the lawn.

"Where is she?" I asked.

Bob nodded along the road behind me.

"I think this must be her now."

A startling figure in a dazzling costume walked towards us.

Instead of blonde hair, she wore a curly red wig topped by a massive yellow bow. Her face was powder white with carefully painted blue swirls across her cheeks and an enormous red mouth.

"Morning!" she beamed at us. "My full name's name's Liza Berlin, by the way, and this is Roly the Wonderdog."

She held up a large ghetto-blaster.

"We have our music and we're ready to perform. Say hello, Roly."

The dog stood on its hind legs, pirouetted, and let out a howl.

I was speechless.

Bob looked as startled as I felt, but he organised the crowd into a circle and introduced our new performers.

Liza soon had the audience's attention.

"Who's good at maths?" she asked.

Children's hands shot up and Liza pointed to a boy at the front.

"Will you help me?"

The boy stepped forwards eagerly.

"This is my dog, Roly. I call him Roly the Wonderdog because he's very clever. He can do sums. If I ask him some sums will you tell me if he gets the answers right?"

The boy nodded, and Roly thumped his tail on the ground.

"OK, then. What is two add three?"

Liza pointed her finger at Roly, and the dog barked five times.

"Is that right?"

The crowd clapped, and the boy nodded.

Liza asked the audience to call out sums, and each time Roly barked out the right answer.

"And now it's time to dance!" Liza announced.

She flicked a switch on the ghetto blaster, and music blared out. At once, Roly reared up on his hind legs and turned in a circle.

Liza began to dance and Roly followed her faultlessly. When Liza lifted her arm, Roly lifted his paw. When Liza nodded her head to the music, so did the dog. When she turned around, he pirouetted on the spot. They moved in perfect harmony and both seemed to be having the time of their lives.

When the music stopped, the audience went wild.

* * *

"It was incredible," I told David later. "You have to see them. Her little dog is superb."

"I heard the clapping from the gift shop. How long is she staying?"

I hesitated.

"She was only supposed to be here until the weekend..."

"There's a 'but' coming, isn't there?" David asked.

"Yes. But Bob has done it again."

"What do you mean?"

"He's made another unilateral decision."

"What is it this time?"

"He's offered her one of the flats in the dormitory block if she stays for the summer."

David laughed.

"If Liza is as great as you say she is that sounds like a good move."

"But what about Mum? Do you think she's going to have another meltdown?"

"Probably. But it might help if you introduce her to Roly first. You know how much she loves dogs."

David was right. The moment Mum met Roly she was entranced and made no objection to him and his human moving into the newly furnished flat.

As I got ready for bed that night Bob had a smug look on his face.

"It's been a funny day, hasn't it?" he said.

"Yes," I agreed, "it was this time last night I said we needed to find another entertainer, wasn't it?"

"And twenty-four hours later our new performer and her Wonderdog have moved in and are ready to start work. You can't say I waste time."

"You can't claim all the credit," I complained. "It was just luck that she turned up when she did."

"No, it wasn't. She turned up because she'd heard about the Clown Convention. I arranged the Convention so I deserve the credit."

"You're impossible!" I laughed. "Now go to sleep. With your luck, we'll probably be woken at dawn by a whole circus turning up."

* * *

Fortunately, there were no more disturbances, and we slept peacefully until the alarm went off.

The next days ran smoothly and Bob made sure he had everything planned for the weekend. The local radio station, DevonAir, were so intrigued by the idea of a Clown Convention they asked if they could send their outside broadcast unit to broadcast from our grounds all day.

We were delighted. Not only would we get a huge amount of publicity on the day, but DevonAir were going to be playing adverts in advance. We were confident we would have a large turnout but still didn't know if any of the clowns were actually going to turn up.

Wednesday was Abbie's day off, and David helped me in the kitchen over lunchtime. When the weather was sunny lots of families brought their own picnics and we didn't have as many full meals to prepare as usual.

David was slicing a cheesecake into portions when he asked if Fred had been behaving himself.

"Everything's been quiet," I said, and David looked disappointed.

"Not even any footsteps?"

"No, not a thing. No Fred, no visits from Duncan Matthews and no word from the solicitor."

"Positively boring then."

"It's just the way I like it. This weekend is going to be exciting enough without anything else going on."

"True. A Clown Convention, a live radio broadcast and the opening of the Motor Museum all on the same day. I don't think we'll notice, even if Fred does make an appearance."

"How are things going at the Museum? Will it all be ready on time?"

"I think so. Ian's got another delivery of cars coming in this afternoon. After that, there's only the fire engine left to arrive."

"Good. Don't forget your walkie-talkie if you disappear."

* * *

As a family of animal lovers, we had always encouraged visitors to bring their dogs with them when they visited Silverlands. I kept a bowl of fresh water on the verandah outside the tearooms, and Phil had a jar of dog treats beneath the counter in the gift shop that she kept for well-behaved doggy visitors.

She had just given a treat to a young family for their chihuahua when she realised Tom the Potter was glaring at her through the shop window.

"He came storming in and demanded to know what I was doing," she told me later. "It was awful. He said I shouldn't encourage visitors to bring animals, and they were not welcome in the craft centre."

I groaned inwardly.

"It was so embarrassing," Phil went on. "He can't behave like that."

"All right. I'll go and talk to him."

I found Tom in his unit.

"I suppose you've come to lecture me."

He sat down at his wheel and switched on the electric motor.

"Can I have a word with you before you get started?" I asked.

"No. I'm running late as it is. People have been distracting me all afternoon and I have orders to finish."

I sighed.

"Tom, I need to talk to you. Phil was very upset by what you said earlier."

"I was merely expressing my opinion."

He threw a large lump of clay onto the wheel and it spun rhythmically as he caressed it into shape.

"She said you told her off for giving out dog treats."

"Don't be ridiculous. The treats are irrelevant. The point is, people shouldn't be allowed to bring dogs here at all."

"But what do you want us to do when a family turns up with a dog? Turn them away?"

"Of course not. They can leave the animal in their car."

"No, they can't! Some families stay all day. If they left a dog in the car, it might overheat."

Tom clicked his tongue as he smoothed the clay into a high mound.

"That's their problem, isn't it? Have you seen how many turds they leave behind?"

I felt my temper rising.

"No."

"Of course, you haven't. Because I clear them up."

His eyes rose to meet mine, then he thrust both his thumbs dramatically into the centre of the clay.

"Well, no more!" he exclaimed and squeezed the clay so hard it spurted between his fingers.

"If you encourage the beasts, you can clean up the crap!"

* * *

"Has anyone had any problems with dog poo?" I asked at closing time.

"I have cleared a bit up occasionally, but I wouldn't say it was a problem," Dad said.

"It's funny you should mention it," Phil said thoughtfully, "I came through the craft block just now and there was a little pile on the grass."

My heart sank.

"The strange thing was…" she added, "it had a flag in it."

"A flag? What do you mean a flag?"

"Just that. It had one of those little flags kids use on sand castles stuck in the top."

It was true. A small, steaming turd lay next to the path and was topped with a tiny flag.

I found Tom in his unit.

"Why?" I demanded.

"I would have thought that was obvious. I wanted to draw attention to the problem."

"Really? With a Union Jack?"

"I'm sorry. Would you have preferred a Welsh dragon? Or the cross of St George?"

"This isn't funny."

"Come now, have you no sense of humour?"

"Not if it involves dog poo."

Tom turned his back on me and began rearranging a display of pots.

"In that case, I can only say that I was trying to make the owner feel guilty."

The following day Phil arrived in the kitchen halfway through the morning.

"You'd better come and have a look," she sighed.

This time there was no flag. Instead, a large round turd sparkled beneath a layer of purple glitter.

"You have to admit it looks much prettier now," Tom said sweetly.

"It looks ridiculous!" I seethed. "If you don't want to clean up yourself can't you just let us know when you spot something and I'll send someone over to deal with it."

Tom frowned at me.

"But that's not the point. This is about education. We have to teach these people that letting their animals poop wherever they choose is completely unacceptable."

"And so is decorating dog turds!" I snapped, but Tom was unmoved.

"If you stop them pooping, I won't have to do it anymore, will I?"

"It's getting ridiculous," I muttered to Bob that evening.

"What's he done now?"

"Feathers."

Bob laughed, but I didn't see the joke.

"It's not funny. There must be something we can do."

"Like what?"

"Do you think Mum could say something to dog owners when they turn up at the ticket box?"

"That would be a bit awkward, wouldn't it? What do you want her to say? Welcome to Silverlands, but don't let your dog poop while it's here."

"Not those exact words. But we've got to do something."

* * *

The Clown Convention was due to take place on the first Sunday in June and we had offered to provide camping facilities or Bed and Breakfast for Saturday and Sunday night, but by Friday evening we still only had three clowns who had confirmed they would be coming.

"It will be four if you include Liza," I reminded Bob.

"There are still a lot I haven't heard from. We might get a couple more if we're lucky,"

He sounded flat, and I knew he was disappointed by the low turnout.

"Whatever happens, I'm sure they will make a lot of noise so it's bound to sound good on the radio," I said brightly.

The next morning, I made sure the cleaning was finished early, and I was settling Claire into a playpen in the kitchen when the baker arrived. I had ordered a lot of extra cakes for the weekend and I hoped I was not going to regret my decision.

"Wow! Look at all those doughnuts," Abbie said as she eyed the first tray. "I love doughnuts."

"They may be your lunch for the rest of the week if we don't get enough customers."

"Sound good to me," she grinned.

Suddenly, the door flew open and a giant figure in a tartan suit with a painted face, floppy hat and enormous feet bounced into the kitchen.

Abbie screamed.

"Hello, my darlings!" The clown wrapped his arms around me and began to sing, "Nellie the Elephant, packed her trunk and said goodbye to the circus..."

Gasping for breath, I pulled away and disentangled myself.

"Daffo! It's lovely to see you."

He turned and beamed at Abbie, who had retreated to the other side of the table.

"Hello, young lady, we haven't met, have we?"

Abbie shook her head and took another step backwards.

"It's OK, Abbie, this is Daffo. He's one of the clowns for the convention. Why don't you get the coffee going in the servery? I'm sure we're going to need lots."

Abbie hurried out of the kitchen as another clown appeared behind me.

"Circo! You're here too!"

Circo was tastefully dressed in a massive pair of yellow shorts, a polka dot shirt and an aviator's helmet with goggles. He greeted me with another bear hug that lifted my feet off the ground.

"It's so long since we saw you," Circo boomed, "and this must be Claire. My goodness, she was only a baby back then."

He knelt down and wiggled his gloved fingers at Claire through the side of the playpen. To my relief, she didn't cry but picked up a teddy and held it out to her strange new friend.

"For me?" Circo's face creased into an enormous smile. "Thank you!"

Claire immediately withdrew the teddy, and Circo's face sagged into a sad expression.

Claire giggled and held out the teddy again.

"It looks like you've made a friend," I laughed.

"He's doing better than me. Your assistant looked terrified. Maybe I'd better go and help her with the coffee," Daffo suggested.

"No, she'll be fine," I said quickly. "Have you seen Bob yet? I don't think he's expecting you."

"He must be. He invited us."

"I know he did, but I don't think he heard back from you."

"Didn't he? Never mind, we're here now. Where is he? We'd better go and say hello."

As soon as Daffo and Circo had gone I checked on Abbie. She was putting out fresh tablecloths at the far end of the tearooms and looked shaken.

"It's safe to come back in the kitchen now. Haven't you ever met a clown before?"

Abbie shook her head.

"I didn't expect them to be so big."

"They can be a bit overwhelming," I agreed, "but they're lovely when you get used to them."

By lunchtime, several more clowns had arrived.

"Why do they all look so different?" Abbie asked as she watched a group walk past the window. "I thought clowns just had white faces with red mouths and noses."

I laughed.

"Clowns really aren't like that. You could never get them all to do the same thing. Every clown has his own make-up. It's called motley. Once a clown decides on his motley, he never changes it. It's like a trademark."

"So that people know it's him?"

"Yes, that's right. The Clown Association registers what they look like, and it's strictly against the rules to wear another clown's motley."

"Wow. I didn't know clowns had rules."

"They do. And they take them very seriously. They're not allowed to swear when they're wearing motley, and they're not supposed to smoke either."

"Can they get arrested if they do?"

I laughed again.

"No. I don't think so. They might get a custard pie thrown at them."

Abbie looked at me seriously.

"Oh dear, I don't think they'd like that."

* * *

By Saturday afternoon twenty-two clowns and their families had arrived. We had expected them to turn up and relax before the convention on Sunday, but all of them arrived in full motley and extravagant costumes ready to perform.

Bob did his best. He arranged improvised shows on the lawn all afternoon, but the clowns who were not involved simply went on performing to any visitors they could find.

"It's chaos out there," David said happily as he passed through the tea rooms. "Giggles and Bingo have got an enormous pair of plastic scissors and are pretending to cut people's hair in the shop. Jim and Gertie are giving guided tours of Down in Devon. Goodness knows what they are telling everyone, and Filpot is teaching kids how to walk a tightrope."

"Is that safe?" I demanded.

"Don't worry. The rope is lying on the ground, but they're all having a wonderful time."

"OK. You had me worried for a moment."

"Don't panic. It's all going really well."

"I suppose it is, but do you have any idea where they're all going to stay?"

David shrugged.

"No idea. Don't worry, I'm sure Bob's got it all sorted."

I was touched by his confidence.

* * *

There was no point in doing a search when we closed as groups of clowns and their families were still spread throughout the building, chatting and laughing and generally enjoying themselves.

"What happens about food?" I asked Bob when I saw him.

"I was going to ask you about that. I hadn't expected to have so many staying tonight. I think we ought to offer them a meal, don't you?"

"How many are there altogether?"

"With the kids, it must be about fifty."

I sighed.

"OK. I'll see what I can manage."

Abbie and Martha had already gone home, but Dad and David joined me in the kitchen.

Fortunately, most of the clowns were easy to please. A lot of them were vegetarians and were happy with mixed salads and warm crusty bread and the rest tucked into an improvised curry and rice. Only one clown, an elderly man who went by the name of Pecky, turned up his nose at everything I offered him.

"I have to be very careful. I can't eat red meat, or chicken, or pork, or flour, or potatoes, or rice, or vegetables, and I don't like fruit. Or fish."

He looked at me expectantly.

"So, what have you got?" he asked.

Eventually, he agreed he could eat a mushroom omelette but when I put it on the table in front of him his large red mouth drooped miserably.

"No chips? You can't serve an omelette without chips."

"You said you couldn't eat potatoes," I reminded him.

"Chips don't count as potatoes," he pouted, "and haven't you got any ketchup?"

* * *

"Could you manage with one less clown tomorrow?" I asked Bob while I waited for the chips to cook.

"Which one?"

"Pecky. I might have to kill him."

"Why what's he done?"

"Nothing really. I'm just tired."

Bob put his arms around me.

"Never mind. I've just got to sort out where they're all going to camp, then let's get an early night. It's going to be a long day tomorrow."

I leaned my head on his shoulder.

"True, but at least you don't have to worry that no-one will turn up."

* * *

As the sun set and shadows crept across the lawn, the clowns brought their cars down from the car park and began preparing for the night.

An assortment of tents was assembled in a rough curve, and two small caravans were parked on the drive.

To my surprise, Liza brought her camper van and joined the crowd.

"I couldn't miss this, could I?" she said. "It's going to be awesome."

"What is?"

"Tonight. Everyone's got their instruments. As soon as it's dark, we'll get started."

I reported back to Bob.

"I think they're going to start singing. What should we do?"

I didn't mind having the clowns to stay, but I was tired and I really wanted to sleep.

"I'm sure they won't be loud. They've got their own kids with them, remember."

"I know, but Claire's bedroom is right at the front. If they wake her up, we'll never get her back to sleep."

"Don't panic. It will be fine."

"I'm not panicking," I grumbled. "I just want to get some sleep tonight."

Once the tents were erected and the younger children were settled in their tents, a collection of folding chairs and benches were dragged into a circle.

Bingo pulled a mobile BBQ from the boot of his car and filled it with a mixture of charcoal and wood. Soon it was blazing, and the others gathered around it like a campfire.

Most of the clowns had changed out of their costumes and washed off their motley, and I was embarrassed to find I could no longer recognise them. In the gathering gloom, I stared at the faces and tried to imagine them with makeup on.

Mum had offered to babysit Claire while Dad was up with Michael so

David, Phil, Bob and I were able to socialise.

To my surprise, I found I was enjoying myself. The clowns were a happy bunch, and it was impossible to listen to them teasing each other and telling jokes without smiling.

Liza was the first to sing. She accompanied herself on a guitar and her voice was pure and clear. When she finished, others took turns and, in between, they told stories about their lives and experiences.

"I got a really well-paid job last month," Gertie laughed. "It was a birthday party for a six-year-old. I got there, and it turned to be a family of naturists. Not a stitch on any of them. Even the grandparents. I've never felt so over-dressed in my life. And I had badges to give away as prizes. Lots of badges and nowhere to pin them! It was a nightmare."

Her expression was priceless, and I laughed out loud.

Bottles of beer were passed around, and the wood crackled on the BBQ. Looking up, I saw the sky was bright with stars and a sliver of moon was already high in the sky.

"We ought to be going," I said to Bob.

"Yes, I suppose so," he agreed reluctantly.

We left the clowns and headed up to the flat. Claire was sleeping soundly and Mum was watching TV. I kissed her goodnight while Bob took Dino down for a last run outside.

"It's been a funny day, hasn't it?" Mum said.

"Yes," I agreed. "Another one."

* * *

As soon as my head hit the pillow, I was asleep, and it only felt like moments later that I was woken by a high-pitched wailing outside.

I sat up in bed to see the first glow of morning lighting the curtains.

"Quiet, boy," Bob said as Dino barked.

"Whatever is that?" I demanded.

"That will be Scotty," Bob murmured without lifting his head from the pillow. "Sorry, didn't I tell you about him?"

"Tell me what?"

"He plays the bagpipes. At dawn."

"Why? It's horrible."

Bob's eyes were still closed.

"Just ignore it. He won't be long."

I lay down again and tried to forget the wailing music outside, but it was impossible.

Climbing from the bed, I pulled back the curtain and peered out. A short figure wearing a dark green kilt, a pink waistcoat, a battered top hat and a pair of wellies was marching around the edge of the lawn. A set of bagpipes were tucked beneath his arm and the drones spread proudly across his shoulder.

"Did he come all the way from Scotland?" I asked.

"No, Southampton," Bob replied sleepily.

I watched for a while, but Scotty showed no sign of stopping, so I wrapped my dressing gown around me and headed to the bathroom for a shower.

By the time I returned Bob had Claire in bed with him and Dino was pacing the room demanding to be allowed downstairs.

"Mummy!" Claire trilled as she saw me.

The pipes were still wailing outside.

"Do you realise it's not even six o'clock yet?" Bob muttered.

"Don't blame me. This was your idea, remember?"

I picked Claire up and cuddled her as Bob and Dino disappeared downstairs.

"That's better, isn't it?" I said as the bagpipes stopped. "Now wc can go back to sleep."

"Want to play My Little Pony," Claire complained.

"Yes, of course you do."

I yawned widely.

"I guess we might as well get dressed."

* * *

I settled Claire in her highchair in a corner of the kitchen and gave her a bowl of cornflakes. A few minutes later Dad appeared.

"You're up early, couldn't you sleep either?" I asked.

"With those pipes going? Not a chance."

"They were a bit of a surprise, weren't they?"

"I take it I'm baby-sitting again today?"

"If you don't mind," I said. "I think it's going to be busy."

"Yes. I hope so," he grinned.

* * *

We were still encouraging the clowns to clear the lawn when the DevonAir Roadshow turned up. They parked the broadcast unit at the side of the lawn and were soon busy trailing cables across the ground and running sound tests.

The presenter was eager to meet the clowns, and Bingo invited her to join him for bacon and eggs, which were already sizzling in a frying pan on his BBQ.

"You'd better not be too long," Bob reminded them. "We'll be opening soon."

While David and Phil arranged straw bales into a circle on the lawn to represent a circus ring, Bob and I made sure the last of the tents were removed.

By the time Dad carried Mum's bags down to the ticket box, a small crowd were waiting and a steady stream of cars were winding their way up the hill to the car park.

Martha and Abbie had come in early to prepare everything in the tearooms and Sue, a new recruit, was ready for her first day in the kitchen. I felt guilty that she was being thrown in at the deep end, but I was glad we would have an extra pair of hands.

Sue had come in for an induction session earlier in the week, and I was reminding her how to operate the dishwasher when a voice reverberated through the building.

CHAPTER 5

"Good morning! Today we are broadcasting from Silverlands in South Devon…"

"That's deafening!" Abbie squealed, and Sue clapped her hands over her ears.

The piercing announcement vibrated the glass in the windows until the sound level dropped abruptly.

"I hope they don't do that again," I gasped.

Once they had tweaked their levels, the radio broadcasts went well, and the weather was perfect all day.

Families flooded through the gates and the clowns performed to excited crowds in the ring or put on their own impromptu performances wherever they could. Balloon animals abounded, and laughter and giggles filled the air.

There was a constant queue in the tearooms and Martha, Abbie, Sue and I never stopped for a moment. When the clowns came in for morning tea, they could see we were under pressure, so Bingo and Giggles decided to help clear the tables.

Their intentions were good but clowns with size twenty shoes carrying trays loaded with plates, cups and saucers was never a good idea. Abbie rushed to clear the broken china but bumped into Sue and sent even more crockery crashing to the floor.

Bingo borrowed a mop from the kitchen to clear the spilt milk but only managed to spray it everywhere. Fortunately, the customers seemed to think the accident was some form of performance because they all clapped wildly.

Normally, I would have been horrified by such a disaster, but in the circumstances, I laughed until I cried.

I need not have worried about the doughnuts. By lunchtime we were running low on all our cakes and buns and I had to pull emergency supplies of scones from the freezer.

"Is it always like this?" Sue asked with wide eyes.

"No," I assured her, "sometimes it's quite boring."

I had hoped David would arrive to help clear the tables, but there was no sign of him. Abbie and Sue were doing their best, but the piles of crockery waiting to go through the dishwasher grew higher and the list of orders grew longer.

"Are you Diana?"

The voice made me jump. A middle-aged woman was standing by the dishwasher, looking around at the chaos.

"Yes, can I help you?" I asked.

"Actually, I was wondering if I could help you," she said. "I'm Belinda Circo's wife. I used to work in a tearoom myself."

I felt I should refuse, but I didn't.

"Really? That would be awesome."

I was showing her the controls for the dishwasher when a loud explosion came from outside. It was followed by laughter, so I decided to ignore it.

None of us got a break that day. Martha manned that server counter like a sergeant major, sending Sue scurrying for fresh supplies and dealing with customers at a remarkable speed while still appearing calm and welcoming. I was in awe of her.

In the kitchen, Abbie and I prepared meals and rushed them out to waiting customers. Each time I hurried through the servery, I glanced at the length of the queue. It was long, but it never became unmanageable. Finally, late in the afternoon, it began to shorten, and I felt a surge of relief.

"Thank you so much, Belinda," I said earnestly. "I don't know how we would have coped without you."

"My pleasure," she smiled as she wiped her hands on a towel. "It reminded me of the old days. Are you sure you can manage now?"

"Yes, we'll be fine. You might just catch the last clown show if you hurry."

She laughed.

"No thank you, dear. I know all their jokes off by heart already!"

"Then let me get you a cream tea. You've earned it."

Shortly afterwards David arrived, looking exhausted.

"I'm sorry," he apologised, "but I've been running all day. Every time I tried to get here, someone else needed something. Gertie's clown car blew up on the lawn. Did you hear it?"

"I heard a bang. Is it OK?"

"It is now. I had to fix it. And I had to stitch one of Daffo's boots back together. And find something Freddo could use as a flowerpot because he'd forgotten to bring one. And Devonair needed a wooden screen put up to block the noise from the car park. And..."

"OK, you're forgiven," I conceded. "Have you seen Dad recently?"

"Not for a while. He had the kids over in the Animal Meadow earlier, but I haven't seen him since."

"Can you keep an eye on Abbie and Sue if I pop down to the ticket box? I want to make sure Mum's OK."

* * *

As I carried a tray along the drive, a few visitors were still arriving. I waited for Mum to unlock the door of the ticket box.

"I thought you might need a drink," I said. "I wasn't sure if Dad had a chance to bring you anything."

"No, he hasn't, but I'm fine. It's been manic, hasn't it?"

I poured the tea and flopped into the chair. Music was floating in the distance and I could hear voices and laughter, but everything sounded wonderfully far away.

"One good thing happened up today."

"What was that?" I asked.

"A family arrived with a dog this morning so I did my little speech about cleaning up after it and the man said, 'Don't worry – I always go prepared. I have my own Pooper Scooper.'"

"His own what?"

"Pooper Scooper. He showed me a little plastic bag. It had a cardboard scraper and a pair of disposable gloves."

"Amazing. If only all the dog owners were that well prepared."

"But that's the point. They could be. How about we charge visitors a token amount to bring a dog with them and in return we give them a Pooper Scooper kit?"

"That's brilliant! I love it!"

Mum looked pleased with herself and I longed to sit and chat, but I knew there was still a lot to do in the kitchen.

"I'd better be getting back," I said.

Mum nodded sadly and locked the door behind me.

* * *

Back in the kitchen, David helped me get everything cleared away. Sue was still working, but she looked shell-shocked.

"How did everything go for Ian's opening at the Motor Museum?" I asked.

"How should I know?" David retorted. "I haven't had a chance to breathe all day, let alone go up there."

"I wasn't suggesting you had. I was just curious."

"I'll find out tomorrow, but if the traffic going up to the top car park is anything to go by, they must have been packed out too."

"Good. That's what I want to hear."

By the time the kitchen was sorted, Mum and Dad were in the tearooms with the children and the last families were making their way towards the exit.

Martha finished wiping down the counter in the servery and switched off the power to the drink dispensers.

"There, all finished," she said. "Now, if you'll excuse me, I'm off home to put my feet up."

Chapter 6

The last of the clowns didn't leave until lunchtime on Monday. Lovely though it was to have them around the place, I breathed a sigh of relief when they went.

Without them, the house felt quiet even though music was playing in the exhibitions and families chattered everywhere.

When Abbie went for her break, the kitchen felt wonderfully tranquil.

As I loaded plates into the dishwasher, a milk jug toppled from the draining board and splashed into a bowl of water in the sink.

The draining board was wet and slippery and the milk jug was round and had been balanced on a pile of cutlery. It was not surprising it had slipped, but I smiled.

"Is that you, Fred?" I whispered. "I hope you enjoyed all the entertainment. Or do you like it better when it's quiet?"

I waited for a moment, but nothing else happened.

"Did the clowns frighten you? Is that it? Have you been hiding until they left? Please don't start playing up now. I've been looking forward to a bit of peace."

I looked around the kitchen, but everything was as it should be. I fished the jug out of the bowl of washing-up water and dried it on a tea towel.

"That's great, Fred. You keep behaving yourself and we'll get on just fine."

* * *

The rest of June passed smoothly, and we were kept busy as the flow of visitors steadily increased.

Sue's first experience in the kitchen had not put her off, and she turned up promptly the following weekend. I was amused to see Abbie instructing her on where everything went and how important it was to tidy up after herself. It was clear Abbie saw herself as the Senior Kitchen Assistant, even though Sue was two years older than her.

One afternoon I asked Abbie if she would like to take responsibility for making sure all the kitchen surfaces were clear and had been washed down before she left each night. She beamed at me as if I had given her a bunch of flowers.

"Does that mean you trust me to do things by myself now?" she asked.

"Yes, Abbie. Of course, I do. You've been working very well."

A few moments later she disappeared into the servery and I heard her telling Martha what I had said.

"I don't think the girl's ever been praised before," Martha said to me later. "She was like a puppy with two tails. Mind you, I'm not surprised. She doesn't do much that deserves it."

"Oh, come on, she hasn't broken anything for days. I thought it would be good to give her a little responsibility."

"A wee bit, maybe," Martha agreed doubtfully, "just as long as she doesn't start thinking she's Queen of the Kitchen."

* * *

Liza soon became one of the crew. To my surprise, Uncle Waldo took to her at once and the two became firm friends. Liza loved having a flat on site and spent hours wandering around the grounds between shows, chatting to visitors or practicing her routines with Roly.

David soon discovered she had made an impression in Chudleigh too.

"I don't think they're used to having a clown walking through town," he told me. "Did you know she often pops up to the shops in full motley wearing her clown outfit?"

"No, I didn't, but I'm not really surprised. I've hardly seen her out of costume since she arrived."

"The locals think she's mad."

"Like the rest of us," I smiled.

"Yes. Maybe that's why she fits in."

We were standing at the bottom of the stairs waiting for Mum to arrive so we could start our nightly search.

"Have you put the bin up yet?" I asked.

"No, I'm doing it this evening. I have to cement the post in, so I thought it would be better to wait until the visitors have gone."

"Good thinking."

David had acquired a special disposal bin for used Pooper-Scoopers and was going to put it on a post at the side of the drive. Next year it would be marked on the map on our leaflets but for now it would have a sign with a cartoon dog holding a shovel so everyone knew what it was for.

David and Phil had volunteered to assemble the Pooper Scooper packs and had been stuffing disposable gloves and cardboard scrapers into plastic bags between serving customers in the shop.

"As soon as the bin is up, I'll take some packs over to Tom the Potter and suggest he keeps them in his unit. That way he can make sure everyone coming into the craft block with a dog is properly equipped."

David laughed.

"You're making him the Dog Poo Monitor, are you?"

"Yes, I suppose I am, but please don't tell him I said that!"

* * *

By now, Claire was three-and-a-half years old and Michael was two-and-a-quarter. Although they were both developing strong personalities of their own, we were lucky they were well behaved most of the time and were not prone to temper tantrums. From the moment they were born they had been with us constantly and were used to fitting in with our work.

They both spent a lot of time sitting with a colouring book while I prepared meals around them in the kitchen or tucked behind the counter in the shop with their toys while David and Phil served customers.

They were very patient, but I worried we weren't being fair to them and I knew the others felt the same.

"They shouldn't be cooped up all the time," I said to Bob, "but everyone's so busy. It's ridiculous, really. We've got all this space for them to run around, but nobody to keep an eye on them."

Bob was thoughtful.

"We need to get better organised. We're all busy at different times. Phil has lots to do first thing, but not so much later on. You're busy at mealtimes. I'm tied up when the shows are on, but I have quiet times in between. We should be able to work out a schedule between us, shouldn't we?"

It seemed a simple idea to set up a child-minding rota, but it proved to be more complicated than I expected. Everyday something happened to disrupt my carefully laid plans. Phil needed to be in the Animal Meadow when the farrier arrived for the donkeys or a belt broke on the circus and Dad had to rush off to fix it. We never had enough people to do everything that needed to be done.

"Can't we just take on more staff?" I said to Mum in desperation.

"I'd love to," she replied, "but we really can't afford to just yet."

"But we're full of visitors every day. Our figures are well up on last year, surely we can afford a few more people?"

She didn't answer me, and I felt worried.

"Is everything OK?"

"Yes, it's all fine."

Her tone did nothing to reassure me.

"You would tell me if there was a problem, wouldn't you?"

"Of course, I would. There's no problem, at least nothing new. It's just that we have such a short season. We're open for less than six months of the year and the things we have planned for next winter will all cost money. Things are going well, but we need to be careful what we spend."

In the end, we decided to take Sue on for four hours a day in the kitchen and advertise for someone to work part time in the shop. That should mean one of us would always be free to look after the children.

Dad volunteered to take the kids up to our flat each day to have their lunch. Unfortunately, we hadn't had a chance to build a kitchen up there and were still using the tearooms kitchen to cook all our meals.

Each day, Dad phoned down when he was ready and I would send one of the girls up to the flat with lunch for him and the kids.

Claire loved the arrangement. As soon as I answered the phone, she would give me their orders.

"Do you think this is a mistake?" I asked Bob one night. "Do you think they're going to turn into brats?"

"Whatever do you mean?"

"Claire and Michael. Do you think they'll be spoiled? That they'll expect to order room service whenever they want anything?"

Bob burst out laughing.

"No, I don't. I admit it's not every child that gets room service, but the kids seem pretty grounded to me. You can always send them over to help Phil clean out the donkey stable if you think they're getting airs and graces."

"OK," I grinned. "I might do that."

The children loved the new routine. Each morning, they waited behind the counter in the gift shop until Phil arrived, then flew out like pigeons released from a loft. After chasing around the Pirate Trail, they arrived on the lawn just in time for Liza and Roly's morning show. Every day the show was exactly the same, but each time Claire and Michael gazed at the same tricks, laughed at the same jokes, and clapped as loudly as the rest.

At lunch time, once Dad had taken Mum her lunch in the ticket box, he would collect the children and take them up to our flat.

Their phone call usually came at about half-past twelve, but one afternoon I realised they hadn't rung. Looking at the kitchen clock, I realised it was nearly three o'clock, and felt a rush of panic.

Something must be wrong.

I rang the phone extension to our flat, but there was no answer.

The tea rooms were still packed and Martha was passing through a steady stream of orders.

"I'm sorry, Abbie, I'll have to leave you to it."

Her eyes opened wide.

"But we've got all these orders to do..."

"I won't be long, I promise."

Grabbing my keys, I hurried upstairs. I let myself into the flat and listened. All was silent and my heart raced. Where were they? What had happened?

"Dad?" I called. "Claire? Michael?"

Only Dino bounded up to greet me.

The door to Claire's room was open. Toys were scattered all over the floor, but there was no sign of anyone. Our bedroom was empty too.

I pushed open the door to the lounge and stopped abruptly. The room was in chaos. The table was tipped on its side and chairs lay scattered across the floor.

Under the table, which was draped with a blanket to make a tent, Granddad, Claire and Michael were curled up peacefully, sound asleep.

I didn't know whether to laugh or cry.

As quietly as I could, I let myself out and returned to the kitchen.

Half an hour later, Claire phoned down and ordered lunch.

* * *

A few days later, Dougal burst into the kitchen.

"Sorry to disturb you, but Phil says a tractor's coming up the back road. They've cut the padlocks off and she can't stop them."

I dropped what I was doing. Bob was introducing a show. I couldn't interrupt him.

"David's in the shop. Tell him too," I gasped and ran out of the kitchen.

As I neared the craft block, I heard the throaty roar of a diesel engine. A tractor pulling a muddy trailer was belching fumes outside the craft block. Families with young children and toddlers were everywhere and Phil was standing directly in front of the tractor waving her arms and shouting.

"You've no right to be here!" her voice was croaky as she strained to be heard above the din.

"What's going on?" I demanded as I ran up.

The driver swivelled towards me. He was young and his face was red and sweaty. A second lad was perched uncomfortably beside him.

"It's no good you lot screaming," the driver growled. "We've got to collect our hay from the top field. The same as every year."

"You didn't collect it last year," I argued.

"Yes, we did! We usually go over Norbrook land, but they've banned us. They say our only right of way is through here. We've got no choice. We've got to get our hay out."

"But this is a tourist attraction!" Phil yelled. "There are toddlers running around behind you and you can't even see where they are! You should be ashamed of yourself!"

David arrived beside her.

"What the hell's happening?"

The driver touched a pedal with his foot and the tractor roared even louder.

"I ain't wasting no more time," he shouted.

"Wait! Let us clear the kids out of the way at least," I begged. "You don't want to be responsible for anything awful."

The driver hesitated.

"OK, but you have to let us through. We can't afford to lose that hay."

"We'll talk about it later. Let's just keep everything safe."

He nodded, and I began marshalling the families who were still milling around and seemed oblivious to the danger.

"We'll have to let it through," I shouted to David. "Phil, can you keep the kids back on your side?"

The tractor edged forwards and ground its way up the road beside the animal meadow.

When we reached the gate at the top of the hill, David unlocked the padlock and swung it open.

"Wait," he called to the driver. "I'm going to lock the gate again. Sound your horn when you're ready to come back and I'll see you through. If you try to drive down on your own again, I'll call the police."

The driver nodded, and the tractor crawled on up the hill.

* * *

A week later, we gathered together after we shut.

Mr Barbary had confirmed that Duncan Matthews was right. A public right of way existed over the back road, but there was nothing to stop us from building a new road and closing the old one.

"Nothing except the cost," David said bitterly.

Dad was as matter-of-fact as ever.

"There's no point in thinking about it. We don't have any choice," he said.

Bob nodded.

"We haven't come this far to give up. We can't run a tourist attraction with a public road through the middle of it. Matthews used the farmer to force our hand, but if that hadn't done the trick, he would have tried something else. This way there won't be any argument."

"But it's so unfair!" I wailed. "We should have been told about the road before we even bought the place."

"I agree," David muttered. "We should sue Barbary!"

"There's no point," Dad sighed. "You'll never win suing lawyers. It's their game. It will only cost a fortune and distract us from the things that really matter."

"This matters...!" David exploded, but Mum interrupted him.

"No, it doesn't. We're coming into the height of the season. We have a few weeks to take as much money as we can. That's the only thing we can think about right now."

Mum was right.

As soon as the school holidays started, we were too busy to think of anything but getting through each day.

From the moment we opened in the morning there was a queue of families at the gate waiting to get in. Crowds filled the exhibitions and watched the entertainers performing on the lawns.

The shop was constantly full, and the tearooms bustled with people. It was what we had wanted. It was wonderful, but it was also exhausting.

One morning, when I took Mum down to the ticket box, a gleaming open-top sports car was parked at the gate with its engine running.

The driver was gazing along the drive towards the house. I guessed he was in his late twenties and he was built like a boxer with wide muscular shoulders and short cropped hair. His skin was deeply tanned, and he wore a gold medallion around his neck and gold rings on his fingers. Beside him, a bored-looking girl in a tiny miniskirt and a low-cut blouse was flicking between channels on the radio.

I helped Mum open the ticket box, then left her chatting to the first customers and crossed to the car.

"Yes, Babes, this is where they sent me..."

"Excuse me, can I help you?" I asked politely.

The man glanced up at me.

"No, we're good. I'm showing my lady where I went. This used to be Stokelake school, right?"

"Yes, it was."

"Someone should have nuked the place. What's happened to it?"

When I explained the old school had been left empty for years and was now a family tourist attraction, the man roared with laughter.

"You mean it's open to the public? This I gotta see! Come on Babes, I'm going to show you round."

"The car park's up the hill," I said helpfully.

"Right you are!"

He was still laughing as the car backed onto the main road and roared off up the hill.

* * *

An hour later I was serving teas when I noticed the couple join the queue.

The man's voice was unmistakable.

"I am soooo glad I came back! When I was here, I swore I would come back one day. I wasn't going to let those bastards destroy me."

Heads turned.

"They were such assholes, but I wasn't going to let them win."

Beside him, the girl was eyeing a plate of millionaires' shortbread.

"Do you know what we did, Babe? The teachers had a common room right on the top floor up a little winding staircase. I had this mate, Sean, he was as messed up as I was. One day, we got a big plank of wood and some nails and hammered it across the door."

The families in the queue fell quiet.

"There was no way they were getting out. Then we piled books and chairs and anything we could find at the bottom of the stairs and set fire to it."

The girl dragged her attention away from the pastries.

"What? With them up there?"

I splashed milk into a jug, slid it onto a tray and moved on to the next customer as quickly as I could.

The man's voice rang out again.

"Yeah! The problem was, we couldn't get it to burn properly. We were just kids. There was a whole lot of smoke, though."

I dropped a tea bag into a pot, filled it with water, and piled cups and saucers onto a tray in record time.

"And what would you like?" I asked the next family.

"Sean reckoned he knew where there was some petrol," the man went on. "So, he went off to get it. We could hear the teachers up there, banging on the door, screaming at us to let them out."

The girl giggled. "Shit, man! That's awesome."

"Yeah, we were going to burn those bastards to ashes! They must have had a phone up there though, because the next thing we knew the police arrived with a fire engine."

"Oh." The girl sounded disappointed.

"That was my last day here."

"You were one bad boy, weren't you?"

The man stopped laughing.

"No, Babe. I was a kid. Just a kid."

The family in front took their tray, and I turned to the couple.

"Hello, again. How can I help you?"

The man recognised me and nodded.

"Do you have any champagne?"

"I'm sorry, we don't serve alcohol. The nearest thing we have is ginger beer."

His eyes narrowed abruptly.

"Are you dissing me?"

He glared aggressively, but suddenly his expression changed.

"OK, I get it. I see what you did. Alcohol. Beer. Ginger beer. Good one."

I breathed out slowly.

"What's the most expensive thing you do?" he demanded.

"Err... that would be a clotted cream tea with extra scones."

"Right. We'll have two of them with two glasses of coke. Bring them outside, will you?"

* * *

When Martha returned from her break, I left her at the counter and took the two cream teas outside.

The couple were sitting at a small table and the man was pointing across to the sculpture on the lawn.

"Jesus! It's still there!"

"What is?"

"That art! We made it. All the kids that were here. This weird old teacher showed us how to make a frame out of wood and fill it with concrete."

His attention was fixed on the sculpture, and he didn't notice me arrive.

"But what's it supposed to be?" the girl asked.

"Nothing. It's just crap." He started laughing again. "We were supposed to express ourselves. There was this blonde kid. He really got into it. He drew everything out on a piece of paper before we started and gave the teachers some line that it was about hidden prejudice or some shit. He was brilliant."

"Two cream teas," I said loudly.

"And you should have seen what we had to do to stand it up," he went on. "First, we dug a great big hole under one end of it until it started to tip, then we tied ropes around it. One of the teachers had a Land Rover, and he dragged the ropes while all the kids pushed and shoved..."

"Excuse me. Can I put this tray down?"

The girl noticed me and lifted her bag out of the way.

"Sorry."

"I can't believe it's still here. I gotta have a snap of this, Babe."

He pulled a camera from his pocket and held it out to me.

"D'you mind?"

The two of them posed, and I managed to get the sculpture in between them. As the camera clicked, the girl flicked her hair and pouted suggestively.

"D'you know something?" the man asked as I handed the camera back to him. "I've dreamed about this place for years. I swore one day I'd come back here and burn it to the ground for real. But I don't think I need to anymore."

An hour later, I watched them leave and breathed a sigh of relief.

I walked down to the ticket box and Mum let me in.

"Was that the couple with the car that just left?"

"Yes."

"Were they any trouble?"

"No. Not really. I thought they might be. I was afraid he was going to say something awful in front of the kids, but he didn't. I'm sure of one thing, though. Stokelake School must have been hell."

* * *

At the beginning of September, Claire started school. She looked adorable in her uniform with her dark curly hair pulled back into bunches.

Michael watched sadly from his bedroom window as I strapped her into her car seat and drove off.

"Will Liza be doing her show today?" she asked.

"Not today, honey. Now the holidays have finished we only have shows on the weekends, remember?"

"What's Michael going to do while I'm at school?"

"Don't worry, we'll keep him busy. And you can play with him as soon as you get home."

I adjusted the mirror so I could see her.

Claire nodded and stared out of the window, watching the fields fly past.

"Are you looking forward to going to school?"

She nodded, but her face looked sad.

My heart ached, and I longed to turn the car around, but instead, I put on a cassette of Disney songs.

When we reached the school, I helped Claire find her peg and hang up her coat and bag. Other parents were shepherding their children and everyone was talking in jolly, 'isn't-this-going-to-be-fun' voices'.

"Hello, Claire! Would you like to sit next to Amy?"

The teacher was round and smiley.

"You remember Mrs Johnson, don't you, Claire?" I said. "We met her last week."

Claire nodded, but her fingers tightened around my hand.

"Come on, shall we find you something to play with?" Mrs Johnson suggested and Claire nodded again.

"You have fun playing with Amy and I'll pick you up later. Is that OK?" I asked.

Claire's fingers slipped from my hand. She gave me a hug and followed Mrs Johnson across the room to meet her new friend.

I waved goodbye and made it out of the classroom before I stopped to pull a tissue out of my pocket.

* * *

Now that summer was over, we had to manage without Sue in the tearooms. It felt strange without her, and Abbie chattered more than usual to fill the silence.

"Would you like it if I brought my radio in?" She offered one morning. "We could have it playing all day."

"No, thank you," I said politely.

The last few weeks of the season were busy, but the rhythm of the days was different. Instead of families, our visitors were mainly young couples and senior citizens.

Zac and Uncle Waldo still joined us on the weekends, but Liza and Roly performed every day. At first, I had been afraid that older visitors might not enjoy her show, but I soon found they loved it.

There was something surreal about a crowd of grey-haired grandparents applauding a small dog dancing with a clown, but perhaps it reminded them of their youth. I always enjoyed the act, so I decided there was no age limit on happiness.

At the end of the month, we closed the doors with mixed feelings. Our second season had been a success. We had increased our turnover, and despite a few obstacles, there had been no major disasters. Now we had to face the challenges that lay ahead.

But first we needed a holiday. I felt guilty taking Claire out of school so soon after she had started, but it was impossible for us to take time off during the holidays. Fortunately, the school was supportive and Bob and I booked a last-minute break in Crete.

We had a wonderful holiday marred only by the fact Claire developed chicken pox on the second day, our bedroom was infested with mosquitoes and it rained so heavily every roof in the hotel leaked and the corridors and dining room were filled with buckets.

Our first task when we arrived home was to get quotes for the new road. Bob and David spent days walking around the site with surveyors discussing different alternatives. Eventually, it was decided the only realistic possibility was to make the new road follow the boundary of our land around the side of the Animal Meadow.

Phil was worried because the route would reduce the size of the donkey paddock, but the gradient of the hill made anything else impossible. We agreed on the plan and waited for quotes to arrive.

A week later Bob brought the morning post up to our flat.

"This must be the first quote," he said, looking at an envelope. "Fingers crossed."

I watched as he unfolded the piece of paper. His reaction was instant.

"Ouch!" He passed me the quote, and I groaned.

"That's ridiculous."

"Never mind. Let's hope the others are better."

They weren't.

We gathered in a dejected huddle around a table in the tearooms. Michael sat on Phil's lap munching a biscuit, but the rest of us weren't hungry.

"What do we do?" David asked, looking at the different quotes spread out across the table. "We can't afford any of them."

There was an uncomfortable silence.

"These quotes are all for a good quality tarmac surface," Dad said at last. "but that's not what we're replacing. The top half of the old road is a mess. It's not tarmac. It's mainly concrete with enormous pot-holes."

"That's true. Matthews can use it in his Range Rover, but I don't think most cars could get up and down it at all."

"I think it was originally meant for tractors and farm vehicles, wasn't it?"

"Has anyone checked with Mr Barbary exactly what sort of road it has to be?"

We shook our heads.

"I'll phone him now," Bob said and disappeared into the office.

He returned a few minutes later.

"I've spoken to him and there are no restrictions on the road surface."

"You mean we can build it however we like?"

"Not exactly. He said it has to be 'suitable for its purpose' but as long as it's as good, or better, than the existing road it will be fine."

"That's great news," Dad beamed. "Let's get the surveyors back."

* * *

The new quotes were less than half the originals. As soon as they arrived Mum put the kettle on.

"It's still a lot of money," she sighed, "and we haven't heard from the water board yet. If they insist we put in a new water main, that might be the same sort of cost. We can't afford both."

"The situation with the water has already been dragging on for two years,"

Dad pointed out. "There's no reason to think it won't drag on for a lot longer."

"I don't like it hanging over our heads," Mum complained, but Dad patted her on the shoulder.

"One problem at a time, love."

"Even with the new quotes, the cost of the road is going to wipe out everything we made this summer, isn't it?" David said dejectedly.

"Pretty much," Bob agreed.

"Does that mean we won't be able to do anything at all this winter?" Phil asked.

We had been hoping to move the model circus into a more impressive space and use the area it was currently in to create an indoor entertainments room.

"We won't be able to do as much as we had hoped," Dad admitted, "but we can still do things that don't cost too much."

David groaned.

"That's exactly what you said last year."

"True," Dad admitted, "but complaining about it isn't going to make the situation any better. We can't move the circus to a different building, but we could move it to the far end of the room it's in."

There was silence as we thought about the suggestion. The room was enormous, and we had partitioned off the section with the circus to make it look more attractive. Behind the partition was a large area filled with nothing but dust and spiders' webs.

"If we move the circus up to the end nearest the kitchen, we could still use the rest of the space for an indoor entertainments room."

"That's a brilliant idea," I agreed.

Suddenly, David was all enthusiasm.

"We could make it look like a tent. All we need to do is put posts up around the walls like tent poles and cover the ceiling with striped material."

Dad nodded approvingly.

"Then I suggest we get started."

It was strange working through the autumn without any builders in the house. For the past two years, we had become accustomed to hearing their voices in the distance or the constant drone of radio one.

While Claire was at school, I often worked alone, and sometimes I found myself listening to the silence. Was I waiting for the sound of footsteps? It occurred to me that I associated the arrival of the builders with 'Fred' events. I knew if I raised the subject with Bob, he would pounce on my observations as proof that Fred was just a trick played on us by the builders.

I didn't believe that. I still wasn't sure what I did believe, but I was certain Fred was real. And yet it had been months now since anything had happened.

I went to find Dad. As usual, he was busy in his workshop filing a piece of metal held in a vice and whistling along to the radio.

"What's up?" he asked as I settled myself on a spare stool.

"Nothing," I replied.

"OK."

He went on filing and I watched him work. Eventually he put down the file and looked at me.

"What is it?"

I hesitated.

"It sounds silly."

"Go on."

"I miss Fred."

His eyes twinkled as his mouth curved into a grin.

"You're missing a ghost?"

"I told you it was silly."

"You did. And it is. Why are you missing him?"

"I don't know. It just feels as though the house is empty. And if he's not here, where does he go?"

"I'm afraid you're asking the wrong person, love. I'm still not sure I believe in this ghost of yours, and even if he does exist, I've no idea how the whole ghost thing works."

"That's the problem. I don't understand it either. I wish I did."

Dad leaned across and put an arm around my shoulder.

"Don't worry about it. There are lots of things we'll never understand. It's just how it is."

"I suppose so."

"If there are such things as ghosts, I think they are more like owls than canaries."

"What?"

"I think they're things that flit around in the night and do what they want to do. If they give us a fright sometimes that's just how it is. You'd never be able to put one in a cage and make it sing to please you."

"I would never have thought of putting it like that."

"But you know what I mean?"

"Sort of. You mean Fred will turn up if he feels like it."

"That's about it."

I nodded.

"I guess I'd better get back to work then, hadn't I?"

* * *

Clearing the void area behind the circus, dismantling the model, moving it, and putting it back together in its new position took longer than we had expected.

Part of the ceiling collapsed when we removed the partition and, in the absence of builders, Dad and David had to carry out the repairs.

Once the ceiling was patched David fixed timbers around the walls just above head height and I was given the job of fixing striped material from the timbers up to the middle of the ceiling to give the impression the room was really a huge circus tent.

As I stood on a ladder with my arms above my head, holding the material taut with one hand and shooting thousands of staples from a staple gun with the other, I realised I had taken on a bigger job than I had anticipated.

Matching the stripes where the fabric met and stitching the lengths of material together so they didn't float in the breeze and reveal the ceiling above were also interesting challenges.

By the time I had finished and we were ready to assemble the circus in its new location, it was nearly Christmas.

This year, Claire and Michael were old enough to enjoy the excitement. Each afternoon, when Claire arrived home from school, she and Michael bounced with excitement as they opened the doors of their advent calendars.

"What's Santa going to bring you for Christmas, Claire?" Phil asked one day.

I listened with interest.

"I'm going to have a baby."

"You mean a baby doll to go in your pram?"

"No." Claire said calmly. "I'm going to have a real baby from Mummy's tummy."

"I don't know how Mummy will feel about that!" Bob laughed.

"And it has to be a girl," Claire continued. "I only want a sister. If it's a boy, you can leave it at the hospital."

Everyone laughed, and I tried to join in. It was only later, when Bob and I were alone, that I brought the subject up again.

"You know what Claire said earlier, about me having a baby?"

"Yes."

"She might be right."

He looked at me in shock.

"I wasn't going to say anything until I was sure."

"Oh my God. Wow. Let me get my breath back. Why did you tell Claire?"

"I didn't."

"Then how did she know?"

"I have absolutely no idca. And I might not be pregnant, anyway. It's too early to know for sure."

"But if you are…"

I could see him doing the math in his head.

I nodded.

"Yes. If I am, it will be due in August. Right in the middle of the school holidays."

We looked at each other.

"The busiest week of the year. Perfect."

* * *

We decided not to share our news with the others until after Christmas.

As the big day approached Claire and Michael talked of nothing but mince pies, presents, flying reindeer and hanging up their stockings.

They watched with eager eyes as we moved tables and chairs out of the tearooms and brought in a huge Christmas tree. The remaining tables were lined up in the middle of the room, and Dad and David carried in a sheet of plyboard and laid it over the top.

"There. Now we're ready for the banquet," Dad announced.

As Mum spread a cloth across the table, the rest of us pulled open a pile of cardboard boxes and began rummaging through the decorations.

"Here Michael, do you want to help me put some tinsel on the tree?" Phil asked.

"I think we need some music to complete the atmosphere," Bob said and slipped a cassette into the tape player.

The holidays were wonderful. On Christmas Day we forgot everything but cooking, eating and playing games with the children. Then Boxing Day dawned bright and crisp and we took the dogs for walks in the woods and warmed ourselves with hot punch and too much food.

For a short while, Silverlands was all ours and it was magical. Bob played endless carols and Christmas anthems and the happy sounds drifted through the old building. It felt so perfect we extended our break until the New Year, but once we had welcomed in 1989, we returned to work.

Our first challenge was moving the circus. Even with six of us working together it took several days before the tiny animated figures were all working correctly.

Finally, Dad was satisfied, and we stood back to admire the spectacle. No matter how many times I saw it, the model circus always filled me with pride. I had grown up watching the little figures being carved and had spent many hours working on the tiny pieces that made it unique. The circus was constructed of wood, steel and paint, and yet it had a life and character of its own.

Now that it was settled in its new location, we turned our attention to the rest of the room. Dad and David built a wooden frame to divide the circus from the rest of the space, and Bob and I covered it with more striped material. Once we had fitted the entertainment room with a matching striped tent top and a new carpet, it looked bright and exciting.

"All we need now is more chairs and we will be ready for the first performance," Bob said happily.

* * *

We had been forced to delay the developments we had planned for the winter, but Dad insisted there was one thing we could not postpone.

"We really have to build a proper ticket box for your mother," he said. "She's been coping in that tiny shed for two years now. She hasn't complained but the walls don't fit together properly so it's damp and freezing most of the time and it's infested with spiders. It's really not fair to expect her to put up with it for another year."

He was right, and we all agreed we had to make a change. Dad looked relieved.

"It needn't cost a lot. If I draw the designs, we can get the woodworkers in Newton Abbot to fabricate the panels and we can assemble it all ourselves."

Within weeks, the panels were ready to be delivered. We waited until the weather forecast predicted a few dry days, then we all worked together to prepare the ground and peg out the base.

Ian's team helped us lay the concrete and by the end of the day the flat, grey expanse was smoothed and ready. It looked much bigger than I had expected.

"Are you sure we got the measurements right?" I asked Dad, but he only laughed at me.

I need not have worried. The partitions fitted together perfectly on the base, and the new ticket box was soon assembled. It looked amazing. It was more like a pagoda than a box. It was beautifully proportioned with windows on all four sides and a sloping roof topped by a miniature bell tower to match the one on the main house.

Dad never did anything by halves.

David wired in a power supply, and soon the little building was bright with light. There was a heater beneath the counter for cold days and a kettle to make tea.

Mum was delighted.

"If only there was a toilet I would move in permanently," she laughed.

"That could be arranged," Bob suggested, and I jabbed him with my elbow.

Mum ignored the comment.

"The best thing is, I'll be able to have the children down here sometimes. There's plenty of space so they can have their toys and colouring books and I can phone you if we need anything."

"That's a great idea," I agreed. "You can have your own little playgroup."

"If the kids are going to be down here, you ought to get them working," David joked. "They could help you hand out the leaflets."

"Actually, I think Michael would enjoy that," Phil smiled.

"And Claire won't want to be left out," Bob added.

"This new ticket box is going to make my life a lot easier, but it also gives a much better impression to people when they arrive," Mum said.

"I was thinking that," David agreed. "It feels symbolic in a way."

Dad nodded.

"Let's hope you're right. After all we've been through, maybe this year will be a turning point for us."

Chapter 7

By the time Abbie and Martha returned, I was four months pregnant, and it was like a reunion of old friends. I broke the news that I was expecting a baby and Martha gave me a hug and wished me well, but Abbie's reaction surprised me. She immediately brought a chair and told me to sit down.

"I'm not ill!" I protested.

"Of course not, but you have to look after yourself. That's right, isn't it, Martha?"

"I'm sure Diana doesn't need any fussing from you," Martha replied briskly.

"When Mum was expecting my little brother, she had to sit on the sofa all the time watching telly. She couldn't do any hoovering or washing or anything," Abbie told me seriously.

"I won't need to do that," I assured her. "Everything will be the same as always. You don't need to worry about me."

But she did.

At first, Abbie's preoccupation with my welfare irritated me and I wished she would stop asking if I was tired every few minutes, but gradually I realised her concern was genuine.

She started coming in early each morning so she could check in the deliveries from the baker and greengrocer and carried the vacuum cleaner upstairs for me without being asked.

Martha noticed the change in her too.

"That girl may be a cherry short of a trifle, but her heart's in the right place," she said to me one morning.

I laughed.

"I'm just glad I don't suffer from morning sickness. If I did, I'm sure she'd call an ambulance every time."

"Aye, you're right there," Martha agreed. "Do you know what she asked me yesterday?"

"No, what?"

"She wanted to know if I'd teach her to knit."

"Really?"

"Aye. She thinks this baby of yours is going to need bootees and bonnets."

I was touched.

"That is so sweet!"

"But don't get your hopes up," Martha warned me. "It's taken me two years to teach her to shut the fridge door after her. I very much doubt I'll get her to master 'knit one, purl one' anytime soon."

"Well, you're a brave woman for trying," I laughed.

* * *

The Motor Museum was also due to open on Easter Sunday and we had put out a lot of joint publicity. I couldn't quite believe that we were now in our third year. After all the trauma of our first two seasons, the fact that we were still going felt like a great achievement.

The new road was finished and just to make sure we would not have any uninvited visitors trying to use the old road, David arranged for Alan to dump a pile of granite against the gates at the top and the bottom of the hill.

"That's one hassle we can tick off the list," Dad said as he looked at the massive boulders.

"Yes. I'd like to see Matthews drive his Range Rover over that lot," David grinned. "I wonder what he'll come up with next."

"Nothing! There isn't going to be any next," I said firmly.

Dad laughed.

"I hope you're right, but I wouldn't put any money on it."

* * *

I had hoped Sue would be available to work in the kitchen again that summer but she had found herself a full-time job in a restaurant in Newton Abbot so we advertised for a replacement. After interviewing a row of girls and one young man who applied for the job, we settled on a sensible twenty-year-old called Pamela.

Bob was convinced she would be reliable, and I hoped he was right. She certainly seemed efficient and level-headed.

My only concern was whether Abbie and Pamela would get on together. It was obvious that Pamela already had a lot of experience working in pubs and cafes, but it was equally obvious that Abbie considered herself to be the Senior Kitchen Assistant. I couldn't help but feel apprehensive.

I broached the subject with Bob, but he dismissed my fears.

"I'm sure Abbie will be glad to have someone with more experience to teach her things. They'll both be doing the same job, so there's no reason for her to think either of them is senior to the other."

"I know. I just don't want any tension."

"Stop worrying, there's no point in looking for problems. I'm sure they'll be friends in no time."

A few days before we opened, Pamela arrived for her first day at work. She was wearing plain black trousers, a white T-shirt, and her blonde hair was pulled back in a ponytail. Abbie was scrubbing the work surfaces in the kitchen, so I called out to her.

"Abbie, come and meet Pamela."

There was a clatter as she dropped what she had been doing and hurried through into the tearooms.

"Pleased to meet you. I'm Abigail," she said formally and held out a wet hand.

Pamela looked surprised, but shook Abbie's hand and smiled.

"Hi, I'm Pam. Nice to meet you too."

"As you know, Pam's going to be with us over the Easter weekend then she'll be working part time the way Sue used to do. Are you OK to show her around and make her feel at home, Abbie?"

"Yes, of course."

The two of them disappeared into the kitchen, and I went on preparing orders for the coming weekend. I could hear Abbie's voice giving a tour around the kitchen, explaining where everything was kept.

Martha was behind the counter in the servery, cleaning the jacket potato baker.

"Do you think those two will work well together?" I asked.

"They'd better," she said simply. "If they don't, they'll have me to answer to."

* * *

The Easter weekend went brilliantly. The weather was good but not hot enough to drive people to the beach, and Silverlands was packed with visitors each day.

Silvers Circus was as popular as ever, and I never tired of hearing people telling me how much they enjoyed the exhibitions.

The kitchen was frantically busy all day long but, much to my relief, everything ran smoothly. Pam picked up our routines quickly and Abbie managed not to break anything irreplaceable.

By the time we closed on Bank Holiday Monday, I was feeling elated.

"It's been a great weekend, hasn't it?" Dad asked as Mum counted up the money from the tills.

"Yes," I agreed. "If the rest of the summer goes this well, I'll be happy."

"Forget the rest of the summer," Dad laughed, "can't you just be happy now?"

On Tuesday, David reported that Ian was delighted with the Motor Museum figures and even Tom the Potter smiled at me as he went past the tearooms' window.

Everything was going well, but the thing that made me happiest was seeing how much Mum loved her new ticket box. I knew she felt at home when I spotted her pick a handful of bluebells and put them in a vase on her counter.

In the past, her view had been limited to a clump of bushes opposite the entrance, but now that she had windows on all sides, she could enjoy looking out across the valley and see what was happening on the main lawn.

"It was lovely to see Liza and Roly doing their show," she told me. "Not that I had much chance to watch it with so many customers. I know it sounds silly, because I have lots of people to deal with, but in the past, it's felt a bit lonely down here."

A few days later she told me she had a regular visitor.

"Who is it?"

"I've no idea what its name is, but it's a scruffy-looking dog. It comes and sits under the hedge and watches me."

"Do you think it's lost?"

"No, I don't think so. It doesn't seem hungry or agitated. It just comes and stares at me."

"How strange. What does it look like?"

"Scruffy. It's not young. There's got a lot of grey in its fur, but it looks like a friendly old thing."

"I'll ask David. He knows all the neighbours. I'll bet he can find out who it belongs to."

I was right.

David soon identified the dog and told us it came from the stables at the top of the hill.

"I asked John, the greengrocer, and he told me they bought it as a guard dog after they had problems with teenagers breaking into the stables and frightening the horses."

"A guard dog?" Mum sounded surprised. "It doesn't look much like a guard dog to me."

"John says they lock it in the stables each night. He didn't sound too impressed, to be honest, he said they don't take much care of it."

"I offered it a biscuit yesterday, and it finished the whole packet," Mum admitted. "I thought it wasn't hungry because it's just been lying quietly under the bushes each day, but when I stroked it, I could feel its ribs through its fur."

"That doesn't sound good," I said.

"You'd better not let it in the ticket box," Bob advised. "It's probably got fleas."

"Yes, I'm sure it has, but it's a dear old thing. If anyone's going over to Chudleigh could they pick up some tins of dog food for me?"

"Is that a good idea?" David asked. "Should you really be feeding someone else's dog?"

Mum frowned at him.

"The animal is skinny. It needs feeding. If you don't get me any dog food, I'll just have to feed it sausages, won't I?"

David knew when to give up.

"All right. I'll get some tins later."

"Good. And perhaps you'd better get some flea powder at the same time."

After that, the dog became a daily visitor to the ticket box. Inevitably, Dad christened him Scruffy, and each morning he would be waiting when Mum and Dad arrived to open up.

Scruffy behaved beautifully, lying on the floor beside Mum's feet most of the time and only rousing himself occasionally to wander around, rise up on his back legs and balance with his front paws on the edge of Mum's counter.

He never barked, but when he opened his mouth, he showed a row of white teeth that gave the comical impression of a smile. The public loved him.

Each night, when it was time for Mum to close the ticket box, Scruffy would stand up, stretch himself, then wait patiently for Dad to arrive and open the door. He would give Mum a little lick on the hand, then trudge back up the hill to the stables.

* * *

Once the rush of the Easter holidays was over, the last weeks of April were wonderful. By now we were all familiar with our daily routines and had enough visitors to keep us busy without being under too much pressure. Pam joined us in the kitchen every Friday and Sunday as well as any days when we had coach trips booked and Abbie was as hardworking as ever.

On quiet days, I was able to escape for a few hours to tend to the grounds.

My baby bump was beginning to make its presence felt but I could still cope with most gardening tasks and I loved being on my own in the fresh air.

I found it satisfying to clear the fading wallflowers from the beds and replace them with pansies, marigolds and petunias ready for the summer.

If it had been possible, I would have spent all my days outside. I loved the trees and bushes and the unexpected wildflowers that sprang up in the long grasses where the lawn blended into the woodland.

An ancient oak tree grew outside the new entertainments room, and under its spreading shade the grass was shorter and finer than in sunnier areas. Here, tiny purple violets, blue speedwell and golden celandines carpeted the ground.

It was a beautiful spot, and I had been afraid when we first opened to the public that the delicate blossoms would be trampled by careless feet, but I had been wrong. It seemed our visitors loved the wildflowers as much as I did because the children played on the grass and adults picnicked on the benches nearby, but the tiny blossoms were left undisturbed.

Unfortunately, the bedding plants were not always so fortunate.

Late one afternoon, when nearly all the visitors had gone, and I was trundling a wheelbarrow along the road at the front of the tearooms, I was amazed to see an old lady kneeling down with a teaspoon in her hand.

I had only finished planting petunias around the edge of the tea lawn a few days before, and there were two muddy holes where plants had been.

"Excuse me!" I said indignantly as the old lady wrapped a petunia plant in a napkin and popped it into her handbag.

She looked up at me and smiled sweetly.

"You don't mind, do you?" she asked. "They're such a lovely colour."

"But you can't just take them," I protested. "They're here for everyone to enjoy."

"But no one will notice a few, will they dear?"

She wiped her fingers on another napkin and stood up.

"After all, I did pay to come in."

I was so taken aback I just stood and watched her walk away.

"Why didn't you demand them back?" Phil asked me later. "She was stealing. You could have had her arrested."

"I know, but she didn't seem to think she'd done anything wrong."

"Some people are impossible," Phil muttered. "Do you know those white toy rabbits that come in gift boxes?"

"The really fluffy, expensive ones?"

"Yes, that's them. A couple of days ago a woman took one off the shelf in the gift shop, tore open the box and gave it to her little boy. Then, when he'd drooled all over it, she said 'I don't think he likes it' and dumped it back on the shelf."

"What did you do?"

"I asked her to pay for it. I pointed out there was no way I could sell it after what she'd done and she got all aggressive."

"What happened then?"

"Luckily her husband, or boyfriend, or whoever it was with her, got embarrassed. He could see the rabbit was covered in chocolate and dribble, so he paid for it."

"I don't understand how people can behave like that."

"Some people are just horrible. Luckily there aren't many of them."

* * *

My favourite moments were still in the early evenings when all the world was quiet and I could water the flower beds and hanging baskets in peace.

House martins had built nests around the eaves of the house, and it was wonderful to watch the fledglings emerge and take their first quivering flights.

I always knew when the young birds were about to leave their nest for the first time. Instead of swooping through the sky after insects, the parents would begin flitting along the eaves in anxious loops while the high-pitched squeaks of the youngsters built to a crescendo until, finally, tiny heads appeared over the rim of the nest and the fledglings took their first great leap into the air.

If the weather was warm, we often left the flat windows open and occasionally the baby birds would misjudge their directions and fly straight into the room.

One evening, as Bob and I were eating our meal, a tiny bundle of grey and white feathers zoomed through the window, crash-landed on the sofa and sat, gasping, for a full minute before fluttering manically around the room.

Bob watched as it bounced off the walls and ceiling before finally finding the window and disappearing outside.

"I guess every family has a klutz!" he laughed.

As the weeks went by, I could no longer fit into my jeans and was forced to dig into my wardrobe and unearth my old maternity clothes. I hated having to wear flowing smocks and billowing dresses. Now that the initial shock of discovering I was pregnant had faded I was looking forward to having another child, but I hated the restrictions that came with being pregnant. Some women positively glow when they are expecting, but I was not one of them.

I would gladly have given birth to an egg and left it locked in an airing cupboard for nine months if it was possible. Sadly, it was not possible, so I did my best to ignore everything connected with my pregnancy. I worked in the tearooms and kitchen as usual and tried to pretend nothing had changed.

I managed to avoid most of my antenatal classes by using the excuse that I had already had one child and was far too busy to attend. Fortunately, my midwife was a lovely lady who was used to dealing with awkward customers. She insisted I turn up for essential measurements and tests, but otherwise left me alone. To my surprise, I came to see her as a friend.

Whenever I could, I escaped to the wildest parts of the grounds, strapped on my strimmer, revved the engine to a roaring fury and sliced through the undergrowth.

"Should you really be doing that?" Bob asked me one evening as I returned to the house covered in dust and tiny shreds of greenery.

"Why not?" I challenged him.

"Don't you think you should be slowing down a bit?"

"No. I'm fine."

I wanted to tell Bob how much I hated being pregnant, but I didn't think he would understand. I couldn't bear sitting still. I hated people fussing over me, and I hated not being in control of my body. As my weight increased my appetite disappeared and every meal became a struggle. I tried not to let it show because Bob cooked me wonderfully tasty, healthy food, but I didn't want to eat any of it.

I didn't really know what I did want except to be on my own.

* * *

The nursery that supplied our plants sent me regular brochures, and the latest one had a full-page advert for ridiculously cheap hedging roses. Since we had moved in, I had dreamed of having a bank of roses along the drive leading to the entrance but had never been able to justify the expense. I convinced myself that this was my chance and sent back an order.

"But why?" Bob asked when the roses were delivered. "Surely you're not going to plant all those by yourself?"

"Of course, I am. There's only two hundred of them. They're not much more than cuttings, so they won't need big holes."

I could see Bob didn't approve, and I expected him to lecture me, but instead he only frowned and turned away. I contented myself that I was right. The roses were little more than half a metre tall and had bare roots. Planting them would hardly take any effort at all.

As soon as Claire was settled in bed I headed out of the flat.

"Don't worry, I'll take a walkie-talkie with me," I called over my shoulder.

I piled a fork, a spade and a heap of roses into a wheelbarrow and trundled them down to the entrance. The air was cool and a hint of honeysuckle drifted on the breeze. Happiness.

It was dark by the time I climbed back upstairs to the flat. Bob was asleep on the sofa and I felt a pang of guilt.

"Do you want a cup of tea?" I asked as he stirred.

He opened an eye and looked me up and down.

"No. I'll get it. You'd better go and have a shower."

By the time I came back, the tea was waiting for me. I could tell Bob was trying to be patient.

"Did you get all the roses planted?" he asked.

"Not quite, I'll finish them tomorrow."

"Can't I give you a hand? We could ask your mother to babysit."

I shook my head.

"There's no need. I'm perfectly happy doing them by myself."

The following night, when I finished stomping the earth around the last rose, I straightened up and admired my handiwork. In the fading twilight the line of thin, prickly stalks followed the fence from the ticket box to the point where the land dipped down to meet the woodland.

The individual plants looked small and straggly but, in my mind, I could already see a glorious hedge of dark green leaves and fragrant red flowers.

Deep inside my bump, the baby moved.

"I wonder if you'll be a gardener?" I murmured as I loaded the fork and shovel into the wheelbarrow.

I let myself into the house, made a pot of tea and carried the tray up to the flat.

"I would have made that," Bob said when he saw it.

"I know you would."

"Then why won't you let me help you?" The exasperation was clear in his voice. "You can't keep doing everything. You're going to wear yourself out."

"No, I'm not. Don't tell me what to do."

He took the tray, put it down on the table and poured out the tea.

Kicking off my trainers, I flopped on the sofa and let a wave of tiredness sweep over me.

Bob handed me a mug.

"I forgot to mention it earlier, but I spoke to Ian this afternoon. A couple of his men are applying for jobs and they need to be able to use strimmers. He asked if he could borrow ours for a few days so he can train them."

"No," I said without thinking.

"But why not? Ian's offered to get them to clear around the paths and verges for us if we agree. Let's face it, you won't be able to do it for much longer, anyway."

I glared at him, but I was too tired to argue.

"OK, if you insist, but you'd better make sure they insure it."

* * *

Abbie's face lit up when she saw me the next morning.

"I've got something for you," she beamed and handed me a tube of ointment.

"Thank you. What is it?"

"It's for stretch marks. My Mum swears by it. She says it works for wrinkles too, so I thought you'd like to try it."

"Right."

I didn't know what else to say.

"You weren't around when I finished yesterday so I didn't get a chance to tell you," Abbie chattered on, "but Fred's been up to his tricks again."

My heart sank. I didn't have the energy to think about Fred.

"Really? What happened?"

"I was putting jam into little pots for the cream teas and the jar of strawberry jam just went. One moment it was there and the next it was gone."

"Couldn't Pam have taken it?"

"I don't think so. She wasn't in the kitchen. I looked everywhere. I had to open another jar in the end."

"OK, well thanks for telling me. You remember what we agreed?"

"About not making a fuss?"

"Yes, that's right."

Abbie nodded.

"Don't worry, I won't say anything, but you'd better order some more jam in case he gets a taste for it."

Before I could answer David appeared from the kitchen yard.

"Do you have a minute?"

He looked excited, so I put my tea towel down.

"Yes, I could do with a break. Will you be OK for a bit, Abbie?"

Zac was at the far end of the kitchen balancing a juggling club on his fingertips.

"Yes, I'm fine," she said dreamily.

I followed David outside, and we sat on a bench in the sunshine.

"What is it?"

"I just wanted your opinion on something. Phil's been getting worried about the donkeys. All they do is stand around in their meadow eating grass all day long and she thinks they're getting fat."

"Really?"

"Yes. She's spoken to the people at the sanctuary and they told her that Moses and Victor are both used to being ridden. They've suggested rides would be a good way to keep them fit, and it would stop them getting bored."

"You mean that Phil should be riding the donkeys?"

"No, not Phil. They suggested we give donkey rides to the children that come to visit."

The penny dropped.

"That's a great idea. I'm sure the kids would love it."

"It would only be for the little ones, obviously, and it would only be for a couple of hours at a time."

"Of course, we don't want to wear them out."

"The only problem is that Phil couldn't do it on her own. She's happy to lead the donkeys, but she would need someone else to get the kids on and off and walk beside them."

"Who were you thinking of?"

"Me, I suppose, but then we'd need someone else in the shop."

"So, what you're really saying is that we need another person to help in the shop?"

David looked apologetic.

"There's only so much we can do with just the family, isn't there? Let's be honest, I was hoping we'd be able to afford cleaners by now. If we want this place to run smoothly, we really need more staff."

"He's right," Bob said when I told him about the conversation that evening, "and we're going to need someone else in the kitchen too."

I opened my mouth to object, but he hurried on.

"You're having a baby, for goodness' sake. You can't pretend it's not happening. It might not be for long, but we will need someone to replace you for a while at least."

I couldn't argue with him even though I wanted to.

* * *

We always tried to serve locally sourced food in the tearooms and small producers often approached us asking if we would be interested in stocking their products.

Bob was delighted when he had a phone call from an estate near Exeter that had a herd of wild boar and was starting a new range of pies and pates.

"They sound amazing. The estate manager's called Simon Piper, and he explained all about them. I've agreed to take some samples to see how they go," Bob told me.

I think Bob was as surprised as I was when the first pie arrived. It was enormous.

"What am I going to do with it?" I wailed. "It's filled the whole top shelf of the fridge."

"It will cut into a lot of portions," Bob said, trying to look on the bright side.

"I don't think it would be wise to let Abbie do it."

"Good point," Bob agreed. "This isn't just an ordinary pie. It's something really special. We ought to put a sign up on the counter explaining about the boars and how they've been raised."

There was a note of pride in his voice, and the pastry looked very crumbly.

"Tell you what, why don't you cut it up yourself? You're always good at portioning things." I suggested.

Bob nodded.

"Yes, you're right. I have to get ready for the next show now, but I'll do it as soon as I've finished."

As he left, I noticed Ian and some of the team walking back along the side of the lawn. Ian was carrying the strimmer. The baby wriggled, and I felt a niggling discomfort.

"I won't be a minute," I said to Abbie, "I want a breath of air."

Without knowing why, I walked along the drive to the entrance. A sweet smell of fresh-mown grass drifted towards me and my sense of unease grew.

As I reached the front gate, I gasped in horror. The grass verge that followed the fence from the ticket box to the point where the land dipped down to meet the woodland had been strimmed to destruction. Not one of the young rose plants had survived.

I wanted to cry. Or hit someone.

"How was I supposed to know they were going to massacre your roses?" Bob protested.

"You should have found out what they were going to do before you gave them the strimmer," I yelled.

Abbie stared as she brought in a tray and I realised our voices must have carried into the tearooms.

"We'll talk about it later," I snapped.

"Fine!"

Bob turned away and pulled a large knife from the block.

"If you've finished screaming at me, I'd better portion up the pie."

I didn't trust myself to be polite, so I was silent as Bob opened the fridge door.

"Where is it?" he asked.

"Where's what?"

"The pie. Someone's taken my pie!"

He was right. The top shelf of the fridge was empty.

"It wasn't me," Abbie said quickly.

"Then who was it?" Bob thundered. "Who's taken my pie?"

"I don't know..." Abbie stuttered.

"Could someone have sneaked in?" I suggested.

"How?" Bob demanded. "The door to the corridor's locked. The only way in is through the kitchen yard."

"There has to be an explanation."

"Could it have been Zac?" Bob challenged me.

Abbie's eyes filled with tears.

"No. It wasn't him," I replied.

"How can you be sure?"

"Because he's a vegan."

Bob prodded at the bowls on the lower shelf of the fridge as if expecting to find the pie lurking behind them.

"Are you're sure you didn't move it somewhere?" he growled. "You might have moved it and forgotten about it. Women get forgetful when they're...tired."

"Stop treating me like an idiot!" I yelled. "I haven't moved your pie and I don't have baby-brain if that's what you're implying!"

Abbie ran out of the kitchen, and I swore under my breath.

"I think you'd better leave us to it," I muttered to Bob. "If I find I've put the pie in the dishwasher by mistake, I'll let you know."

He stalked off without a word, and a few minutes later Abbie reappeared.

"Are you all right?" she asked.

"Yes, I'm fine, but Bob's not going to calm down until he finds out who took his pie."

Abbie hesitated.

"Then don't you think we should tell him who it was?"

I looked at her in disbelief.

"You mean you know who took it?"

"It's obvious. It was Fred."

I smiled despite myself.

"Abbie, ghosts don't eat pies. Not even wild boar pies."

"Of course not. They don't eat strawberry jam either. He just took it to mess with you."

Her words made no sense to me. I had come to accept that something in the house made things vanish occasionally, but I was not ready to believe that Fred did things on purpose.

"I don't think that's likely, is it?" I said. "I'm afraid Bob's right. Someone must have crept in through the yard when we were both busy. The only sensible thing to do is to keep the yard gate locked from now on."

* * *

Bob was still grumbling the following day.

It was Sunday morning and Abbie and Pam were laying out cakes in the servery before we opened.

"What am I supposed to tell Simon? He's going to phone me at some point and ask how the sales are going. And I was supposed to have tasted the pie myself. I can't even tell him what I think of it."

"Why don't you phone him and explain what happened?"

"And what am I supposed to say? That we left his pie unattended and let someone walk off with it?"

"That's not fair. You know it wasn't like that."

Bob glared at me.

"Have you tried the pate?" I asked.

"No, not yet."

"You might as well. At least then you can tell Steve you've tasted something."

"I suppose," Bob muttered.

He opened the fridge and let out a gasp.

"Is this someone's idea of a joke?"

The wild boar pie filled the top shelf.

Bob's voice rang out like a foghorn.

"I want to know who's responsible for this. Now!"

At once, Abbie and Pam ran in from the servery.

"Do you know anything about this?" Bob demanded.

They both shook their heads.

"This is not funny! I'm going to get to the bottom of it. Just you wait and see!"

For added emphasis, he slammed the fridge door shut and marched out of the kitchen.

Abbie and Pam stared at me in confusion.

"I'm afraid he's a bit upset," I said lamely.

"But what's it all about?" Pam asked and Abbie jumped in before I could explain.

"It was Fred. He took Bob's pie when we weren't looking, but now, he's put it back again."

Pam looked bewildered.

"Who's Fred?" she asked.

"Abbie!" I tried to stop her, but it was too late.

"Fred's the ghost. He haunts this whole house. He moves things and sometimes he breaks glasses and cups."

"You're joking!" Pam's face was white.

"Yes, she's joking," I cut in. "We don't know who it was. Let's not talk about it anymore. Abbie, I want a word with you."

"I thought you agreed we weren't going to talk about Fred?" I said as soon as I had Abbie on my own.

"I'm sorry. I thought you just meant we couldn't talk about him in front of Bob."

"I don't want you to mention him at all. Not to anyone. Right? You heard how upset Bob was earlier."

Abbie looked at me with innocent eyes.

"But wouldn't it be better if he knew the truth?"

I shook my head.

"No. Just promise me you won't mention Fred again."

* * *

Abbie's words went round and round in my head. She was right. It would be better if Bob knew about Fred, but knowing was one thing, believing was another.

It was clear he already thought the pregnancy was affecting my judgement. If I told him I believed in ghosts, he would just think his worst fears had been confirmed.

There was nothing I could say that would convince him Fred was real and

I couldn't bear the thought of being labelled an over-emotional, irrational female.

So, I said nothing.

Chapter 8

Flaming June lived up to its name. As the temperature rose and my bump grew, I felt increasingly uncomfortable.

Beryl, a middle-aged lady with tightly permed hair and huge, owl-like glasses began working in the shop and Millie, a quiet teenager with crinkly red hair joined Abbie and Pam in the kitchen.

Bob expected me to be pleased.

"You don't have to worry anymore," he said on the day Beryl and Millie started work. "You can put your feet up whenever you like."

I knew he meant well, but I was so tense I could have screamed. The majority of our income came during the six weeks of the school holidays. I couldn't put that truth out of my mind. I wanted to keep checking everything was running smoothly and lead by example. Having a baby in the middle of August was a disaster. I was sure I was letting everyone down.

Now that we had more help, I was not needed in the kitchen in the mornings, so I began spending time in the office catching up on book work.

As I entered our income and expenditure, I wondered how the extra staff costs would affect our profitability. The margins in the gift shop and tearooms were not as high as I would have liked and at peak times, they became so crowded it was hard for visitors to get inside. Were we losing sales?

I decided to calculate our average spend per customer, and the results were depressing. On our busiest days, the spend per head went down considerably.

I went looking for Dad and found him with the children in David and

Phil's flat. He gave me a hug and made me a mug of tea.

"What are you up to?" he asked. "I don't seem to see much of you these days."

I explained what I had been doing, and that I was worried our figures for the summer were not looking good.

"But I thought the figures were up on last year?"

"They are. At least the amount of money we're taking each day has gone up, but our outgoings have gone up almost as much."

"Have you spoken to your mother about this?"

"No. I haven't spoken to any of the others. They're all working flat out and it doesn't seem the right moment."

"No, I see your point," Dad agreed, "but it's a good idea for you to keep an eye on the figures and see where we can improve things."

After that, I analysed everything.

I kept records of how much stock we sold, the average cost of the items in the gift shop, the busiest times at the ticket box, when visitors started to leave, the approximate number of people watching the shows and many other things.

It felt good to have something to keep me busy, but the patterns I saw emerging worried me.

On wet days families left earlier than on sunny days, even though we were advertising Silverlands as an all-weather attraction. There was so much space in the old building that it never felt crowded, but it soon became clear that our new indoor entertainment room was far too small. On busy days Bob persuaded the entertainers to put on extra shows, but there were still families crowding outside trying to get in.

The tearooms were just as bad. I had thought if we increased the number of staff and cut down on queuing times, we would be able to cater for more customers, but now I saw I was wrong. It was not the speed of preparing food that limited the amount of meals we could serve. It was the number of seats.

On wet days when we couldn't use the tea lawn, we only had forty seats available inside. The queues in the servery quickly became unmanageable, but there was no advantage in serving people more quickly if there was nowhere to eat their meals.

To make matters worse, there was nowhere inside for families to eat the picnics they had brought with them.

Fortunately, we only had a few wet days that year, but it was clear that in a bad summer we would have serious problems.

I realised that since we first opened, we had all been so busy dealing with the day-to-day running of the attraction that we hadn't had time to step back and see the bigger picture.

One day I walked up the hill and watched the cars filing into the car park. I had assumed that our visitors were mainly families and was surprised by how many couples arrived on their own. That meant the average number of people per car was far lower than we had anticipated when we planned the number of parking spaces we would need.

Also, I was horrified by the careless way drivers parked. Most left huge spaces between their car and the next vehicle. The result was that all the levels of the car park were full well before lunchtime.

I stopped at the ticket box on my way down the hill.

"Do you ever see cars drive up the hill to the car park and come straight back down again?" I asked.

Mum frowned at me.

"How could I tell? Cars go up and down the hill all the time."

I wanted to talk to her, but there was a queue of customers.

"Never mind, I'd better let you get on."

The more I thought, the more I realised our business plan had big holes in it. Apart from the rent from the craft block and the Motor Museum, all our income came from ticket sales and the turnover of the tearooms and giftshop.

Without making major changes, all of them were limited. We had hoped to develop Silverlands from the profit we generated each year, but now I realised that was never going to be possible.

The more I thought about the situation, the more stressed I became. I felt responsible. I knew it was illogical to believe everything that went wrong was my fault, but I did.

* * *

When a letter arrived reminding me of my next antenatal check, I was tempted to throw it in the bin. The last thing I wanted was to be poked and prodded.

"The things I go through for you," I muttered to my bump as I drove up the hill to Chudleigh.

The midwife greeted me with a friendly smile.

It was only when she took her usual measurements and weighed me that her smile faded.

"What is it?" I asked.

"You haven't put any weight on."

"Is that a problem?"

"Not necessarily, but it's a sign we need to keep a closer eye on you. Have you been eating properly?"

"Yes," I lied.

"And getting plenty of rest?"

"As much as I can."

She gave me a sharp look.

"I'll take some extra blood tests and see what they tell us. And I want to see you again in seven days."

"Really? That soon?"

"Yes. I'll phone you tomorrow with the results of your tests."

I was in the office poring over figures when the midwife called.

"I'm afraid you're anemic. It's not unusual, but it's important we get it under control. I've left a prescription for you in the surgery and I want to see you again on Wednesday. If you haven't gained any weight by then we'll have to talk about your options."

"OK. I'll see you then," I said obediently.

* * *

After the success of the Clown Convention, Bob was keen to put on more special events, and I encouraged him as it seemed a good way to attract more visitors outside of the peak season.

He had already arranged for a local re-enactors group known as The American Eagles to put on a display in August but I was taken aback when he announced that he wanted to stage a week-long run of Open-Air Shakespeare performances in the middle of September.

"It will be perfect," he said. "There's often a last burst of warm weather then, just before the start of autumn, and we'll have had a couple of weeks to get our breath back after the school holidays."

"I suppose that makes sense," I agreed hesitantly, "but how will we advertise it?"

"That's not a problem. I've got lots of contacts in local newspapers. I'm sure they'll give us plenty of coverage."

"But won't it cost a lot to stage?" I asked.

"Not necessarily. We won't have to pay for theatre hire, or rehearsal rooms or building scenery. I'm sure David can rustle up whatever props we need. And we can offer meals before and after the performances in the tearooms and keep the gift shop open. I think it's going to work out really well."

David loved the idea of staging a play on the lawn, but I'm not sure Phil or our parents were quite so keen.

"What will happen if it rains?" Mum asked doubtfully, but Bob was unconcerned.

"We'll just move everything indoors. I doubt we'll sell so many tickets that we couldn't fit everyone into the entertainment room."

"I suppose so, but it all seems rather rushed to me," Mum said.

"Not at all," Bob replied confidently. "We have twelve weeks to prepare. That will be plenty."

* * *

Even though I had no appetite, I had plenty of nervous energy and constantly needed to be doing something. It was simply not possible for me to sit down and relax. Despite my increasing size, I still ran up the stairs if no one was watching me.

Unless I was in the office, I spent all day on my feet, either behind the counter in the servery or in the kitchen. By the time I fell into bed, my body was exhausted, but my mind refused to rest. Each night I lay awake wondering how we could make the business more profitable.

When I returned to see the midwife, she weighed me and tutted. She marked a point on a graph and held it out to me.

"You see this? That's where your weight should be by now."

"But I've put on a bit since last week," I said defensively.

"Not enough. Have you been taking your iron tablets?"

She bombarded me with questions about my health and eating habits, and I tried not to lie too much. Finally, she took some more blood samples and made another appointment for the following week.

"I thought I only needed to see you once a month?" I protested.

"That was when you were hitting your targets. Once you get back on track, I'll be glad not to see you so often," she assured me.

When I got back to Silverlands, I slipped into the kitchen and helped myself to two large pieces of chocolate flapjack. I popped them into the microwave for a few seconds, then dolloped a pile of clotted cream on top. As I picked up a fork, I noticed Millie watching me.

"It's OK," I said, "I have to gain weight somehow."

After that, chocolate flapjacks with clotted cream became my regular breakfast. Sometimes I managed a doughnut at lunchtime and, in the evenings, Bob prepared me a home-cooked meal as always. I checked my weight each day and felt virtuous as the needle crept slowly upward.

* * *

We decided our Outdoor Shakespeare production would be A Midsummer Night's Dream.

"It will be perfect," Bob declared. "The trees around the lawn will make a stunning backdrop and the laurels at the side will hide actors waiting to come on stage. We can bring all the chairs from the entertainments room and line them up along the road, or if people prefer, they can bring blankets and cushions and sit on the grass. It's going to be spectacular."

It was good to see him so enthusiastic. He soon found a director and spent every evening arranging auditions, planning rehearsals, and writing press releases.

The play had a large cast, and we decided to add a community element by asking the local school if they would like to provide children to play the fairies. The headmaster was delighted, and we soon had a team of adorable youngsters eager to flit in and out of bushes dressed in floaty white outfits.

One night, Bob had a phone call from a friend of ours called Barbara who worked for a well-known children's charity. She explained that she was responsible for promotions and asked if we would consider holding a grand opening on the first night of the show in aid of her charity.

"It would be great for everyone," she explained. "I can invite all the local dignitaries and celebrities who support us and you'll get a lot of extra press coverage."

We agreed at once.

As I was putting Claire to bed she reached out and put a hand on my bump.

"Has she been kicking today?" she asked.

"Yes, this afternoon, but the baby might not be a girl, you know. It might be a little boy."

Claire's nose wrinkled in disgust.

"It's can't a boy."

"It might be. Wouldn't it be nice to have a little brother?"

"No. I don't need a brother. I've got Michael."

I sniffed as a sudden surge of emotion brought tears to my eyes.

"But you will still love the baby if it's a boy, won't you?"

Claire shook her head, and a flurry of curls flew around her face.

"No. I only want a sister."

* * *

My next checkup went badly.

My weight had increased, and I expected the midwife to be pleased with me, but she was not.

"I only got your test results back this morning," she said. "If I'd had them before, I would have phoned you."

"Why? Is something wrong?"

"Yes. You're a lot more anaemic than you were. In fact, your level has dropped so far it could be considered pernicious."

"What does that mean?"

"It means you have to take your health seriously. I'm prepared to give you one more week but if your levels don't improve drastically, I will book you into hospital for a blood transfusion."

I was shocked.

"How long would that take?"

"It depends. You could be in and out in a few hours, but if the doctor is worried about you, he might want to keep you in until the baby is born."

"No! I can't do that. I'm not staying in hospital!"

"Not even for your baby?"

I felt sick. I looked down at my bump and felt tiny feet kicking me.

"Yes, of course. If it's really that serious, I'll do whatever I have to do. It's just that I'm very busy right now."

The midwife looked at me sternly.

"As I said, I'll give you one more week."

When I got home, I told Bob what the midwife had said.

"Then no more arguing. You have to rest."

To my surprise, he shared the news with Mum, and she backed him up.

"Bob's right. You have to slow down."

"But I can't just sit around all day. My head would explode."

"Then you can take over the ticket box for a while. I can help out in the shop or in the servery for a while. The change will be good for me."

"That's a great idea," Bob agreed. He put an arm around me. "Just for a while until you're feeling better."

"That's the problem, I feel fine..." I began.

"Then until the midwife says your blood levels have improved," Mum cut in.

"OK," I sighed. "It doesn't feel as though I have much choice."

"I used to suffer from anaemia when I was young," Mum said to Bob. "I found eating lots of spinach and red meats helped."

"Really? OK, I can arrange that." Bob nodded.

"And drinking plenty of milk can help too," Mum added.

There was no point in objecting. I was outnumbered.

Being in the ticket box wasn't as bad as I had anticipated.

Although I had to speak to lots of people, it was mainly repeating the same questions to everyone that arrived.

Mum often added a few cheerful comments about the weather or asked visitors if they had travelled far to visit us, but I soon found that if I smiled at people when they arrived, they would tell me how many there were in their party. Then I just had to tell them how much they needed to pay.

If I smiled at them again when I gave them their change, it was easy to convince myself that I had been friendly and welcoming.

The only problems I had were with senior citizens. We offered a discount to anyone over retirement age, but I have never found it easy to judge people's ages. Inevitably, I made mistakes.

On my first day a couple appeared in front of me and the man simply said, "Two, please."

I hesitated. They both looked as though they might be in their sixties, but I didn't want to offend them if they were younger than they appeared.

I took the note the man offered and charged him for two adults.

"Where's the rest?" he challenged me when I handed him the change. "I'm eighty-four and my wife's eighty-three. Surely you can see we're senior citizens?"

I apologised and made an excuse about how young they looked, but I knew he thought I had tried to short-change him.

Later, a single woman arrived with three young children.

"Can we go in now, Granny?" One of the children asked.

"I'm paying for me and three kids, please," the woman said, so I charged her for one senior citizen and three children.

Wrong again.

"Are you saying I look like an old age pensioner?" she demanded.

"No, of course not. I'm so sorry."

"I should think so. I'm not even fort-nine until next month."

"And I hope you have a very happy birthday," I said.

The woman gave me a strange look and shooed the children ahead of her through the entrance.

By the time Mum arrived to take over at lunchtime, I was exhausted.

"How do you do this all day?" I said. "They're all so difficult."

"Don't be silly, dear," she smiled. "They're just people."

* * *

That evening Bob served up a large steak with an enormous pile of spinach. I winced when he put the plate down in front of me.

"Do I have to eat this?"

"Unless you want a transfusion."

The baby twisted, and I sighed.

"OK." I muttered and patted my bump. "I hope you appreciate this."

Every day that week Bob made sure I took my iron tablets and fed me steak, liver and piles of leafy green vegetables. I felt I was being punished.

I had expected all the extra iron to give me a surge of energy, but I felt no different when I returned to the midwife.

She took a blood test and promised she would phone me as soon as she got the results.

As I walked into the kitchen, Abbie was having her break and I smiled to see she was wrestling with knitting needles and a ball of yellow wool. I pretended not to notice as she hastily shoved everything into a carrier bag.

"I was just wondering," she said, "would it help if I came in on my day off tomorrow and did some weeding for you? Some of the flower beds have got dandelions in them."

She was right. Dad had taken over most of my gardening duties but the combination of blazing sunshine and night time showers had made it perfect growing conditions and he was struggling to keep up with the weeds.

"I help Mum with the garden sometimes so I know what I'm doing and you don't have to pay me," she went on.

"That's very sweet of you, but don't you have things to do on your days off?"

"Not really, I just get bored at home."

"In that case, I would really appreciate it." I smiled, then added. "But we will pay you."

To my surprise, Abbie turned out to be a sensitive gardener and made an excellent job of weeding the borders around the tea lawns.

I was even more surprised to find Tom the Potter helping her when I took her out a mug of tea.

"That's very kind of you," I told him.

"We all have to do our bit, don't we?" he said.

* * *

I was dreading the call from the midwife, but the moment I heard her voice I knew it was good news.

"Well done," she said. "Your levels are much better. I'll see you at the same time next week, but until then just keep doing whatever it is you've been doing."

"Ok. Thanks for letting me know."

I should have been pleased, but I felt deflated as I put the phone down.

July was over and since the beginning of August the temperature had edged higher every day. I could still squeeze behind the counter in the servery, but bending down for cups was awkward. Carrying trays was awkward too, and so was lifting the lid on the dishwasher. Simple things had become challenging and my patience was running out.

Whenever I was alone, I talked to my bump. I was afraid the baby would sense my mood and feel guilty that I was miserable. I wondered if it liked being inside me or if it was as eager for the birth to be over as I was.

I talked to Fred quite often too. I told him that I needed him to behave. Everything had been quiet for weeks and I was worried that something might happen while I was in hospital.

As my due date approached, I grew increasingly emotional and struggled to hide how I was feeling. One evening I walked into the kitchen as Bob was feeding Dino.

"There you go, boy. Maybe we won't be the only males in our little family for much longer."

He patted the dog on the back as he wolfed down his food, and I felt tears spring to my eyes.

As well as Claire, Bob had Lynda, Julia and Penny from his first marriage. He adored all his daughters, but I knew how much he would have loved a son. It seemed that either he or Claire was going to be disappointed.

I wiped away the tears and told myself I was being ridiculous.

I was still feeling emotional a few days later when Phil walked into the tearooms with something in her hands.

"Look what I've found," she said and lifted a finger to give a glimpse of a tiny kitten. Blue eyes stared up at me from a white face covered in downy fur.

"Oooh! It's adorable!" I exclaimed.

"Don't be fooled by the cute looks. It's vicious," Phil warned me, and I noticed spots of red on her fingers.

"Where did you find it?"

"On the tea lawn. It was wandering around mewing."

Phil opened her hands to reveal the little creature. Its body was white and tortoiseshell, and its stumpy legs ended in pink paws that seemed far too big.

"It hardly looks old enough to be away from its mother," I said.

"That's what I was thinking. Can you do something with it? I was just on my way to the donkeys."

"Yes, of course," I said and carefully took the bundle of fluff into my own hands. "Like what?"

"I don't know. Whatever you think."

Bob was getting changed into his ringmaster outfit when I found him.

"You'll never guess what I've got," I said.

"You're right. I won't. What is it?"

"Ouch!"

I jumped as needle-sharp teeth sank into my fingers.

"Little beast!" I declared and held the kitten out to Bob.

"Where did that come from?" he asked in surprise.

"Phil gave it to me. It just appeared on the lawn. I'm not sure what to do with it."

Bob peered at the kitten and put out a finger to stroke it. At once, a tiny paw rose up and waved miniature claws at him.

"Feisty little thing, aren't you?" he smiled.

"Yes, it is. It's got teeth like razors."

"It's probably scared, poor thing. It's tiny. It can't have walked far. Surely someone must know where it's come from?"

As usual, it was David who discovered the answer.

Eric told him that one of his visitors had noticed a cardboard box dumped at the side of the car park. When he investigated, he found three tiny kittens inside. A local family who were leaving the Motor Museum had offered to take the animals to the cat rescue centre.

"So, our kitten must have walked all the way from the car park by itself," Bob said when David recounted the story to us. "I told you it was a feisty little thing."

"But what are we going to do with it?" I asked.

"Take it to the rescue centre, I guess," Bob replied.

"I suppose so."

I could feel Bob looking at me.

"Or do you want to keep it?" he asked.

I smiled for the first time in days.

"Yes, I do."

"I thought so," Bob blew out his cheeks and sighed. "Perfect. Just what we need right now. All right, I guess it can stay, but God only knows what Dino will think of it."

* * *

Later that day I took the kitten to our vet and discovered it was a girl.

"The vet thinks she's older than she looks," I told Bob when I got home. "He said she's a bit malnourished, but other than that there's nothing wrong with her."

"Good. Then we'll have to feed her up a bit."

"Yes. I bought some tins of kitten food on the way back."

As I opened the top of the box I had used to take the kitten to the vet, a tiny white head popped out.

"Have you thought about a name yet?" Bob asked.

"Not really."

He watched the kitten scramble out of the box and slither to the floor.

"How about Sammy?"

"Maybe..."

"She reminds me of the cat I had when I was little. She was called Sammy."

"OK," I agreed. "Sammy it is."

Sammy immediately took possession of our flat. I had expected her to be frightened by Dino but when they first met and the dog put his nose down to sniff Sammy ran straight towards him. She fluffed out her fur until it stood on end like ginger and white thistledown, then opened her tiny mouth and hissed.

Dino's ears pricked up, and he backed away in surprise.

"It's all right," Bob reassured him, "I won't let the kitty savage you."

At first glance, Sammy seemed frail and defenceless, but she was full of courage and personality.

She didn't like being stroked, and she hissed and spat whenever anyone tried to pick her up. She was fiercely independent but occasionally, when she was in the right mood, she would butt her head against my ankle or rub her head against my hand.

Dino was not impressed that we had allowed a kitten into his flat.

I had been worried that he might not like Sammy, but I had no concern that he would be aggressive towards her. He was always gentle with small creatures.

One morning, soon after he arrived, I had seen him lying on the ground in the garden with his head under a bush.

When I went to investigate, I was horrified to see that he had a bedraggled baby bird between his paws. At first, I thought he had killed it but then, when it let out a little chirp, I realised it was unharmed and he had merely been licking it.

I was much more concerned that Sammy might hurt Dino. She was a tiny in comparison to him, but she had no reservations about using her teeth and claws.

On the first day we kept her shut in our bedroom so that Dino had the run of the rest of the flat but, in the evening, we let Sammy out and the first thing she did was run towards the dog.

Dino put his head down to say hello, but Sammy showed him no respect whatsoever. She reared up on her hind legs and waved her claws at the dog towering over her.

The kitten's lack of fear seemed to intimidate Dino, and he soon retreated. Sensing victory, Sammy hissed and chased after him.

"That's not very nice, is it?" I said as I picked up the little ball of fluff. "You're supposed to be friends."

Sammy bit my finger, and I put her down on the sofa.

"You need to learn some manners," I said sternly as Dino hid behind Bob's legs.

Sammy was fascinated by Dino's long, hairy tail. Whenever she got the chance, she would launch herself at it and cling on tightly while Dino raced round in circles trying to shake her off. Sometimes she lay in wait on a chair, hoping that Dino would walk past. If he did, she would jump on him, run along his back to his head and chew his ears.

It was clear we couldn't leave our pets alone together until they became friends. It wasn't fair on the dog.

"It's rough on the poor old boy," Bob complained. "He had a lovely life until that thing arrived."

I couldn't argue. I felt sorry for Dino, but there was something about

Sammy's fearless independence that captured my heart.

* * *

The American Eagles were booked to stage their re-enactment on Saturday 12th August. We had advertised the event as a battle from the American War of Independence, but it was really more of a skirmish as the armies only had twelve soldiers on each side.

"It will be impressive though," Bob assured me. "They are going to put up authentic tents and camp on the lawn. In the morning there will be Living History displays so people can ask them about their clothes and their weapons and how they lived. Then, in the afternoon, they will have the battle."

"It sounds exciting. I'm sure people will love it."

"And there's another thing. The re-enactors cook an authentic army meal whenever they camp out and they've asked if we'd like to join them."

"After the battle? When the public have gone?"

"Yes, that's the idea."

"Why not?" I agreed. "It sounds as like fun."

The American Eagles arrived on Friday morning.

I knew they would be setting up their camps on the lawn, so I was not surprised when they arrived in the tearooms. What did surprise me was that they were already wearing authentic eighteenth-century costumes.

"Who are those weird people?" Abbie asked as she stared through into the servery.

"They're re-enactors. The ones that are going to fight the battle tomorrow."

"But why are they dressed like that? They must be boiling in this heat."

She was right. The sun was blazing outside, and I had felt hot and sweaty from the moment I stepped out of the shower that morning. I tried to explain that re-enactors liked to make their performance as authentic as possible, but Abbie merely snorted.

"They must be mad," she said. "We've got much nicer clothes now. Why would anyone want to go around wearing old-fashioned stuff like that?"

I was not surprised to hear the re-enactors needed help with their equipment. Their costumes, tents and cooking apparatus all came from a former era and it seemed their public address system did too.

"It's ancient," David muttered as he passed through the kitchen. "It's not working and even if it was, it's far too small to use here."

"Then what are we going to do?"

"I'll have to set up the system we used for the Clown Convention, but I wish I'd known in advance. It's going to take me ages."

A few minutes later, Bob called in on his way to introduce Liza's morning show.

"I thought I'd better warn you. Your mother's got three coaches queued at the gate."

"Thanks for the warning. I'll get Abbie to put some extra jacket potatoes in," I smiled. "See you later."

It was Pam's day off, but Abbie and Millie were already busy toasting teacakes and taking orders through to customers.

"Be good today, will you?" I whispered as I stroked my bump. "It looks like we're going to be busy. Remember, only one more week and you'll be out."

By lunchtime, the queue in the servery stretched out into the corridor. Between shows, Bob took off his red coat and joined Martha behind the counter taking orders.

"Shouldn't you be resting?" he asked each time he passed a pile of orders into the kitchen.

"Honestly, I'm fine," I assured him. "I'll let you know if I need a break."

The lunchtime rush was underway when I felt a twinge. I told myself it was indigestion. A while later, I felt it again.

Abbie was struggling to get a tray of potatoes out of the oven, and Pam was washing lettuce. I knew there were tables waiting to be cleared.

I went to the office and phoned through to the shop.

"Is Phil there?" I asked when Beryl answered.

"No, she's gone to look after a boy that's hurt himself on the pirate trail."

I swore under my breath.

"Never mind. Can you ask her to phone me when she comes back?"

I thought about calling Dad, but I knew he had the two children.

As I stood wondering what to do the twinge stopped. I waited for a few minutes, but nothing else happened.

"Can you slice some ham for me, Diana?" Abbie's voice floated in from the kitchen. "And we've run out of grated cheese."

"OK, I'm coming."

I ran a hand over my bump.

"If you're planning on making an appearance, could you leave it until we finished the afternoon teas?" I whispered.

* * *

"Are you all right? You look a bit flushed," Bob said an hour later. "I've had to leave Martha on her own. The next show's due any minute."

"Yes, I'm fine," I assured him, "but if you see David or Phil, can you get them to call me?"

By the time David arrived, the lunchtime rush had given way to the afternoon rush.

"Can you clear some tables?" I asked him.

"Of course. Phil's still down at the Pirate Trail. A little boy twisted his ankle and his mother fainted."

"Really?"

"Luckily, the boy's OK. Phil strapped his ankle up but the mother's laying on the ground demanding we call an ambulance."

"Can Phil deal with it?"

"Don't worry, Dad's there too with the kids and he's got a walkie-talkie in case he needs us."

"It's all go today, isn't it?" Abbie beamed as she rushed past with a plate of food in each hand.

"It certainly is," I agreed.

I looked at the clock. It was nearly thirty minutes since the last twinge.

"Clear as many tables as you can," I said to David. "We'll be starting on cream teas any time now."

The queue never eased all afternoon. By the time Bob finished the last show we had run out of scones and the cake stands were empty.

"I think there are some tea cakes in the freezer if you want me to defrost them," he suggested, but I shook my head.

"The girls can manage now," I said. "I think you'd better get me to the hospital."

* * *

A few hours later, another girl joined our family. Lucy was healthy and beautiful with a full head of black hair. I wanted to take her straight home, but the doctor insisted we stayed until the morning.

"But there won't be anyone to come and get me tomorrow. Can't I go home with my husband now?" I pleaded.

"Don't worry. I'll arrange an ambulance for you," the doctor said.

I was about to protest when Bob put a hand on my arm.

"Don't argue this time. Just rest."

I gave in.

The pillow was soft, and I was exhausted. With Lucy in her cot beside me, I was asleep before Bob left the room.

The next morning a nurse helped me take Lucy down to a waiting ambulance. I had offered to catch a bus, but the nurse explained that a new mother was not allowed to take her baby home unaccompanied.

"Your doctor will be in touch to arrange a home visit," she reminded me as she closed the ambulance door.

We arrived home to a barrage of congratulations. All the family were eager to meet Lucy, and Abbie pushed a package into my hands the moment she saw me.

"Here, I wanted to be the first to give you something for the baby."

I tore open the wrapping paper and a shawl of yellow wool tumbled out.

"It's lovely, Abbie, thank you so much," I said as she hugged me.

"I made it myself," she beamed.

"Did you?" I admired the uneven stitches. "I would never have guessed."

"I started as soon as I knew you were expecting. Martha showed me how."

"Well, it's beautiful, thank you so much."

Claire was delighted to meet her new sister and Michael peered at his cousin as she slept in a carrycot.

"Is she ever going to wake up?" he asked.

"She will as soon as she's hungry," I told him.

The grounds were already filling and families crowded around the two army camps on the lawn.

"Do you want me to help you up to the flat?" Bob suggested.

"No, I'd rather sit here and watch the battle," I said happily. "Pam's in the tearooms today so I'm sure they'll be fine without me. You go and organise your soldiers."

He bent over and kissed Lucy's head.

"Don't wake her up," I said, but the baby didn't stir.

It felt strange sitting at the side of the tea lawn watching instead of racing around serving people.

Luckily, Lucy was a contented baby. She opened her eyes occasionally and demanded food when she was hungry, but mostly, she was happy to sleep.

"Do you think the battle's going to upset her?" Dad asked as he watched her nestling quietly in my arms.

"I don't know. I'm not sure how loud it's going to be."

"They've got a cannon, I know that much, and a lot of muskets," he replied.

We were sitting on the grass bank at the side of the lawn while Claire and Michael rolled down the slope and clambered back up again.

"Is it time for the battle yet?" Claire demanded.

"Ladies and Gentleman…" Bob's voice rang out across the grounds.

I listened as he welcomed everyone and gave a brief introduction to the American Eagles and the history of the War of Independence. When he finished, there was a loud cheer as the two lines of soldiers marched out to take their places.

The battle was much more impressive than I had expected, and the crowd loved every moment.

The re-enactors played their parts with enthusiasm, and the audience gasped at the ear-splitting roar of the cannon. Soldiers shouted, muskets fired, and clouds of blue smoke rolled across the grounds, enveloping the armies and audience alike in a reeking haze of gunpowder fumes.

Children squealed with excitement, and cameras clicked everywhere, but Lucy never flinched. She slept through the whole battle and only stirred when it was time for her next feed.

That evening, when the public had gone, the family and some of the craftspeople joined the re-enactors around their campfire. Liza and Roly were there, and Claire and Michael ran around the lawn in the fading light, protesting that they didn't want to go to bed yet. We all talked and laughed and ate beef and vegetable stew that had been simmering in a steel cauldron all afternoon.

As the light faded one of the re-enactors produced a mouth organ and began to play. Others joined in with the song and I rocked Lucy in my arms. I hoped she was enjoying her first night in this crazy world.

* * *

I took Sunday off.

* * *

On Monday, I persuaded Mum to let me take over the ticket box for a few days.

"Are you sure?" she asked me with a worried look.

"Of course, I am. If Lucy can sleep through a battle, I'm sure she'll be fine sleeping in her carrycot. When it's time for a feed, I'll phone the shop and someone can come down and relieve me."

Bob was less easy to convince.

"You should be having a proper rest," he insisted. "There's no reason for you to be working at all."

"But I want to work. If you make me sit in a room with nothing to do but look after the baby, I'll go mad. I love her very much, but I can't just sit around changing nappies."

Bob's face darkened.

"You do understand, don't you?" I asked.

I could see that he didn't.

"What was the point in taking on extra staff if you still insist on working?" he muttered as he walked away.

The following morning, I was serving customers when a neatly dressed man stepped in front of the queue.

"Excuse me, can you let me through, please? I'm here to see Diana Townsend."

I laughed as I recognised him.

"Good morning, doctor. Can I help you?"

He peered at me through the glass partition.

"My goodness. I wasn't expecting you to be in there. I've come to do your check-up."

"Thank you. Well, as you can see, I'm fine and the baby's asleep," I said pointing to the carrycot beside me.

"Yes, so I see.... Well, this is a bit awkward." He looked at the queue behind him, "Perhaps I should have phoned. Can you make an appointment and bring her up to the surgery?"

"Yes, of course."

"Right, well... I won't keep you, then."

"Goodbye, doctor." I smiled.

The next few weeks were hectic. Lucy was a peaceful baby, but she still kept us up at night and demanded regular attention during the day.

At the beginning of September, Michael started school, and Claire was proud to show him the ropes.

The end of the school holidays meant saying goodbye to Beryl and Millie, but there was little chance for the rest of us to relax as preparations were well on the way for our season of Open-Air Shakespeare.

Rehearsals took place several times a week, and David spent his evenings rigging a lighting system and preparing props.

* * *

Sammy had grown considerably since she had arrived, and we now felt that she was big enough to be allowed out of the flat. I was afraid she would be intimidated by the outside world or might get lost, but I should have known better. She marched around the grounds like a lioness surveying its territory.

I had intended to have a cat-flap installed, but Sammy had her own ideas. Even inside our flat it had been obvious that she was a natural climber. She scaled the curtains in seconds and could shoot straight up the wallpaper thanks to her formidable claws.

To my surprise, when she wanted to go home, she simply ascended the oak tree at the front of the house, jumped on to the entrance roof and squeezed in through our bedroom window.

Being allowed out of the house gave her an even greater sense of independence. She had been content to eat the tinned kitten food we had put down for her, but now she turned her nose up at it.

"Do you think she's ill?" Bob asked me. "She hasn't eaten anything since we let her outside. It's been three days now."

I watched as Sammy raced around the room, jumping from chair to chair, only pausing long enough to sink her teeth into Dino's fur as he passed.

"She looks OK to me."

"Then do you think someone else is feeding her?"

"Maybe. I saw her in the craft block yesterday."

I asked everyone if they had given Sammy anything to eat, but they all denied it. Bob tempted her with boiled chicken, fresh fish and steak, but she wouldn't touch anything.

"I think we'd better take her to the vet," Bob said at last.

I was getting worried myself.

"Ok. I'll make an appointment."

But Sammy never got to the vet.

That afternoon David spotted her dragging part of a dead rabbit through the bushes.

"Look, it's bigger than she is," he said as he showed me.

"Urgh! Can you get rid of it?"

He hesitated.

"I can, but I think she wants it back."

"No! Certainly not. It's disgusting. She must have found it somewhere."

David sniffed the carcass.

"It's fresh. There are lots of rabbits in the grounds. She could have caught it herself."

"Don't be ridiculous." I laughed. "You said it yourself. It's bigger than she is."

Sammy meowed and stood on her hind legs to reach the remains of the rabbit.

"I'm sorry, kitty-cat," David said. "Mummy won't let you have it."

I put down more tinned food, but it was futile. Sammy preferred to provide for herself.

"I suppose it's natural. There are plenty of mice and things around here for her to eat," Bob said one evening as he watched Sammy cleaning her fur. She was always immaculately groomed and her coat was beautifully soft and silky.

"I guess so. I just wish she'd stop bringing things in through the bedroom window," I complained.

Bob grinned.

"Don't be so unappreciative. That's her way of giving you a present."

"Is it? Well, I don't care. I'm never going to be pleased to find half a vole on the carpet."

"Did you hear that, Sammy? Be careful or Mummy and Dino will gang up and send you to the cat's home."

"Does that mean that you're the one that wants Sammy to stay now?"

"I didn't say that," he replied but it was obvious how fond he had become of her.

* * *

Barbara was as good as her word. She arranged the Gala Opening Night for A Midsummer Night's Dream and invited many of her charity's celebrity supporters. Bob was delighted when she told him she had asked everyone to attend in full evening dress.

"Wow! This is going to be a glittering event," he said as he looked at the list of RSVP's she had sent him.

"Who's coming?" I asked.

He passed me the list and I read through it. In addition to the local mayor and his wife there was a long list of VIPs and I recognised the names of several sportsmen, a jockey, a radio presenter and a celebrity chef.

I was impressed.

It was only when Bob asked me if I planned to buy an evening dress that I realised he expected me to help him host the evening.

A wave of panic filled me. It was bad enough having to deal with the public, but making polite conversation with celebrities while being photographed for the newspapers was beyond me. And there would be glasses of wine to spill and long dresses to trip over.

My courage failed, and I searched desperately for an excuse.

"Lucy will need feeding and someone will have to be in charge of the tearooms," I reminded Bob. "You don't really need me, do you?"

"I didn't say I needed you," he said sadly. "I thought you would enjoy it. I thought it would be fun to do it together."

"I know. And it will be fun. I can watch it all from the back of the lawn."

He sighed.

"If that's how you want it."

It wasn't how I wanted it. I knew I was letting him down, but I was relieved he didn't try to change my mind.

And it was true that I was needed in the tearooms.

Millie, Pam and Abbie were all on duty and Barbara had lent us sophisticated black and white uniforms for them to wear.

"My God! I've never been this posh in my life!" Abbie giggled as she did a twirl for me.

"You look amazing," I told her.

Bob was right. The evening was sparkling.

As dusk fell the old house looked magical with golden lights shining from every window. David had lined up chairs on the road that ran around the lawn, and the front row was reserved for our VIP guests.

As they arrived, Bob welcomed them and Pam handed out glasses of champagne. Mum was at the entrance collecting tickets as families arrived and spread out blankets and cushions on the edges of the lawn.

"Don't they all look lovely!" Abbie trilled as she peered out of the tearooms window at a group of women in long evening dresses talking to Bob.

"Yes, they do, but please hurry up, the play will be starting soon."

"Do you need any help?" David asked as he popped into the kitchen. He was wearing a suit, and I stopped and stared at him.

"Wow! I haven't seen that outfit since you got married."

"I know," he grinned. "I'm surprised it still fits."

"You look great. We're fine here. Go and enjoy the show."

* * *

I finished clearing up and was heading outside to watch the play when I spotted David coming towards me.

"Is everything OK?" I asked.

"No!"

"What is it?"

"It's your bloody cat!"

"Why? What's she done?"

"She's been going around making friends with people and now she's giving them presents."

"What do you mean?"

"She must have found a nest of baby mice. She's bringing the bodies and dropping them on people's laps."

"Oh, my God!"

"I tried to catch her, but she's too fast for me."

We hurried across the road and stood at the back of the crowd.

"There she is," David hissed. "She's got another one."

By the glow of the stage lights, I could see Sammy sloping around the edge of the lawn with something hanging from her mouth.

While Oberon and Titania performed in the spotlight and fairies flitted among the bushes, David and I crept between the audience, trying to corner Sammy. She must have known what we were doing because every time one of us got close, she darted off in another direction.

As twilight faded to dusk, the cat merged into the shadows.

"Where is she?" David whispered as we peered into the gloom.

"I don't know. I can't see her... Oh, no!"

A movement caught my eye by the row of VIP seats as Sammy leaped onto a woman's lap.

"Quick!" I breathed. "You go that way."

I pointed to the far end of the seats and David scurried off as I picked my way through the darkness. Perhaps a pincer movement would catch her unawares.

In front of me, Sammy was calmly stepping from lap to lap, her trophy still dangling in front of her.

"Excuse me," I whispered as I edged half-crouching in front of the seats. I could see David's head bobbing as he approached from the other end of the row when a shrill squeal rang out. A celebrity jumped to her feet as Sammy deposited the baby mouse on the lap of her evening dress.

The cat sprang to the ground, and I pounced. Sammy meowed indignantly, but I tucked her under my arm and scrambled to my feet. Every head turned, and from the middle of the row, Bob stared at me in bewilderment.

"Sorry about that," I whispered and scurried back to the house.

"I know you mean well," I told Sammy as I shut her in the office, "but for the rest of the night, you are confined to barracks!"

Chapter 9

At the end of September, we closed for the winter. By the time we opened again it would not only be another year, it would be another decade. The nineteen nineties lay ahead of us.

Without the daily routines of running Silverlands, I could finally get the whole family together to talk. We gathered in the tearooms around the inevitable pot of tea, and Dino and Ossie lay down obediently beside us. I caught Mum looking at them with a glum expression and guessed she was missing Scruffy.

I wasn't looking forward to the discussion. I always hated sharing bad news, but I knew it was important for everyone to have a realistic idea of how the business was performing.

David handed round a packet of biscuits.

"Where are we going to start?" he asked. "I've got lots of ideas to talk about."

Mum cut in.

"Before we get going, I want to update you with our takings for the year. I've tallied everything up and got the final amounts if you want to hear them."

Everyone nodded their agreement, and Mum read out the figures.

"Great. That's a healthy increase on last year," Bob smiled.

I couldn't delay any longer.

"Actually, there's something I need to say."

I felt as though I was cancelling Christmas.

"The figures are good, but I think we need to look a bit deeper. While I've been looking after Lucy, I've had time to do some projections and things aren't as positive as they look."

I avoided looking anyone in the eye while I explained what I had discovered.

"So, what you're saying is that even if we spend a fortune on advertising and get thousands more people here and work ourselves to death, we won't end up with any more money in the bank at the end of the year?" Bob said when I had finished.

I sighed heavily.

"Yes, that pretty much sums it up."

"Then we might as well give up now," David exploded. "what's the point in slaving our guts out if we're never going to have enough cash to finish the things we've been planning?"

"Calm down, everyone," Dad urged, but David was not in a mood to be calm.

"You heard what she said! We'll never make any money until we have more catering facilities and a bigger car park, and we can't get either of them until we have more money. It's Catch 22, isn't it?"

"Can't we attract more visitors in the off season?" Phil asked.

"We can, and it would certainly help," I agreed, "but I don't think it would be enough to make a real difference. It would still take years to get enough finance together for the things we need to do."

We talked for hours, and everyone had a different opinion on what we should do. Finally, we agreed to keeping thinking and to meet again the following day.

* * *

When we gathered again there were fewer smiles than before. It was clear everyone was taking the situation seriously.

Dad spoke first.

"Before we get started, I want everyone to remember how far we've come. When we first saw this place, it was a wreck. Water pouring through the roof, windows missing, holes kicked in the walls. Look at it now. We may still have challenges to face, but we can't let anything discourage us."

"And the value has rocketed," David added.

"Yes, if we look at it as an investment it's been a massive success," Bob agreed.

"But our biggest problem is cash flow," Mum pointed out. "We need to concentrate on the things that will bring us in more money."

David nodded.

"You're right. There are still lots of new exhibitions, I want to add, but they'll have to wait for now."

"Good."

I was relieved there were no arguments.

"I think we're all agreed that we need a proper restaurant." I looked around and everyone nodded. "We're lucky that we have a huge kitchen but we can't make full use of it at the moment. It's great having the tearooms but if we could open up the room on the other side as a restaurant it would make a massive difference."

"And it's not just about catering for visitors during the season. If we had a restaurant, we could hold functions," Bob joined in. "I know some of the other attractions are making a fortune from functions."

"But what about the circus and the indoor entertainments? Where would they go?" Phil asked.

"I've been thinking about that," Dad said. "It seems to me the best answer would be to open up the building behind the dormitory block. The one that used to be the school science lab."

"I'm not sure which building you mean," Mum admitted.

"Why don't we go around there and I'll show you?"

As we walked around to the back of the site, I realised Dad was right. In fact, I couldn't believe we hadn't thought of it before.

The old science lab was built into the hillside and was linked by a corridor to the first floor of the main house. By opening it up we would not only be providing a new home for the model circus and a spacious indoor entertainment area, but visitors would be able to access it all without having to go outside.

"It's perfect!" I cried, "and when it's sunny people can come out through the top doors straight to the Animal Meadow."

Dad pointed to the open space in front of him. "I've got another idea. It wouldn't take much work to level this area and create a little outdoor circus ring. Then, when it's really busy, we could have Punch and Judy or a juggler working here as well as on the lawn."

"That would be great!" Bob agreed. "Especially when it's sunny, but the lawn's too soggy to use."

By the time we got back to the tearooms we had the basis of our plan agreed. We knew what we wanted to do, and we knew it would make an enormous difference to our long-term profitability. All we had to do was work out was how to finance it.

We talked for days. We considered opening during the winter, holding events in the tearooms in the evenings, increasing our prices. We even considered selling some of the undeveloped buildings, but we couldn't come up with anything that would provide the amount we thought we needed.

"We can't go any farther until we know exactly how much it will all cost," Bob said at last.

"Then we'd better start drawing plans, hadn't we?" I said. "As soon as we have everything down in black and white, we can get quotes."

"If we're being realistic about it, our only option is to go back to the bank and borrow more money, isn't it?" Bob said.

I saw a worried expression cloud Dad's face.

"Yes, you might be right," I agreed, "but we don't have to make any decisions yet. Let's work out all the costs first."

* * *

Money was tight, but we had one big extravagance ahead of us.

Dad's birthday was at the end of October and he was going to be seventy-five. At the beginning of the year, Mum had asked if we wanted to plan a special celebration for him and we had all leapt at the idea. He was not particularly fond of parties, so we tried to think of an alternative.

It was David who came up with the idea.

"Why don't we take him to Disney World?"

We had all laughed at first but the more we thought about it the more we loved the idea. Dad was a big kid at heart. He had taken David and me to see every Disney film the moment it was released. We knew he would be thrilled to visit the Magic Kingdom itself.

With hindsight, I was glad we had made the decision and paid for the tickets before we started worrying about money.

When we broke the news to Dad that he would be spending his birthday with Mickey Mouse in Florida, he roared with laughter.

"Are you serious?" he asked. "All of us? That's incredible."

I had never seen him so excited.

Claire and Michael were excited too. They had no idea what Disney World was, but they ran around the house with their arms sticking out like wings making aeroplane noises.

As the holiday drew near the anticipation grew and we all busied ourselves packing suitcases, checking passports and collecting dollars from the post office.

Marion & Elliott, the glass engravers from the craft centre, had become trusted friends over the last three years so we left them the keys to Silverlands and they promised to walk the dogs and look after the animals while we were away.

"I hope this trip is as good as everyone's expecting," Mum said as we finally shut the front door behind us and headed to the airport.

She needn't have worried. The holiday was better than we could have imagined. Dad loved every moment, and the children were so overwhelmed by the constant thrills and distractions they were too tired to misbehave and slept soundly every night.

Even Lucy was content to lay in her pushchair and stare at the wonders around her.

The rest of us were captivated too. The sheer scale of the attractions and the professionalism with which everything was presented was phenomenal.

"That was awesome! Just imagine how much it must have cost," David gasped as he staggered off another stunning ride. "If only we had that sort of money to play with."

"What have you done with the kids?" Bob asked me one evening when Claire went to bed without complaint and Lucy gurgled in her cot. "Have you drugged them with something?"

I laughed.

"No. It's just an overdose of Disney Magic. It's wonderful while it lasts, but I'm sure we'll pay for it when we get home!"

"You're probably right," Bob grinned.

At that moment, home could have been on another planet. Everything around us felt exotic and alien. The air-conditioning rattled as it fought to keep the temperature down, and outside our window cicadas sang and the distant chorus of bullfrogs echoed across the lakes.

"I'm glad we came," I began, "but I'm not sure I want to go home."

"Why not?"

"It's all a bit much, isn't it? I mean, how are we supposed to compete with this? Lots of people can afford to travel abroad for their holidays now. How are we going to impress them with what we can offer at Silverlands if they've been here?"

Bob thought for a moment.

"What strikes me most about this place is how happy people are. I know it's all rather cheesy. Everyone saying 'have a great day!' all the time, but it does create an amazing atmosphere."

"Are you suggesting we should tell Abbie and Martha to give our visitors big toothpaste smiles and ask them how they're doing?"

"Of course not! It wouldn't work at home. I'm just suggesting we concentrate on making Silverlands a magical place to visit."

I understood what he meant, and I knew many of our customers had already commented on how much they liked the atmosphere we had created.

"I know you're right," I said, "but I really wish we could take a roller-coaster home with us. Just a little one."

Bob burst out laughing.

"Sorry, I can't give you a roller-coaster. If you're really good, I'll pop down to reception and get you a bag of chewy cookies."

"OK. That will do!" I grinned.

* * *

We had left England during a mild spell in October, but by the time we returned at the beginning of November we were greeted by near-freezing temperatures.

I pulled out my warmest jumpers, vests and extra socks, but Bob was still wearing a T-shirt.

"Don't you ever get cold?" I muttered.

"No. I eat porridge for breakfast," he replied smugly, but I refused to believe a few oats could make such a difference.

Bob never seemed to feel the cold. He loved warmth and sunshine and his skin always looked freshly tanned, but he loved fresh air even more. He insisted on leaving our bedroom window open unless it was actually snowing outside, and since Sammy had arrived, he used the fact that we didn't have a cat-flap as an excuse to keep the window permanently open.

I tried complaining that it wasn't safe, but he pointed out that only a cat could get in by jumping from the slender branches of the oak tree.

I wouldn't have minded so much, but the open window was on my side of the bed.

To make matters worse, Sammy decided to show her appreciation by bringing us even more 'presents'. I felt a guilty sense of schadenfreude when I was woken by Bob swearing in the middle of the night. Needing to visit the toilet, he had felt for his slippers only for his bare foot to squish onto something wet and bloody on the carpet.

I had hoped the experience would persuade him we needed to make other arrangements, but he simply reminded me I had been the one who wanted a cat. It was hard to argue, but a few nights later my patience snapped.

I was roused from my slumber by something soft brushing against my cheek. I could hear the drone of Sammy purring inches from my ear and realised my hair was sticking to my face.

Jumping out of bed, I saw that our generous cat had left a large, well-chewed mouse on my pillow. I picked it up by the tail and threw it out of the open window.

"That's enough! I can't take it anymore!" I shrieked and stomped off to the bathroom to wash the blood from my forehead.

Bob was sitting up in bed stroking Sammy when I returned.

"She was only trying to please you."

"I don't care," I snapped, taking the cat and dumping her unceremoniously in the corridor. "We have to get a cat flap."

"All right. If you insist."

"I do. And I'm closing the window. I don't care what you say, it's freezing tonight."

I was right about it being freezing. Bob had left our car parked immediately below our bedroom window. The following morning, when he went to take the children to school, he found a large, well-chewed mouse frozen to the windscreen.

* * *

Before we left on holiday, we had already agreed our plans for the next development, but by the time we returned we had lots of ideas for minor changes. We wanted to add more touches of humour to our displays and little details to make people smile.

We already had signposts around the grounds pointing to the Pirate Trail or the Craft Block, but now David added others with the number of miles to the North Pole, Australia, and one pointing straight up to the Moon

Our advertising leaflets featured cartoon clowns, so we added a cartoon version of Bob in his ringmaster outfit and started using the characters on our information boards and menus.

David made some models of the clowns and the ringmaster and hid them around the exhibitions. Then we put up notices saying the little people were hiding and offering a reward of a Silverlands badge for any child that spotted them all.

We also designed an adventure pack to give to each family as they arrived with games and activities relating to each display and a treasure trail that led to the Pirates' Treasure.

We had great fun designing the extra features and were content that although we couldn't move ahead with any major developments straight away, at least our repeat visitors would find lots of new things to amuse them next time they visited.

* * *

At the beginning of December, I felt the familiar tightening in my stomach as I spotted a solicitor's letter in the post.

Tearing open the envelope, I read the letter then passed it to Bob.

"I don't understand," I said.

I waited until he put the letter down.

"What do they want us to do?"

"I'm not sure either. Our neighbours seem to be asking us to guarantee that if their water supply freezes, we will fix it immediately."

"They're mad!" David exclaimed when we showed the letter to the others. "Do they think we can control the weather? If the pipes freeze, what do they expect us to do?"

I couldn't believe it was three years since we had moved in and the battle over the water supply still hadn't been resolved.

In addition to the dispute with our neighbours, I worried we would soon hear from the water board. We had paid a considerable amount in legal fees, but we hadn't yet paid a penny in water rates. The situation couldn't go on indefinitely, and I was sure we would soon receive an enormous bill.

I harangued Mr Barnaby with my fears, but he only made his usual excuses.

"If you're really concerned, why don't you estimate how much your bill should be and pay that amount?" he suggested.

"How on earth can we do that?" I protested. "The meter's broken, so we have no idea how much water is being used."

"The amount is not important," Mr Barnaby said patiently. "As long as you make a payment of some sort, the water board can't claim you are refusing to pay. It would certainly be in your favour if the case does come to court."

"All right, but it will only be a token amount," I grumbled.

"Good. In that case, please forward the letter on to me with the amount you decide to pay and I will take the appropriate action."

Putting the phone down, I tried to put the matter out of my mind. There was nothing to be gained by worrying.

Christmas was upon us in no time, and Claire and Michael were delighted to open their presents and find two identical yellow pedal cars. They soon learned how to drive them and raced off around the corridors. I winced as Michael crashed into the skirting boards at the bottom of the stairs, but David was unconcerned.

"Don't worry, I needed to retouch the paintwork, anyway."

Fortunately, the kids steering abilities soon improved, and they spent the rest of the holidays pedalling from one end of the building to the other.

Soon after New Year, I was working in the office when I heard a crash from the kitchen yard. I went to investigate and saw that a metal dustbin was lying on the ground with rubbish scattered around it. A dark shape, half-hidden by the bin, was nosing through the garbage. It was Scruffy.

Mum and Dad hurried down when I called them.

"He must be starving, poor thing!" Mum said when she saw him.

"Come here, boy!" Dad called.

Scruffy's ears pricked up and his tail wagged as he trotted over. A powerful stink came with him.

"Eew! He reeks," I complained.

"It's not his fault," Dad said evenly.

"I didn't say it was his fault. He's lovely, but you can't let him in the house."

Scruffy let out a friendly yelp as Dad scratched him behind his ear.

"Look, he's got bits of horse poo in his fur," Mum frowned.

"Sorry, old boy, you're not welcome like this. Come on."

I felt a pang of guilt as Scruffy followed Dad out through the kitchen yard.

"Do you think he'll be all right?"

Mum patted my arm.

"Don't worry, dear, your Dad will deal with him."

An hour later, I was disturbed again. This time, a commotion was coming from the downstairs corridor. I could hear Claire and Michael squealing and assorted bangs and thumps.

Leaving the office, I hurried through to see what was going on.

A soaking wet Scruffy was racing around the house, rubbing his ears on the carpet and shaking water and bubbles everywhere.

The children squealed with delight each time he passed them and Dad chuckled as he watched.

"That's better, isn't it? Now he smells of roses," he said when he saw me.

I was horrified.

"You can't just bath other people's dogs. What are the stables going to say when he goes home smelling of roses?"

"Who cares?" Dad shrugged. "It's disgusting the way they neglect him."

He bent down as the old dog came careering back up the corridor towards us, and Scruffy slowed down enough to lick his hand as he passed.

"The poor old fellow deserves better."

I knew he was right. After that, Scruffy came to visit every day. Dino and Ossie accepted him without any problems, and Dad bathed him regularly. Scruffy had an excellent sense of time. Every evening at six o'clock he scratched on the back door to be let out, then plodded back up the hill to the stables.

By the end of February, we were all used to Scruffy's routine, but one night the weather was awful. A heavy wind howled along the valley, and icy rain battered against the windows.

"Come on boy, it's half-past six. You'll be late," Dad said, but Scruffy didn't move. He put his nose on the floor between his paws and wagged his tail hopefully.

Claire and I were in the kitchen while Bob prepared our evening meal.

"He doesn't want to go," I said.

Dad walked to the door and signalled to Scruffy, but the dog only wagged his tail harder.

"What are you going to do?" I asked.

Dad sighed.

"Well, I'm not going to force him out in the cold if he doesn't want to go, am I?"

Scruffy was still there at bedtime.

Bob took Dino down for his last run outside and found Dad raiding the cupboards for a tin of dog food. He had some old blankets under his arm to make Scruffy a bed in the flat upstairs.

The next morning, Scruffy was a different dog. He bounced around the house with his teeth showing in a smile, and his tail never stopped wagging.

"He's grateful to be here, isn't he?" I said.

"I'm not surprised," Phil replied. "I know one of the girls that works up at the stables. She told me Scruffy doesn't even have a bed up there. He has to sleep on the straw and if he's in the way, the horses kick him."

"That's terrible. Poor old thing,"

"But if the stable owners bought him as a guard dog, won't they be looking for him?" David asked. "Surely they'll want him back?"

"Probably," Phil agreed, "and they've got quite a reputation for being tough. If they come down and ask for him, I guess we'll have to hand him over."

I didn't like the idea of Scruffy going back to the stables, but I knew Phil was right.

When we stopped for tea that afternoon Dad was nowhere to be found, and Mum was worried.

"It's not like him to go off without telling me," she fretted.

Scruffy was beside her and thumped his tail on the floor.

I checked if Dad had taken a walkie-talkie with him, but they were all lined up in the charger.

"I'm sure he'll turn up soon enough," Bob said, but there was an uncomfortable silence as we drank our tea.

Finally, the kitchen door clicked open, and Dad appeared. Scruffy rushed over and rubbed his head against his leg.

"Where have you been?" Mum demanded.

"Nowhere special. I thought I'd go for a little walk."

Dad peeled off his coat and scarf before he continued.

"As it happens, I went past the stables so I thought I might as well call in and have a word with them. I explained that Scruffy doesn't want to live there anymore so he won't be going back."

We waited, but Dad merely took the mug Mum offered him.

"But what did they say?" David asked as Dad sipped his tea.

"Not much. I made the situation very clear."

Dad never told us anything else about what happened at the stables. He was always a gentleman, but I would love to have known what he really said.

After that, Scruffy was one of the family. Within a few months he was a healthy weight and his badger-coat was soft and curly rather than matted and dirty. His eyes were bright and his stubby tail never stopped wagging.

Chapter 10

It came as a shock when Ian told us he was leaving.

"But why?" Bob asked.

"I don't have any choice. The government has withdrawn the funding for the scheme. It came out of the blue. I just got a letter saying everything has been cancelled."

"But that doesn't make any sense."

"Tell me about it! I've been on the phone all day trying to get an explanation, but all I've been told is they want to prioritise other things."

"Wow. I'm sorry to hear it, Ian."

"I wanted to tell you guys straight away. Personally, I think it's a mistake, but there seem to be a lot of mistakes right now. I guess the politicians have a lot on their hands."

It was true. The mood in the country was changing. After the optimism of recent years, there seemed to be unrest everywhere. People were no longer satisfied with the status quo. Margaret Thatcher had been Prime Minister for over ten years, and the popular support that had helped her win election after election was waning. Across the country, there was a growing sense that things needed to change.

The recent introduction of a poll tax had caused outrage, dividing opinions and causing rifts in communities and families.

At the end of March, huge numbers of people came out on the streets to protest against the new tax, and Trafalgar Square was the scene of the worst rioting for a century.

We watched the news on television in disbelief. Looters stripped shops, set cars on fire, and pelted the police with bricks and lumps of concrete.

The biggest unrest was in the cities, but even in Chudleigh there were protests and vandalism.

David returned from a shopping trip with reports that the windows of the Conservative Club had been smashed and a group of men had been arrested for threatening local councillors.

"Luckily, it has nothing to do with us," Mum said firmly. "It will all blow over soon enough. These things always do."

* * *

"Will you miss having Ian's team around?" Dad asked me later.

I thought for a moment.

"No. In fact, it might be easier without them. It was great at first when they were being taught brick-laying and they cut the paths through the woodland, but last year they did more harm than good."

"Do you mean your roses?"

I laughed.

"No, it wasn't just the roses. I think Ian has been struggling with underfunding for a while. Last summer the men didn't have tutors with them half the time. They had no idea what they were doing. They were just given things to do to keep them busy."

Dad nodded in agreement.

"The scheme must have cost a lot to set up, but I'm not sure it achieved much. I don't think it helped the men who were on it."

Ian and his team moved out within days. Once they were gone, I went and looked around the building they had used. I was pleased to see they had tidied up before they left and apart from a lot of muddy footprints, everything was in reasonable condition.

Money was still my top priority, and it occurred to me that with a little work the rooms could make useful offices. Chudleigh was miles from the nearest big town or industrial estate, and I was sure there must be local people who would want to rent somewhere to run a business.

Even if we could only charge a small amount for each room, it would help.

As soon as the plans for our next development were finished, I turned my attention to budgeting and finance.

I drew up detailed lists of the work that would be needed and began researching builders, catering suppliers, decorators and interior designers. Finally, I sent off our briefs and waited for the quotes to come back.

I am not a religious person, but I whispered a few prayers that the estimates I had been using were not too far removed from reality. Our budgeting had to be realistic and affordable. From now on, cash flow was going to be the key to our success.

The first quote that arrived was from a shop fitting company that specialised in restaurants. I had butterflies in my stomach as I opened the envelope. Bob was watching me. I tried to hide my reaction as I read the figures, but I failed miserably.

"That bad?" Bob asked as he watched my face. "Never mind. There are plenty of other companies out there."

"But that's nearly half of our total budget," I wailed.

"Don't panic yet. Wait until you hear back from the others."

"I'm not panicking," I said indignantly. "It's just frustrating. I explained to them we're working to a tight budget."

"But everything's comparative, isn't it? When people come here, they see this place looking like a stately home and think we're loaded. It's inevitable."

"Do you think so?"

It had never occurred to me that people might think we were wealthy.

"Of course, they do. Why wouldn't they?"

"Because we're still driving the same car we had four years ago? And I haven't bought myself a new pair of shoes since last summer?"

Bob burst out laughing.

"Cash poor, asset rich. Isn't that the phrase? We may be broke, but people will never believe it while we're living here like the lord and lady of the manor."

* * *

Martha and Abbie came back to work at the beginning of April.

Martha was as unchanging as ever. There was something timeless about her. I guessed she had been born with the same curly hair and inscrutable expression that she wore in the tearooms, and I imagined she would be much the same when she died. Abbie, on the other hand, had blossomed.

Her long hair had been cut into a fashionable bob and her eyes sparkled when she told me she had a boyfriend.

Martha was scathing but amused when she heard the news.

"Madam thinks she's so sophisticated now, doesn't she? But she's still as thick as two short planks."

"Shh! Don't let her hear you say that," I scolded.

"Why not? Who else do you know that can't master a microwave?"

It was true.

Our old microwave had died over the winter and had been replaced by a new, larger version. Abbie had noticed it the moment she walked into the kitchen.

"Ooh! Wicked. Look at that!"

The controls were basic and yet the first time she used it she set fire to a plate of doughnuts.

"For the love of God, what have you done now?" Martha gaped as Abbie pulled open the microwave door and a smell of burning filled the kitchen.

"They're ruined," Abbie wailed. "I brought doughnuts for everyone on our first day back. I thought they'd be nicer if they were warm."

She stared at the plate of shrivelled doughnuts surrounded by a glassy puddle of melted sugar. On top of the pile, the centre of the largest doughnut had melded to a small black lump and a faint curl of smoke was rising from it.

"How long did you set it for?" I asked.

"I don't know," Abbie sobbed. "I just pressed Start."

I explained the controls again while she wiped her eyes with the back of her hand, spreading mascara smudges across her face.

"God give me strength. Is there nothing you can do right?" Martha muttered.

Abbie soon calmed down, and I set her to work clearing out the cupboards beneath the sink while Martha assembled the meat slicer.

Lucy was in a playpen in the centre of the room and I was trying to keep her amused while checking the use-by dates on boxes of sugar sachets.

"She's grown so much," Abbie said admiringly. "I'll bet she'll be walking in no time."

"I'm sure she will, but please don't encourage her. I intend to keep her in the playpen for as long as I can."

"Have you finished that cupboard yet?" Martha called across to Abbie.

"Not quite. I've still got the bottom shelf to do."

"Well, hurry up. I'll be in the servery when you've finished."

"OK," Abbie called after her.

"So, what's this boyfriend of yours like?" I asked as soon as Martha had gone.

Abbie stopped scrubbing, and a dreamy smile lifted her lips.

"He's gorgeous. He's tall, and he plays football, and he's really into his music. We've been going out for weeks now and it's amazing."

"For weeks? That sounds serious."

"It is serious," Abbie said earnestly. "We haven't had a single argument and even my dog likes him."

"That's a good sign. What's his name?"

"Jason. It's not his fault, though."

"There's nothing wrong with Jason. It's a nice name."

"No, it isn't. It's old-fashioned. I call him Jaz."

Lucy burped loudly, and I wondered if it was a comment.

"Does he like that?"

"He says he doesn't mind, but his Mum hates it."

"Be careful. You don't want to upset your mother-in-law."

Abbie giggled, and her cheeks turned scarlet.

"Don't say that! I'm not old enough to have a mother-in-law!"

"But I thought you said it was serious?" I teased her.

"It is serious! He's the one. I know he is, but I don't want to rush things."

She ducked as Lucy threw a plastic cow out of the playpen.

"Is that for me?" Abbie picked up the toy and held it out. "Do you want it back?"

Pulling herself to her feet, Lucy stretched out a chubby hand.

"All right. You can have it. You're such a little angel, aren't you?"

I snorted.

"That's not what I'd call her. She might look cute, but she can be a real little pest when she wants to be."

"Thinking of pests, how has Fred been behaving himself?" Abbie asked.

"Strangely enough, everything's been peaceful."

"You mean nothing's happened at all?"

"No, not that I can think of."

Abbie went back to cleaning the cupboard.

"Good. Maybe he's not here anymore."

"Yes," I agreed and felt a touch of sadness, "I think you might be right."

* * *

As soon as Silverlands reopened on Easter Sunday we were plunged into the chaos of a new season. However, instead of the panic I experienced on our first opening day, I now felt a confidence bred of experience. There was a comfortable familiarity to our daily routines, and it was good to have the house full of visitors again.

The adventure packs were a great success, and it was always a pleasure to see children clutching their completed forms, eager to exchange them for their rewards.

The weeks passed smoothly and as summer approached; I noticed Abbie was taking more interest in how the tea rooms were run.

"How do you do that?" she asked me one afternoon as I was writing out an order for the baker.

"How do I do what?"

"Decide how many cakes and things we need."

I smiled at her serious expression.

"It's really not that complicated. We have a standard order that the baker sends every day, but I always check to see if there's anything we want to change."

I pointed to the list in front of me.

"Like the apple puffs. We've run out of them by lunchtime every day this week, so I'm increasing the number for tomorrow."

Abbie nodded thoughtfully.

"And Danish pastries. Those always go quickly."

"Do you think we should get some extra then?"

"Yes, but not too many. Maybe an extra dozen."

I was pleased to see her growing confidence.

"Do you want to phone the order through?" I suggested.

Her eyes widened in surprise.

"Me? Really?"

I added Danish pastries to the list and handed it to her.

"Go on. All you have to do is ask them to add these to the delivery for tomorrow."

"Abbie's grown up a lot since last year," I said to Bob as we got ready for bed. "I haven't seen her break anything all week, and she's taking a real interest in learning things."

"That's good."

"In fact, I was wondering if we should try giving her a bit more responsibility. Do you think that's a good idea?"

Bob pulled back the duvet and climbed into bed.

"Do you want my honest opinion?"

"Of course."

"Then I think it's a terrible idea."

"But she's trying really hard," I protested.

"I'm sure she is, but she's still a disaster on two legs."

"That's not fair! How's she ever goes to improve if we don't give her the chance to try things?"

I glared at him, but Bob only picked up a book from the bedside table and began to read. I waited for a moment, then climbed into bed beside him and yanked the duvet over me.

"Do what you want," he sighed at last, "but don't blame me when it all goes wrong."

The next morning, I asked Abbie if she would like to take responsibility for checking how the cakes were selling each day. She was ridiculously excited and listened attentively as I explained what she had to do.

When the cakes were delivered each morning those that contained cream or custard were stored in the fridge and the rest were put in the larder. Then, as the cakes on display in the servery were sold, they needed to be replaced with fresh stock.

"Yes, I've got it," Abbie beamed at me.

"And remember, when you're counting how many we have left you have to include everything in the larder and the fridge, not just what's on the counter."

"Don't worry, I won't let you down."

Abbie was bursting with pride, and I wanted her to succeed. I was sure she was capable of doing what I had asked, but I decided to keep a close eye on her just in case.

"When you've made the list up each afternoon, you'd better let me have a look at it before you call the baker," I said.

For nearly two weeks, everything went smoothly. Then, as Bob was passing through the servery one day, Martha asked him if he could fetch a replacement carton for the milk dispenser.

The fridge was an enormous, walk-in relic from the days when the building had been a school and had slatted wooden shelves on each side.

As Bob picked up a carton of milk, he noticed a sickly sweet odour, and after sniffing his way around, he found the smell was coming from a pile of trays stacked high on the top shelf.

Taking them down, he discovered an entire tray of custard tarts and another of cream eclairs.

"But I would never put them on the top shelf," Abbie protested when Bob confronted her with the rancid cakes. "Why would I do that?"

"It's a mistake. That's all," I said. "There's no point in making a big deal out of it."

Bob gave me a look that said 'I told you so'.

"Just make sure it doesn't happen again," he said as he left.

"It wasn't me, you know," Abbie persisted once Bob had gone. "I would never put tarts on the top shelf."

I wanted to believe her, but a niggling doubt made me question whether Bob had been right all along. Perhaps I had expected too much of her.

"I'm sorry, Abbie, but I don't see who else it could have been."

"What about Fred? It could have been him."

I hesitated. I had seen no sign of Fred for months.

"It could have been him, couldn't it?" Abbie repeated.

"I'm not saying it wasn't Fred," I said slowly, "but I don't think we can blame him for everything."

Abbie's face fell as if she had been slapped, and I felt terrible.

* * *

When we received the last of the quotes, I put together the final budget for our planned development. Despite our best efforts to keep the cost down, it seemed a huge amount.

"I don't see anything else we can cut out," David said after looking at the figures.

"If we want to go ahead, that's how much it will take," Bob agreed.

After that, Mum and I spent every evening drawing up cash-flow projections and a business plan.

I was encouraged when Bob came back from a meeting of the Tourist Attraction Association bubbling with enthusiasm.

"I talked to the owners of the Shire Horse Centre today. They told me about the functions they're doing in their restaurant. It's amazing. It's a huge part of their turnover. If we can get anywhere near their figures, we'll be laughing."

"That's good to hear."

"I'm sure we're doing the right thing," he said. "This new development is going to be a challenge, but if we can just get everything up and running,

I'm sure it's going to work out brilliantly."

* * *

After the incident with the custard tarts, Abbie was quieter than usual. I didn't want her to lose confidence, so I tried to find something else that could be her responsibility.

Jacket potatoes were always popular at lunchtimes and it was important they were ready on time, so I decided to put her in charge of making sure the first batch was in the oven by half-past ten each morning.

I went through each step with her and Abbie glowed with pride the first time she took potatoes she had baked herself out to the customers.

The next morning, I watched from a distance as she prepared the potatoes and laid them out on trays.

"It's two minutes to half-past ten and they're all in the oven," she told me proudly.

"Excellent." I smiled. "Can you imagine what would happen if they weren't ready on time?"

"Martha would go ballistic, wouldn't she?" Abbie laughed and managed a passable impression of a Scottish brogue.

"Can you not do anything right, you useless lump?"

We both erupted in giggles and it was only when Martha passed in an order for two jacket potatoes with beans at quarter past eleven that Abbie thought to check the oven.

"They might not be done yet," she said. "I'll go and have a look."

As she opened the oven, she squealed so loudly I thought she had burned herself, but her pain was not physical.

"It's not on!" she shrieked. "The oven's not on!"

I rushed across and gazed at the tray of raw potatoes.

"Abbie! I don't believe it!"

"I turned it on! I know I did."

I put my hand into the oven and felt a faint vestige of warmth.

"Did you turn it off by mistake?"

"Why would I do that?" Tears were running down her face. "What are we going to do?"

"Put them back in and turn the oven up full. I'll tell Martha what's happened."

I picked up four of the potatoes and popped them into the microwave, then went out and faced Martha.

When I got back Abbie was sitting on a stool sobbing.

"I turned it on. I know I did…" she mumbled.

"Never mind that now, there's a massive queue at the counter."

I slapped a pile of orders on the counter and gave Abbie a quick hug.

"We'll have to zap the potatoes in the microwave then put them in the oven to crisp up. Come on. We've got to keep moving."

* * *

That evening I went to find Dad. He was brushing Scruffy in the front room of his flat while Mum prepared a meal in the kitchen next door. I told him about the potatoes.

"So, what are you saying? Did Abbie forget to turn the oven on or do you think there was more to it?"

"The oven had been on. It was still warm. It must have been turned off."

"Was there anyone else in the kitchen?"

"No. Martha came in a couple of times to pass over orders, but she never went near the oven."

"Then I've no idea what happened. Maybe we should get someone in to check the gas supply."

"It worked perfectly well afterwards. I don't want to say this to anyone else, but I think it was Fred."

Dad stopped brushing and looked at me with a puzzled expression.

"Why would a ghost mess about with the oven?"

"I don't know!" I moaned.

Scruffy turned around and lay his grey muzzle on my knee. I stroked the old dog's head, and he looked up at me with shining black eyes.

"I know it sounds crazy but… I think he was playing a joke on us. I think he did it to wind us up."

Dad was silent, and I realised how insane I must have sounded.

"I can't think of any other explanation," I went on. "He heard us saying how much trouble it would cause if the potatoes weren't ready, so he turned the oven off."

Dad nodded seriously.

"You mean we've got a ghost with a sense of humour?"

I glared at him.

"Except it wasn't funny. Not for us. Abbie got herself in a right stress and Martha had to deal with a row of hungry customers and no jacket potatoes."

"And all the time Fred was floating around laughing at you?"

"I know it sounds ridiculous, but that's what it felt like."

I expected Dad to laugh at me, but instead he shrugged.

"Maybe you're right. If there is a ghost, he must get bored hanging around watching other people live their lives."

I leaned my head on his shoulder, and he put his arm around me.

"Thanks, Dad. You don't think I'm crazy, do you?"

"No." He grinned. "At least, no more than you've always been."

* * *

Over the next weeks, Fred often crept into my thoughts. When I was alone in the kitchen, my eyes were drawn to the shadows in the corners. I found myself listening for tiny sounds or watching for faint movements, and I became hyper-aware of everything around me.

One evening after we closed, Michael accompanied David and me on our nightly search of the house. Claire was happy playing in the gift shop with Phil, but Michael enjoyed helping us switch off the displays.

We finished the exhibitions on the first floor and I held Michael's hand as we came down the back staircase. As we reached the ground floor, I noticed a white figure disappear into the Enchanted Forest.

"Who's that, Auntie?" Michael asked.

I hadn't seen the figure clearly, but a shiver ran up my spine. I remembered seeing a similar vision in the same spot shortly after we moved in.

"I expect it was Grandma," I said quickly. "You stay here with Daddy and I'll go and see."

I walked slowly through the indoor playground, checking every space and making absolutely certain there was no one there. By the time I came out, David was alone.

"You took your time," he complained. "Michael got bored. He's gone to find Phil."

I told David about the figure.

"But what did it look like?" he asked eagerly.

"I told you. It was just white. I only caught a glimpse of it."

"Did Michael see it too?"

"Yes, but I told him it was Mum."

"Why did you do that?"

I looked at him in surprise.

"Because he's a little boy."

"But we can't just pretend it hasn't happened."

"Yes, we can. I'm not having the kids being scared."

David gave in grudgingly, but I knew he thought I was wrong to hide what we had seen.

A few days later he caught me on my own.

"I've been thinking about what happened the other day. We can't just ignore it."

"What do you mean?"

"This place is haunted. We both know it. I don't want the kids to be upset any more than you do, but isn't it better to be honest and talk about it?"

"No! You wouldn't take them to see an X-rated movie, would you? How much scarier would it be for them to have something weird going on in their own home?"

David's face was a picture of confusion.

"But that's my whole point. It's not scary, is it? A ghost isn't a monster. It's just a glimpse of something from the past. We should try to explain it to them."

"It's not that simple."

I didn't want to talk about it. I turned to walk away, but David wasn't going to let the subject drop.

"Lots of people that are fascinated by ghosts. If we really have got a ghost here, it would be crazy not to make something out of it. We could have ghost tours and talks and animated displays..."

I couldn't control myself.

"No! We're not doing that. Fred was here long before us. What right have you got to bring people in to interfere with him?"

David stared at me in disbelief.

"We're talking about a ghost. Not a person! It's not real, is it?"

He didn't wait for me to answer, but hurried on.

"I mean, it is real. We've all seen things, but that doesn't mean it's real like we are. A ghost doesn't have feelings, does it? It's just some sort of image. Something that can be seen sometimes. Like an optical illusion..."

"You don't know what you're talking about."

"And you're some sort of expert, are you?" he demanded.

"Of course not! I don't understand any of it. The only thing I know is that whatever Fred is, we shouldn't upset him."

"Why? What do you think he's going to do? Bang on the water pipes and turn the lights off?"

"Of course not. I can't give you any sensible answers. It's just the way I feel. I think we might regret it."

* * *

By the end of August, the business plan was complete, and I had drawn illustrations to show exactly how the new developments would look when everything was finished.

Bob suggested we should arm ourselves with as much information as possible before going to see Mr North again, so he arranged for a surveyor to come and do a full valuation of the property. When the written valuation came back, we were all astounded.

"I don't believe it! That's nearly ten times what we paid for it," David exclaimed.

Dad looked more relaxed than I had seen him look in ages.

"If there's one thing you can be sure about, it's property values. Other things change, but in all my life I've never known property values go down," he said.

"Yes, it's fantastic news," Bob grinned. "That should convince Mr North."

A week later Mum and I were back at Torrington Bank explaining our plans.

Mr North welcomed us and listened intently as we explained the progress we had made since we last met. We had sent regular copies of our accounts to the bank, and it was clear the banker had kept himself updated.

He asked lots of questions and seemed satisfied with our answers. When I explained our reasons for wanting to expand as quickly as possible, he nodded.

"I think you're right. It makes sense to concentrate on the areas that will help you maximise your income. It's a sensible plan, and I am delighted to hear things are going so well."

He leaned back in his chair and put his fingertips together under his chin as he considered us. I was starting to feel uncomfortable when he suddenly straightened up.

"Well, ladies, in view of the remarkable increase in the value of your property I have no problem agreeing the additional funding you ask for. However, there is one thing you are going to have to consider."

My heart fell as I waited for him to go on.

"At this point we will need to refinance your borrowing. That means you will have to decide whether you want to go ahead with a fixed interest rate, as is the case at present, or if you would rather opt for a variable rate?"

I glanced sideways at Mum, but I couldn't read her expression. I had no idea what to say.

"The choice is entirely up to you," Mr North continued. "If you remain on the fixed rate, you will have the advantage of knowing exactly what your repayments will be. However, if the Bank of England rate goes down, you will be tied to paying higher fees than your competitors."

We decided to take the variable rate.

I waited to hear what other restrictions there would be, but Mr North merely smiled at us.

"I will arrange to have the paperwork sent over and I hope the building work goes smoothly."

He stood up and held out his hand.

"It was lovely to see you both again. And good luck."

"That was easy!" I giggled as we drove back to Chudleigh. "Maybe we should have asked for more."

"No!" Mum laughed. "Don't say that. I can't believe he actually agreed. On the spot. We walked into his office and asked for all that money and he agreed."

"Of course, he did. He's a banker and we've got a very valuable property to put up against the loan. Let's face it, even with the extra borrowing, what we'll owe them is less than half of the value of the property."

"I know, but let's not get carried away. What we're taking on is massive. Next winter is going to be a nightmare. It will be like living through the first year all over again."

"Yes, and we have no one to blame but ourselves," I laughed.

* * *

As soon as we could arrange babysitters, we all went out for a celebration dinner. By then there were only two weeks left until we closed. Normally, we would have been looking forward to relaxing once the season was over, but this year was different. This year there would be no time for a holiday.

We had scheduled the building work to start on the first of October, and we knew we were enjoying the calm before the storm. It was going to be another crazy winter and we could only trust everything would work out as well as we hoped.

As we ordered our meals, we chatted happily about nothing in particular.

Life was good, and we had everything ahead of us.

By the last day of September, our visitor numbers had reduced to a trickle.

"Is it worth putting any potatoes in do you think," Martha asked me half-way through the morning. We had seen hardly any customers in the tearooms since we opened.

"We might as well," I replied. "It will be embarrassing if customers turn up unexpectedly and if they don't, we can always eat them ourselves!"

I opened a box of potatoes and took out enough to fill a tray.

"Here you are, Abbie, as it's our last day you can do them."

"Do I have to?"

She looked at me reproachfully. She hadn't prepared the potatoes since the day the gas had been turned off.

"Yes, it's not a big deal. You prepare them and I'll turn the oven on."

When the potatoes were ready, I held the door open as Abbie pushed the tray to the centre of the oven.

"There. I'll be disappointed if we get a lot of customers now," I said. "I quite fancy a potato for lunch."

Abbie managed a smile.

"Me too. Especially if there's any of that garlic mayonnaise left."

"You're not having garlic, are you?" I teased her. "I thought you were seeing Jaz tonight?"

It amused me that Abbie still blushed whenever anyone mentioned her boyfriend.

"He won't mind," she said. "He likes garlic too."

An hour later Martha bustled into the kitchen.

"It's just as well you put those tatties in," she said as she put an order on the work surface. "There's an old couple turned up and they want one each."

"No problem," I replied. "Abbie, can you see if the potatoes are done?"

Abbie pulled on a pair of gauntlets, bent down and open the oven door. At once, a haze of smoke surrounded her, and she jumped back.

"Oh, my God!" she wailed, "What's happened?"

I was beside her in a moment and grabbed a pair of oven gloves. As the smoke cleared, I could see the tray of potatoes was right at the back of the oven directly over the gas jets.

"I didn't move it!" Abbie protested. "It wasn't me! You know it wasn't!"

Leaning into the oven, I managed to reach the tray and drag it out. Half of the potatoes were black and charred, and the side of the tray was practically glowing.

"It's all right Abbie, calm down. The ones at the front are fine."

But Abbie wasn't listening to me. Her shoulders were heaving and her breath came in great shuddering sobs. Dropping the gauntlets on the floor, she rushed out into the yard.

I was about to rush after her when I remembered the order.

By the time I had taken the potatoes out to the old couple, Abbie had stopped crying, but her face was streaked with tears.

"Why does he pick on me?"

She was sitting on a dustbin, looking dejected. I put an arm around her shoulder.

"I don't know."

"But it was Fred, wasn't it? You saw I put that tray in properly,"

"Yes, I saw. I know it wasn't your fault."

Her shoulders started quaking, and I searched through my pockets for a tissue.

"Please don't cry."

"I can't help it. It's so unfair..."

"I know it seems that way, but I don't think Fred does things on purpose."

I found a tissue and passed it to her.

"I don't even know if there really is a Fred or if these things are just random, but I'm sure they're nothing to do with you."

Abbie wiped her eyes, and the sobs slowly subsided.

"I've been trying really hard."

"I know you have. I'm very proud of how well you've done this year."

She looked up at me and blinked.

"Are you?"

"Yes, I am. In fact, you deserve a reward. Stay there. I'm going to get you a doughnut."

She smiled at me through her tears.

"Thanks."

I walked into the kitchen and was half-way to the larder when I froze.

A familiar stench filled the air, and a low hissing sound issued from the ovens. Every burner was turned on full, but none were lit. The room was full of gas. Struggling to hold my breath, I ran along the row of ovens, turning off the gas taps.

Tears streamed from my eyes, and my lungs ached. Choking and spluttering, I flew to the windows, threw them open and gulped in the fresh air.

Turning back, I stared around the empty kitchen. My heart was pumping so hard my ears rang.

"For Christ's sake," I screamed, "this isn't a joke anymore!"

For the first time, I was afraid.

Let's keep in touch!

One of the best things about being a writer is being able to build a relationship with my readers.

Every month I send out a newsletter or two with details of my next book release, special offers and insights into my other writing projects.

If you choose to join my mailing list, I will welcome you with a free download of my latest novella, Gin on the Rock, which tells the story of an unexpected adventure Bob and I had soon after we got married. We thought we were going on a two-week working holiday in Spain but things turned out very differently indeed!

You can join my Readers Group and download Gin on the Rock on my website www.dianatownsend.co.uk.

Did you enjoy Summer Days?

If so, I'd like to ask you something.

As a new writer, my success depends largely on being able to draw attention to my work.

Much as I would love to take out full-page ads in magazines or put posters on the underground those options are simply not available to independent authors without the backing of a large publishing house.

However, reviews from readers can have a huge impact on the amount of exposure a title is given on online.

If you've enjoyed reading this book, I would be very grateful if you could spend a couple of minutes leaving a review (it can be as short as you like) on the book's Amazon page.

You can jump right to the page by clicking below.

Click here to leave a review

Thank you very much,

Diana

Coming Soon!

DIANA TOWNSEND
Me
My Family
and the
Poltergeists
How it all ended...

About the Author

While growing up in Exeter, Diana worked with her family to build a remarkable animated model circus. When she left school, she helped display the model to the public then went on to buy a derelict school and transform it into a tourist attraction.

Later, she formed a company specializing in designing and installing Christmas displays for shopping centres and local authorities.

After writing several plays which were staged by schools and community groups, Diana began writing and producing short films.

Two of her feature film scripts, Deadly Intent and Scareycrows, have been produced and distributed by Inspired Toad Productions.

Diana lives in Devon with her husband Robert.

You can connect with me on:

- http://dianatownsend.co.uk
- https://twitter.com/Diana_Townsend
- https://www.facebook.com/dianatownsendwriter
- https://www.instagram.com/diana_townsend13

Subscribe to my newsletter:

- https://landing.mailerlite.com/webforms/landing/f6t6a0

Also by Diana Townsend

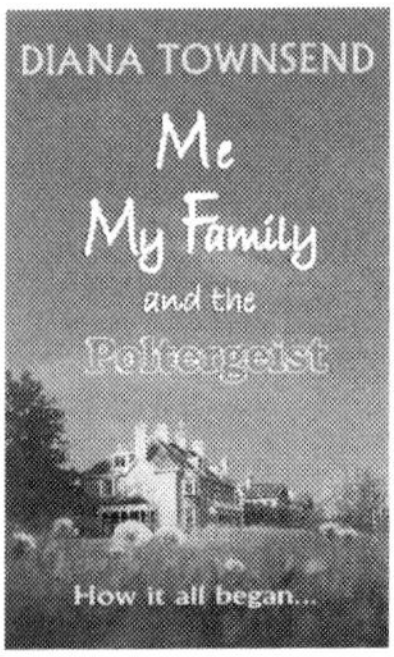

HOW IT ALL BEGAN...

For Diana Townsend, life was never boring. Her mother was a writer, her father was an artist and her grandmother was insane.

As teenagers, she and her brother, David, helped their father build a magnificent, animated model circus and display it to the public.

While trying to keep their Grandmother out of the local asylum, the family grew their model exhibition and dreamed of opening their own tourist attraction.

Hearing a derelict school was up for sale, the family made an impulsive decision to sell their house, pool their savings and risk everything on making their dream a reality.

Not believing in ghosts, Diana was amused to hear local people claim the old building was haunted. However, once renovations began, she realised strange things were happening.

As their opening day approached and unexpected problems threatened the family with ruin, Diana became convinced they were dealing with a poltergeist. But was she right? And would the rest of the family believe her?

GIN ON THE ROCKS

Diana Townsend discovers she has much to learn about her new husband, Bob, when they arrive in Spain to find their business trip has been cancelled.

With two weeks to wait until their flight home, Bob suggests they visit his favourite bar in Gibraltar. Expecting a relaxed holiday, Diana quickly agrees but soon finds her husband has a very different trip in mind.

Oblivious to Diana's growing alarm, Bob leads her from a confrontation with armed police in Tangiers, to a power-cut in the Kasbah, an illicit visit to a private palace and a near-riot in a ferry port.

As the date of their return flight approaches, Diana realises they are stranded. Bob assures her he will find a way to get them home safely but is he right?